YOU THINK I'M DEAD

LOUIS ROMANO

ISBN: 9780 9860 4703 9

Printed in the U.S.A.

First Edition, 2015

Also by Louis Romano

Detective Vic Gonnella Series

INTERCESSION

Gino Ranno Series

FISH FARM

BESA

Poetry Series

Anxiety's Nest

Anxiety's Cure

This book is dedicated to all those who kept the life and memory of this little boy alive so that I have now, 58 years later, had the privilege to write about him.

"Louis Romano weaves an intricate emotional tapestry filled with suspense and intrigue as former Detective Vic Gonnella embarks on a search for justice in the case of a ravaged innocence that echoes through time."

— Jerome Elam

Staff Writer/Columnist at Communities Digital News, LLC. Classified USMC, child sex trafficking survivor, public speaker and advocate.

Acknowledgements

Let me get one thing out of the way first. I want to thank no one at the Philadelphia Police Department. They couldn't care less about solving this poor child's case.

I do owe a debt of gratitude to Bobby Jordan and his wonderful son, Jeremy Jordan

To Marc Brown at the DNA Diagnostics Center in Ohio; He schooled me on DNA testing

To "M" for her bravery and honesty in coming forward with invaluable information about her brother

To Jim Hoffman, my new friend and author of The Boy in the Box

Many special thanks to Danny Rivera for all things cop

To cover models Olga Nieves aka Raquel and Anthony Zunno aka Detective Vic Gonnella

To Fiton Gjonbalaj for his incredible photography for the book's cover and my mug on the back cover

To all my pre-readers whose opinions I find valuable

To Jeanne Rebillard my publicist who works hard keeping my foot in the door

To Sr. Editor, Pamela Fuchsel, whose input is priceless

To Christian and Lisa Cook for their help with production of the book

And to my publisher and editor, Kathleen Collins of Vecchia Publishing, for her total commitment to the story, without whom this book would have never been written

*"There can be no keener revelation
of a society's soul
than the way in which
it treats its children."*

—Nelson Mandela

CHAPTER 1

New York City - 2014

Detective Vic Gonnella's decision to retire from the New York City Police Department was not a very difficult one to make. After what had happened in the John Deegan case, he was catapulted into the world of global notoriety and became an overnight celebrity. Vic had put in his retirement papers with the Bronx Homicide Division to no surprise of the NYPD brass.

Appearances on every major television network variety and talk show throughout the world made Gonnella a household name. Offers came in for television series from HBO, Showtime, Netflix, CBS, NBC, ABC, and a host of other mass media outlets. The offers were so lucrative that his lifetime pension from the NYPD, which included lifetime healthcare coverage, was nothing more than chump change. Vic quickly hired an agent, a publicist, and an entertainment attorney to advance his persona and protect his financial interests. From his average annual income of around one hundred and seventy-five thousand dollars, Vic was now making millions. After all, what he had done in the John Deegan case was simply heroic.

Speaking engagements with various law enforcement agencies and product endorsements for everything from automatic pistols to cereals brought Vic and his advisors to start an international private corporation, headquartered on Park Avenue and 56th Street in Manhattan. Financing was not an issue. Investment money flowed like water from hedge funds and pension funds around the world.

Centurion Associates LLC, of which Vic was chairman and CEO, had long-term plans to operate offices in several major cities, employing the best personnel in global law enforcement. From marital investigations to worldwide anti-terrorism, Gonnella and his associates were demanding huge fees--and getting them--from high-profile clientele.

Vic asked Raquel Ruiz, his live-in girlfriend, to leave the NYPD with him and head up his New York office. They were no longer living in Raquel's Radcliffe Avenue home in the Bronx. The company was renting a magnificent duplex apartment on East 59th Street and Third Avenue within walking distance of their luxurious and high-tech office. A sizeable down payment on an estate in Armonk, New York, would be their escape-from-the-madness country home.

Vic and Raquel were deeply and madly in love with each other. Raquel, along with advanced psychoanalysis, had opened Vic's personality like a blooming flower. Gone were the horrid feelings of guilt and despair from the sexual molestation Vic had experienced in his childhood. He was dealing well with his past, and, now, he was flourishing both financially and emotionally. Raquel had become Vic's untiring teacher and mentor. She had helped him to remove the suppressed anger and the wall of emotional emptiness that was slowly eating away at his life. Gone also were the recurring nightmares with visions of his family priest molesting him, which Vic had tried to repress for over forty years. Now, it was his time to enjoy life and bask in the limelight of success. Vic could think of no better person in the world to enjoy and share his life with than Raquel.

Raquel's Columbia University education was now going to help her reach her full potential as a business woman. That, along with her time as a NYPD police officer, was the perfect recipe for her success as a partner of Centurion Associates. Her summa cum laude status from an Ivy League school and the street smarts she learned in the Bronx enabled her to compete with the best in the world of high-end private investigation. The only thing that was missing in Raquel's life was a child.

Raquel's biological clock and an amazingly strong maternal instinct were up against Vic's been-there-done-that attitude toward having more children. Raquel felt a need to confront Vic with her feelings for the last time. She had no plans to end their relationship over this life-changing issue, but she needed to find out once and for all if she would ever be a mom. Raquel made a date with Vic to have dinner at a quiet, dimly-lit, Italian restaurant on the Upper East Side. She was going to make her case, and she had no intention of walking away with his usual "Let's see," put-off answer.

"Honey, I know it's probably going to make you roll your eyes, but we need to talk," Raquel said.

"Let me guess, you want the Armonk house to have horses. I hate horses." Vic laughed.

"Well, that's a topic for another day. I love horses, and the time will come that you will, too. No, we need to discuss having a child, Vic."

"Can we discuss this when I get back from Virginia next week? I'm working on that speech for the NRA annual meeting. I have no idea what I want to say to those people."

"Vic, no. Sorry, no flight and avoidance behavior right now; I want to let you know how I feel."

"I know, baby. I know you want children. It's just that I did that already and I didn't do it very well. With our business growing like mad, I may be a worse dad to our children than I was to my first kids. Christ, I hardly see them at all anyway," Vic retorted.

"Did you love your ex-wife?" Raquel asked, looking deeply into Vic's eyes. The candlelight made her chestnut-brown eyes sparkle. Vic was thinking about how truly beautiful she was.

"I have no idea. I'm not sure I even knew what love was then. I think I went through the motions because it was the thing to do at the time," Vic said.

"Do you love me?"

"Ah, come on, baby. What kind of question is that?"

"Answer the question, Gonnella. Do you love me?"

"Of course, I love you. You know I do. That's not even a question you should have to ask. I tell you I love you every day, and I mean it."

"Don't you think having children with someone you love would be an incredibly amazing thing in your life?" Raquel asked, her eyes filling with tears.

"Raquel, please don't start that now. If you cry, I will cry and my veal will get even more salty," Vic said.

Raquel ignored Vic's attempt at distracting humor.

"I will not cry. Listen to me for a second. You have to admit that, in the last year, you have become a totally different person than you were when we met. You are more loving, more open, more relaxed. You are now a famous person, a damn celebrity for Christ's sake! You make the world a better, safer place. Why not share that world with our children?" Raquel said as she sat back in her chair awaiting the answer to the toughest question she had posed to Vic on the issue.

"Baby, it's not such a great world to bring kids into...and..."

"Don't hand me that crap, Vic. That is such a cop-out. You are going to let me become an old Spanish lady without children? There is nothing sadder than a woman who wants children and cannot have them. You will turn me into a bitter, old hag. In my world we call that a *machota*. I will not be a machota. I don't want to be *sin decendientes*--alone in the world with no children. "

"Will you leave me if I say, 'No, I don't want any more kids"?

"You know what, Vic? Fuck you. You know I will never, ever leave you. Are you serious? I love you like you are my own blood. I have found my soul mate, and you are him. But to think that you know that I want children so desperately and you will let me go to my grave without that experience of love is just totally unfair," Raquel said. Her eyes were clear. No tears welling up.

"So, should we get married first?" Vic asked.

"Is that a yes, Gonnella?"

"I just want to know if we need to get married to have children."

"Why, are you looking to have a big wedding at the Pierre?" Raquel asked. She smiled for the first time since they had started the conversation.

Vic loved her dimples and took in the whole picture of his beautiful lover.

"Baby, the way you put it finally opened my eyes. Your need to have children is greater than my need not to have any more. You deserve a chance at being a mommy."

"And my answer on the wedding bit is no. It's a silly piece of paper. I have no need for a piece of paper when I have the best man on the planet," Raquel said.

"So, when do we start?" Vic asked. He raised and lowered his eyebrows up and down a few times to get a laugh from Raquel.

"Get the check," Raquel said. She slowly licked her lips around her open mouth.

CHAPTER 2

Vic and Raquel left the restaurant and walked back to their apartment. Vic's arm was gently around Raquel's waist the whole time.

"I'm really very proud of you, honey," Raquel said.

"Really? Just because I agreed to make a baby?"

"Don't be silly. You are so much more relaxed now. It seems all the pent-up anger and baggage that you were carrying is virtually gone. That's made me very happy, Vic."

"And, now, we are rich. That ain't so bad either. I've been poor, and I've been rich. Rich is a lot better," Vic laughed, his voice echoing off the buildings.

"I don't think about that so much. I do think about the future a lot more now than I ever have before though. What we can achieve together is all because of you."

"Lucky, I guess," Vic said.

"Way beyond lucky, my love. More like destiny. *La forza del destino*. The power of destiny."

Vic and Raquel entered the building lobby and strolled past the security desk with Raquel smiling politely at the two men on duty. They entered the elevator. Vic pressed the PH button, and the door closed slowly on the outside world. Raquel moved closer into Vic, and they began to kiss, both conscious of the two men watching them on the monitor at the desk. Vic looked up at the camera in the corner of the elevator, smiled, and shook his finger back and forth as if he were admonishing their snooping. Raquel put her head back and laughed at her boyfriend's joking wittiness.

The couple entered their home, and Vic headed for the wine cabinet while Raquel moved toward the entertainment system. She loaded a few CDs, and he selected a nice, bold California Cabernet. Within a few minutes, they were in their bedroom, Raquel lighting a few candles and Vic pouring the wine into two long-stemmed, crystal glasses. In a flash, they were both undressed and on the bed.

In the morning, Vic lay there, propped up on his side. Raquel lay next to him on her belly, welcoming sleep, her dark, long hair splayed about haphazardly on the cream, satin pillowcase. They had been together almost a year now, and he still found himself insatiable for all that was her. As he watched her, the slight rising of her shoulders as she breathed softly and her bottom jutting out from the small of her back as if teasing him began to turn him on, and he felt himself harden.

They had already been at it earlier, but he wanted her again now as if for the first time. He lightly began to trace his name on her back, his finger drawing a "V" and then an "I." Before he started the "C," she began to stir. She sensed him near, his soft breath on her. Turning her head on the pillow toward him, she let out a soft "Mmmm." He moved his lips over her cheek.

"Good morning, detective," he said in a playful tone.

"Screw you," she said softly, smiling. He grabbed a fistful of her hair and again whispered softly.

"You meant to say, 'I want to fuck you,' right, Ruiz?" With that, he moved on top of her, straddling her voluptuous butt.

Vic even wondered what had gotten into him. He felt twenty again. Raquel made him feel that way, keeping his real age at bay. He felt like a kid in a candy store, and she was his sweet, sinful treat. Her body instantly welcomed him; she was still wet as she pushed her ass out more toward him, opening herself up further.

"Oh, god," she muttered, and her soft moaning began. Vic did her slowly at first, waiting for her to build her orgasm. He knew how she worked, yes, knew her well. He could feel her shudders, her moaning becoming louder as she would build towards her climax.

Vic pulled himself out of her and, with his right hand, grabbed her hip and turned her body over. He wanted to see those chestnut eyes with her second orgasm. Before he entered her again, he began to kiss her breast lightly then slowly suck and nibble it. He could feel her nipple harden even more in his mouth.

"Baby, oh, god," Raquel breathed, and, with that, she grabbed him and pushed him deep inside of her. She wrapped her legs around his rear, and he began to have her, faster, feverishly, as though she would disappear if he dare stopped. He wanted her, needed her as never before, and, as she began to build her orgasm, his cell rang.

"Shit!" He could see the number highlighted from the bed stand.

Though it had been awhile, he recognized it instantly.

"Christ, Vic, if this isn't the cop cliché. In the middle of sex, and the phone rings. You are not on the job anymore, remember? Leave it alone. You can call back," Raquel said.

"I have to take this, Raquel...it's John Deegan."

"Areyoukiddenmeorwhat???" Raquel bolted up to her knees on the bed.

Vic gathered his thoughts then pressed the green button on the phone.

"Hello, Vic Gonnella," Vic said.

"Long time!" Deegan exclaimed.

"Hello, John. This is a surprise. Never thought we would be talking again."

"I just wanted to check in and catch up a bit."

"That's what *friends* do, John. I hardly think we are that," Vic said, his voice betraying neither annoyance nor friendliness.

"Well, we do have history, Vic. The kind of past that changed the world, don't you agree?"

Ignoring the statement, Vic calmly said, "What are you up to, John?"

"Loving my life, loving my one and only love, Gjuliana. But, I must say, I don't like reading all the news reports about kids being molested by their family members, their teachers, priests, rabbis. Do you know how difficult it is for me to hear those things?"

"It's a cold, hard, harsh world, John. You did your thing. Now, it's time to move forward, don't you think?

"I'm getting a bit bored with the good life, Gonnella. Maybe it's time for me to make another statement," John said. His voice sounded like he was joking.

"Do you remember our deal, John?"

"As I recall, if I ever did another vengeance killing, you are going to hunt me down and kill me. Am I close?"

"Bingo," Vic said abruptly.

"Don't worry, I'm living up to my part of the deal so far, tough guy. I'd like to spend the rest of my days donating my money and helping the world be a better place in spite of the riff-raff that surrounds us."

"Really, John, why the call after all this time?" Vic asked.

"I owe you my life, Vic. Well, my freedom anyway. I just wanted to say thank-you for making the decision not to kill me or arrest me and put me in a cage. Is there anything I can do for you in return?"

"Such as?" Vic felt they were getting to the real reason for Deegan's call.

"Do you need investment funds for your company? I can direct whatever you require through off-shore accounts that will not lead to me."

"I'm good, John. Nice thought, but I have to decline."

"I know you do, but I thought I would at least ask. There will be funds set aside for your children. Two boys if I'm not mistaken."

"No need for that, John, we are fine," Vic said. His mind was racing, trying to figure out if John had an angle with the talk of money.

"Already done, my friend. Where would you expect for me to leave my money, the Church?" John said with a hearty laugh.

"John, I'm not your friend. If I needed a friend, I would get a dog."

"Hahaha...the jaded child of the NYPD."

"Anything else, John?"

"Vic, I just have to ask you...Are you planning to have any more children? I would hate to leave any of your progeny out of my estate planning."

"Good night, Mr. Deegan. I wish you a long life and happiness."

"Call me anytime, Vic. I'm always here for you."

Vic pressed the red button to end the conversation. He looked at Raquel who was simply gorgeous in the flickering light of the candles. Her mouth was agape from listening to Vic's side of the conversation.

"Can you believe what just happened, baby?" Vic asked.

"Holy shit, Vic. Is he at it again?"

"I don't think so. He sounded different this time. More relaxed, more at peace. I just can't figure out why he called."

"What was that he said when you asked him, 'Anything else, John?'" Raquel asked.

"He asked, get this, if I was planning to have any more children!"

"I just got chills, Vic. That's crazy!"

CHAPTER 3

A few days later, Vic Gonnella and Raquel Ruiz had an important appointment up in the boogie down Bronx. Raquel made the meeting with a woman famous throughout all of New York City, at least among people of Caribbean descent. There was a six month wait list to see Tia Carmen Auffant, a clairvoyant of great reputation for being balls-on accurate. She could tell a person their past and future, that is, if there was a future to tell. In that rough neighborhood, death from sudden heart failure and murder were common occurrences. The locals were nutritionally challenged and living in harm's way at all times, so, being a clairvoyant had some natural advantages.

Tia Carmen lives alone in a second-floor, one-bedroom apartment on Southern Boulevard and East 180th Street in a tough Hispanic and black neighborhood in the Bronx. At eighty-one, she has shrunk down from five foot three to just a hair over five feet. She has never married or had any children of her own but is the mother to many. Tia Carmen's salt-and-pepper hair is kept pulled back in a tight bun tied with small, red rubber bands. Her housecoats are wool in the winter and cotton in the summer, and she wears no adornments; no earrings, no finger rings, no necklaces, and there are no religious icons in her cramped but very clean apartment. There is always an aroma of something delicious in the air, although Tia Carmen never uses her stove. Neighborhood women and restaurant owners provide her with a steady flow of the foods she enjoys in payment for her services. The local women clean her apartment in thanks for the many years of advice and warnings she has provided them.

Her entire life, Tia Carmen was surrounded by Catholicism, the Yoruba beliefs of Santería, Jehovah's Witnesses, Palo Mayombe, the Mita Congregation, and a variety of obscure Taíno religions. Regardless of this exposure, religion has had no influence on her whatsoever. Her gift of seeing the future came from her grandmother, her *abuelita*, who told her that the secret to their clairvoyant sight was from pure energy. No man on a cross, no god with a face, no ceremonies, no *Casa de Santos*, animal sacrifices, healing mass, holy water, scripture, no nothing.

Tia Carmen, like her *abuelita*, did not disrespect people's beliefs; she just dealt in the facts of the past and of the future, unless people altered their prospects by their present behavior. Tia Carmen would give advice on how to prevent bad things from happening in the future to those who asked. Sometimes, there would be no advice as the future she saw was certain. She would simply say, "The energy is sleeping right now." There was no price list. Her services were whatever her patrons could afford. Coins from returning bottles and cans were fine. Folding money, checks, whatever the person wanted to give was placed in an old, yellow and red *Cafe Bustello* can that sat on her stove in the tiny kitchen.

Tia Carmen called her readings her *cuenco de arroz,* her bowl of rice. Her younger sister Idalis kept the appointment book. A strict five hours a day, 9 in the morning until noon, then after her supper from 6-8 in the evening. Carmen needed her rest and her daily walk to Arthur Avenue to shop for incidentals and some pastries to satisfy her sweet tooth. Occasionally, Tia would walk around to see a few exhibits at the Bronx Zoo, whose main entrance is a few blocks from her apartment. She never had to pay the $14.95 senior citizens rate. There was always someone at the gate from the neighborhood who knew her and her reputation as a seer.

Tia's sister Idalis was an old and dear friend to Raquel's mother. They were from the same town in the hills of central Puerto Rico, Naranjito, and had attended school together. Naranjito had all of sixteen hundred people, so, everyone seemed to know each other and his or her business. Raquel's mom was able to get a time for her and Vic to see Tia Carmen without waiting for months. But they had to be there today, and they had to be on time. They needed to bring a few personal items. A piece of jewelry, a watch, a scarf from the woman, and a belt from the man. Tia would handle the objects, sometimes sniff at them, and read their future.

Vic Gonnella was skeptical about this whole process. He thought it was the foolish rants of Raquel's Hispanic heritage and nothing more than Puerto Rican voodoo as he laughingly called it. His mentality didn't permit the foolishness of an old woman who told fortunes. But Vic would do anything in the world to please Raquel, and, if it meant a few hours in his old stomping grounds, what the hell. Maybe they could even have lunch at Dominick's restaurant. It would be good to see his old pal, Charlie, who owned the place.

Raquel was very excited and chatty on the drive from 59th Street.

"Honey, don't say anything to Tia Carmen about a baby or anything like that, okay?" Raquel said.

"Can I ask if you will lose that great ass of yours?"

"C'mon, Vic, that's not nice." Raquel fake punched Vic's arm.

"How about a question about the lotto numbers for next week? I hear it's up to three-hundred billion or some crazy number. Okay, I have a serious question though, honey. How come there aren't any rich Puerto Ricans in that neighborhood if this lady is that good at telling the future?"

"Seriously!" Raquel squealed and laughed.

"Yankee's chances next year for number twenty-eight?" Vic asked.

"Who is number twenty-eight?"

"Their twenty-eighth world championship, Raquel. C'mon, will ya?"

"It's important that you just listen, and no faces or negative vibes, okay, honey? This is important to me," Raquel said.

"Will they kill a chicken and attach the head to a cat's body?"

"Shut up, stupid," Raquel said trying not to laugh.

"Is Momma Ruiz attending this séance ceremony?"

"It's no séance or ceremony. Just say hello, smile, be nice, hand her your stuff, and listen."

"Sure, baby. I'm only kidding. But can she tell me if Dominick's has the pork chop *pizzaiola* on today's menu?"

"Of course, make a complete fool of yourself, and the next time we have sex will be in the fall," Raquel said as she feigned annoyance.

Vic pulled his shinny black Mercedes 550 up to the curb in front of the apartment house where Tia Carmen lived. The building was a five-story, brick walk-up with an intercom system on the side of the graffiti-scarred entranceway. The car looked out of place during the day. At night, pimps and drug dealers circled the neighborhood in similar luxury, but, during the day, it was a rarity to see such an expensive vehicle actually park and its occupants have the nerve to exit. Vic still carried a Glock .22, a heavy caliber automatic. Raquel had her trusty Beretta PX4 Storm Compact, also .40 calibers. Like her, the gun was small and left nothing to chance. Vic opened the car's glove compartment and placed his eight-by-ten park-anywhere-in-the-city-for-free card given to him by the mayor on the dashboard.

A morbidly obese, Spanish guy in a wheelchair pulled up to Vic. One of his legs was gone, and they were working on taking the second one away bit by bit.

"How ya feeling, dude?" Vic asked.

The fat man's teeth were brown, black, missing, or twisted and looked to be very painful.

"Okay, poppie. This diabetes though, they keep cutting me up, man. Pretty soon, nothing to cut, you know what I mean? You got some change for my cup, poppie?"

"Tell you what. You're not really busy right now, are you?" Vic asked.

"No, poppie, I have all day."

Vic took a twenty-dollar bill from his pocket and tore it in half.

"You keep this part, and, when I come back and the car is good, I give you my half. Deal?"

"Ay, poppie, I will wash and wax the motherfucker for twenty."

"No, just watch it. Okay, my friend?"

"You got it, poppie. And I have to say...she fine," the guy said, pointing to Raquel.

"That she is, my friend, that she is," Vic said, leading Raquel to the building entrance.

Idalis buzzed them in after Raquel said her name. The hallway smelled like a cross between fried plantains and urine. The urine was winning. These two former NYPD cops wouldn't find anything offensive though. As a matter of fact, the aroma was familiar from their vast catalogue of hallway odor experiences. They walked up two flights of stairs and found apartment 2E, letting themselves into the room through the partially opened door. The kitchen was to the right. Vic and Raquel could see the *Cafe Bustello* can prominently displayed on the small, white stove, and a small kitchenette table with several aluminum-foil-covered dishes. The living room contained a couch with end tables on either side. Matching lamps with painted butterflies sat on the tables. There was also a two-person loveseat and a winged chair with a brown, wooden coffee table. Only the tables did not have plastic covering. The floor had a small area rug on top of speckled linoleum.

Tia Carmen Auffant sat in the winged chair. Her face did not betray any mood. It would have been a perfect demeanor for the world championship of poker on ESPN.

"Hello, Raquel, you have grown into such a beautiful woman. Just like your momma when she was your age. Very pretty indeed," Idalis said in Spanish.

"Thank you, Idalis, my mother talks of you fondly and often. May I present...."

"Not necessary, dear. I know who you both are," interrupted Tia Carmen. "I will speak in English so Victor can understand me. My English is not perfect, so, if I don't know a word, I know you can both help me," Tia Carmen said nodding to Idalis and Raquel.

Idalis began serving piping hot coffee into cups that were set on the coffee table. There were cakes and cookies on small plates, milk in a creamer, and a sugar bowl. Tia Carmen opened her hands and pointed toward the table for Vic and Raquel to partake in the hospitality.

"Thank you, Tia Carmen. We appreciate you seeing us and for the coffee and nice treats," Raquel said.

"It's nothing, my dear. I knew your mother, too. I am older than she and Idalis. They were in school, and I was learning my gift from my dear *abuelita*. I knew your *abuelas*, too. Good and honest people. Raquel, we are all very proud of your achievements in school and then in the police department and now with your new life."

"Why, thank you, Tia Carmen. It's nice to hear all this from you. Would you like to have the things that we brought along?"

"Victor, you are a handsome man, and you love our Raquel," Tia Carmen said, ignoring Raquel's question.

"I do love her very much. And thank you for the compliment," Vic said taking in the whole experience. He now had a sense of the serious nature of Tia Carmen. She had a certain aura about her that intrigued him.

"Tia Carmen, I would like to ask you if you see a child in our future. I would like to have a baby, and we have some concerns," Raquel said.

"Ah, yes, indeed, a child. I definitely see a child in both of your futures. A child that is not yours."

"Oh, Tia Carmen, are we going to adopt a child? Perhaps I cannot have one of my own?" Raquel was feeling emotional.

Tia Carmen smiled at Raquel and then turned her attention to Vic.

"I do not need to hold your objects. Victor, you gave me tremendous energy when you came into my home. You make a clear reading. Your business will be very successful, but you will need to make it famous. It will not be famous only because of what you have done in the past. I can see your secret of what occurred in Rome. You did a good thing for the energy of the entire world. Now, there is a soul that you need to help. This soul is in the form of energy. The energy is caught in a place where it cannot be released. It has been in my view for many, many years. It came to me when our family came here from Puerto Rico. I was a young woman in my twenties then. A very sad story. A little boy left in a box--already dead. No one knows who he is or who took his physical energy. He was beaten, abused, and murdered. He alone has the answers that no one could discover for many years. You may be the one who, perhaps, can solve the mystery and free his energy. I do not believe in coincidence, Victor. Raquel brought you here, and I feel the boy's energy reaching out to me in a powerful way. Your energy will grow quickly from this. The boy has no name, but I can tell you his energy is still in Philadelphia, where his body was found and where his bones are now buried. Go, release him, and, then, come back to me," Tia Carmen said. She motioned at Idalis to fill her coffee cup.

"Can I ask you for more details, Tia Carmen? Philadelphia is a big city. Where do I start?" Vic asked.

"Victor, you should know that he is called the Boy in the Box. Many policemen have tried to find his killer before you. They have all failed because they lack your drive, your energy, your past. The rest is your world. You are a detective. Do what you do best. My advice for you is to follow your instincts," Tia Carmen said. She now turned her attention to Raquel.

"Raquel, I know why you are here. Victor will do this first, and then I will tell you what you want to know. You should help your man with this. You have helped him come out of great despair, but, be warned, that anguish can return to him at any time. You must be strong, my little girl. The life of any child is precious. Be like a mother to this wondering boy's energy. You cannot take care of your child until you first take care of this child. I have to take my walk now. Give my hello to your mother. Her life energy is still very, very strong."

"Thank you, Tia Carmen. I was hoping for other news. You have your reasons though, and I respect you. Please stay well," Raquel said.

"Oh, one more thing. Victor, you should start immediately. Time is growing short. I cannot explain why I see the boy's energy flickering," Tia Carmen said and quickly left the living room for the solace of her bedroom. Idalis said her goodbyes. Vic put a hefty wad of cash into the coffee can just before he and Raquel left the apartment in stunned silence.

"Hey, poppie, the car is still here, look," The wheelchair guy said. His wide, gross smile awaited his reward.

"Now look at that. Good job, my friend. Let's make a trade. You give me that half a twenty, and I give you a whole hundred. But you have to do something for me," Vic said.

"Anything for you, poppie."

Vic handed him his cell phone set on camera.

"Take a picture of me and my lady."

"You got it, poppie."

The wheelchair guy took the phone and looked into the view finder as Vic and Raquel held each other.

"Okay, poppie *chulo* and mami *chula*...ready...say cheese!"

21

CHAPTER 4

Raquel and Vic spoke a bit about their reading with Tia Carmen on the way back to the city. Vic thought it was interesting and still referred to it as voodoo, but Raquel felt a bit cheated. After all, she wanted to hear about a baby and not some child who was killed in the fifties, sad as it was. Raquel was on the verge of tears and in no mood for dinner. When they arrived at their apartment, Raquel took a shower while Vic's curiosity sent him to Google the Boy in the Box case.

"So, what do you think about that boy she was talking about?" Raquel asked. She was drying her long, silky, dark brown hair with a towel.

"Look at this, honey. There is an entire web site dedicated to this case. See, they even have the kid's morgue shots. There is an awful lot of information that's exposed. Evidently, the pieces weren't put together in spite of what looks to be some solid detective work by the Philadelphia PD," Vic said, never taking his eyes from the PC.

"How old did she say he was?"

Vic ignored Raquel's question. "He was left in a cardboard box in a not so remote area. It says that a young man called it in and then another young guy later called and said he saw the body as well."

"How did he die?" Raquel asked. She sat next to Vic, her damp hair and perfume arousing Vic's attention.

"Man, you smell great," Vic said. He leaned over and kissed her neck sending a shiver down her arched back."

"Okay, detective, you've got my attention. I'm all yours," Raquel said.

Vic refocused on the screen. "Poor kid was battered a bit. It says he died from a fractured skull. No signs of sexual molestation. Lots of bruises."

"And no idea who he belonged to or any positive leads?"

"A few theories, a few dead end leads. I need to read more about the case. Do me a favor, Raquel; make some coffee. I want to study this a bit. It's fascinating--how all these people worked on this for years and never found the perp or perps is incredible."

"Can I help?" Raquel asked.

"If we decide to take on the case, you certainly will."

"If?"

"Honey, I'm not sure if it's something we can spend time on. We need to discuss this," Vic said, still reading the facts.

"I guess it's too cold for you," Raquel said.

"Well, it happened in 1957. That's not cold; that's a friggin' iceberg."

"Hmmm…I seem to recall you working on the John Deegan case, which started in 1956, and you busted that one wide open." Raquel sounded a bit testy.

"I know what you're thinking. If we don't take the case on, you can't get another reading from that Tia Carmen lady. C'mon, honey, this is a long shot at best. We can't live our lives based on superstitions and some old clairvoyant in the hood."

"And, if you took the case and were able to solve it, don't you think we could get some great recognition?"

"I don't want to do it for that reason, Raquel. Cashing in on a dead kid from the fifties is not what I want to do. There are so many cases like this in the United States. Listen, let's read up on this one. It could be a challenge, sure. Let's spend some time on it and make a decision based on what we see and the likelihood of solving the murder. Chances are, whoever did this is already dead."

"So, if they are alive, they skate. The perfect murder."

"Why are you so intent on doing something like this?" Vic asked.

"Why? Tia Carmen didn't just pull this out of her ass. There is a reason that maybe we just don't understand right now. Maybe she's heard from the kid's energy like she said. The challenge can put the company in the limelight like the Deegan case did for you. I think it's good business."

"And, if we come up empty?" Vic asked.

"Big fucking deal. So, we wasted two weeks."

"Let's do the research and make a decision. I promise to keep an open mind. I'm gonna read for a while, take a nice shower, and…" Vic said. He winked at Raquel.

"And have wild-monkey sex. That works for me."

Vic spent most of the evening reading everything he could find online about the Boy in the Box case. He knew a few Philadelphia detectives from a long-ago case and thought about calling them, but the hour was too late. He would save that for the next day after he'd gathered his thoughts. In Vic's mind, he was apprehensive about jumping into a case that was picked apart by many Philly homicide detectives, a volunteer sleuth organization called the Vidocq Society, whose members were retired FBI agents and other law enforcement experts, and a Facebook page full of theories and conjecture on the subject. The society is appropriately named after a former criminal Eugène François Vidocq, who became the founder of the famous crime detection *Sûreté Nationale* in France during the early 1800s. Vidocq started his own private detective agency, the first of its kind. He is considered by many to be the father of modern criminality.

As planned, Vic took his shower, added a splash of his favorite cologne, and snuggled up to Raquel who was sound asleep. On her hip she left a Post-it note. "Open for business." Vic stifled his laughter. He adored Raquel's sense of humor and sexy playfulness. His gentle touch on Raquel's firm butt and kisses on the back of her neck were enough to get the low moaning started. Another intense lovemaking session kept them both awake for hours. When they finished, they embraced in the middle of the bed and began to fall asleep in each other's arms. Just before going under, Raquel said, "Baby, I love you. You were fabulous as always. I'm just surprised the smoke alarm didn't go off." Vic was already asleep.

A few hours later, Vic awoke and bolted upright on the bed. He looked around the room for a few seconds until he realized that what he had just experienced was a dream.

Vic shook Raquel gently. "Honey, honey I need to talk to you."

"Just talk? Or are you ready to go again?" Raquel joked.

"Raquel, we are gonna take this case, no doubt about it," Vic said.

"What? You wake me from a dead sleep to tell me what I already know?"

"What do you mean already know?"

"Baby, you could never walk away from a challenge, especially when it involves a child. I know you too well, my love."

"Well, that little boy was here. I don't mean only in my dream. He was fucking standing right here with us."

"Shut the fuck up!" Raquel said. She pulled the sheets over her head.

Raquel thought that Vic was poking fun at Tia Carmen.

"No bullshit, honey. He was here, I tell you. I could sense something more than a dream. He's about five, maybe six years old. He looks just like he did in the morgue shots:still bruised; no clothes on but he was wearing the blanket they found on top of him in that cardboard box. Holy shit," Vic said as he placed the bottom of both palms on his eyes and rubbed them as if to polish the memory.

Raquel pushed the sheets off and sat upright on the bed.

"Did he say anything?" Raquel asked.

"Yes...yes he did," Vic said. He paused and felt a bead of cold sweat on his forehead.

"Well, what did he say, baby?"

"He said, 'Mister, would you please help me?'"

"That's it?"

"That's all he said to me. His eyes were dark with an artificial blue color surrounding them like it said in the autopsy report. I have to do this. Fuck that it's good or bad for business. This kid was here. He is searching for justice or something. Maybe that energy thing is real. I don't know. That crazy Tia woman of yours just reopened this kid's case."

CHAPTER 5

In the morning after his startling Boy in the Box dream, Vic reached out to Philadelphia Homicide Detective Collin Frank. They had met a few times over the years, and Vic had developed a fast friendship with Collin. A murder case had brought them together way back when Vic was first promoted to homicide detective. They kept in touch from time to time, exchanging e-mails and frequent telephone calls.

The telephone rang at PPD.

"Homicide, Frank."

"Well, my old friend, catch any bad guys lately?" Vic said.

"Ahhh…the famous Vic Gonnella. I'd know that New York accent anywhere."

"Getting close to retirement, Collin?"

"Are you kidding? Kids in school, wife not working. I need a second job," Collin said.

"Bullshit, I'm told you have your communion money wrapped around your baptism envelopes."

"Whoever told you that is a lying sack of shit, Vic. What's up, pal?"

"First of all, my offer for you to work for my company is always open. When you retire, I will have a place for you. Unless you want to sit around and get a big belly," Vic said, laughing at his own remark.

"No big belly for me, Vic. I'm working out and running. I may do the New York Marathon this year," he said jokingly.

"Then you and your wife will stay with Raquel and me."

"You're on!"

"If you're interested, I have something for you. That's if you are up for a cold case challenge," Vic said.

"Shoot."

"Know much about that Boy in the Box case in your town?"

"Who doesn't? Don't tell me you want to chase that down," Collin said.

"I do. I need help though, and I would like you to assist Raquel and me."

"I'll work with her anytime," Collin said, laughing.

"I'm part of the package, you hornbag. Do you need approval?"

"My CO will think I'm nuts. That case is colder than a witch's tit, Vic. It's been picked apart by the best of 'em. Obviously, it's still an open case. Why the interest?"

"For now, let's just say personal reasons. I've read what's online. It's a captivating story, and I want to see if there is anything that was overlooked. Can we get access to the files?"

"Not a problem. When my CO hears it's you, he will be out of his mind. Since that Deegan case, you're a cult figure down here," Collin said.

"What's your schedule like? We'd like to come down in a couple days and stay a while. I have rooms at the Loews Philadelphia Hotel. We can discuss your pay when we see you."

"I'm not interested in taking your money. On second thought, my wife just told me that my daughter Angela needs braces. Just kidding, Vic. I'd love to help. I can take a few vacation days and pour over the case with you. I know a bit about the case, but, I have to admit, I'm not an expert on the subject by any means. I'm friendly with the detective sergeant in charge of that case. Great guy."

"I'll make it worth your while. How about day after tomorrow?"

"No problem. I'll text you my office address. Is 10 o'clock too early for you?"

"We'll be there at 8:30, wise ass."

Little did Detective Collin Frank know he was soon to be immersed in Philadelphia's oldest open murder case in modern times.

Vic and Raquel spent the rest of the day reading over the case and taking copious notes. The more they read, the more entrenched they became. Vic's Type A personality was in overdrive.

"Listen to this, honey. The guy who found the body, a Frederick J. Benonis, student at LaSalle College, was asked why he was walking through the thicket when he found the body. There was a school for wayward girls that was run by nuns nearby. Can you imagine? They actually called them wayward girls back then. He said he would drive by the school and park his car to look at the girls. He said he saw a rabbit run past, so, he pulled his car over and chased it into the field," Vic said, pointing to his PC.

"So?" Raquel asked.

"The guy was twenty-six years old. What kind of twenty-six-year-old stops his car to chase a fucking rabbit?"

"Hmm, maybe the kind that jerks off in his car, watching young girls in their uniforms?"

"That doesn't make him a killer," Vic said.

"That just makes him a creep," Raquel said.

"I hope this guy is still around. Oh, and listen to this. He didn't report seeing the body until the next day. He saw the Boy in the Box the day before and was afraid to report it. His relative was a priest. The priest told him to report seeing the dead boy to the police immediately. Strange."

"Interesting. Now listen to this, honey. This report says that there was the school for girls and also another place that unwed pregnant women went to have their babies nearby. Maybe the boy came from there." Raquel was reading from the web site on her iPad.

"He wasn't an infant," Vic said.

"There could be a tie in," Raquel said.

"I can't wait to get down there. By tomorrow night, we will have some questions for Collin. His badge will open some doors, I'm sure."

"I found this Facebook page. It's a few years old. I'm going to read every post and jot down any plausible theories," Raquel said.

"Good idea. Discount any of the lunatic stuff. Some of those Facebook posts may be conspiracy theorists."

"Gotcha."

"Once we see what the Philadelphia PD has on file and their follow up to any leads, we'll know a lot more than simple conjecture," Vic said.

"That's assuming they did a thorough job. It seems like they became emotionally involved. Look at this photograph." Raquel flipped her iPad for Vic to see a photo of men carrying a small casket.

"These are the detectives on the case taking the boy from the church to his grave. And this one shows them at the funeral home with the closed casket."

"Why is that an issue?" Vic said.

"I'm not sure. It seems to me that they cared a lot for this poor kid. Sometimes, emotions can cloud judgment."

"Conversely, it can make cops work even harder," Vic said.

"Maybe. But, sometimes, you can't see the forest for the trees."

CHAPTER 6

Vic and Raquel took the next day to wrap up some loose ends in their office. As far as anyone knew, they were taking a much-needed, impromptu vacation. A week or so is what they told their staff. Unless it was a dire emergency, they were not to be disturbed. The staff was all former law enforcement professionals who knew not to ask any questions or form any speculation on the sudden absence of their bosses. What was assumed was there was no vacation in the offing. If Vic and Raquel needed assistance for whatever reason, the staff would act accordingly.

The trip from New York to Philadelphia was uneventful except for the awful smell on the New Jersey Turnpike near Elizabeth.

"Jesus, Raquel, couldn't you hold that one in? Should I pull over to find a rest room? Damn, my eyes are watering," Vic said.

"The one who smelt it dealt it, Vic, you foul man." Raquel waved her hand in front of her face.

"How can anyone live here?" Vic asked.

"Remember your first DOA? Mine was dead for about seven days. When I walked into the building, I threw up in the lobby. And he was on the third floor. I guess people get used to stink after a while," Raquel said.

"This is nasty, and our windows are closed. Can you imagine if they were open?"

The rest of the ride was filled with discussions about current events in New Jersey. How embarrassing it must be to live in a state that boasted Snookie, *Jersey Shore*, the bully governor, that Bridgegate nonsense, and *Housewives of New Jersey*. Vic saved the state by hitting play on the car's CD player. *The Best of Bruce Springsteen* made the state look like a better place, and the couple sang a few of the songs together--and loudly. Vic and Raquel intentionally avoided discussing the case as everything they could possibly know so far was found on the internet.

They arrived at Philadelphia's police headquarters in under two hours at 8:15 a.m.

Vic and Raquel were escorted to the homicide unit where Detective Collin Frank was already at his desk.

"She gets hotter, and you get older, Vic." Collin went right to a beaming Raquel and hugged her.

"So, this is where the oldest municipal police department in the country has their HQ? Pretty fancy digs if I may say," Vic said. He and Collin exchanged a friendly handshake and shoulder bump.

"Yeah, it's pretty new. We call it the Round House. I'm happy to be here. I'm happy to be anywhere at this point. Half of my friends and family are out of work. Times suck. But you guys are doing great, I see," Collin said.

"Lucky," Vic said.

"Lucky is once. You guys are the model for all detectives in the country. Great careers, solve a high profile case, start an investigation company; now, that's what I'm talkin' 'bout."

"Family all good?" Raquel asked Collin.

"Wonderful, thanks for asking. Now, I have to embarrass you two and bring you into a conference room upstairs. The commissioner, police chief, my boss, the inspector, and some other brass all want to meet you guys and take some shots for their desks. They need a bit of a diversion. It was announced yesterday that Philadelphia has the highest per capita murder rate in the country," Collin said.

"Oh, Christ. Sure, pal. How about we sign a few baseballs while we're at it?" Vic said.

Collin brought them down a long, sterile corridor and up a flight of stairs. Along the way, Vic shook a few hands and winked at a few female cops and some secretaries. He was aware of all of the men checking out Raquel. It made him proud that his lady was so appealing and sexy. Raquel was used to the attention and ignored it, making little eye contact with the men and smiling broadly at the women. This was serious business and, by no means, a public relations or social call to Raquel.

They entered a large conference room, which had an enormous, cherry-wood table with at least twenty plush, leather chairs all pushed neatly at attention into the table. A crowd of uniformed and suited men and women were standing, waiting for the celebrity cop visitors. Collin made the introductions.

Vic and Raquel were caught up in a whirlwind of smiling faces and flashbulbs, something they had gotten used to after the Deegan case came to an end. After their cordial photo opps with the big brass, Collin walked back to his office with Vic, Raquel, and his boss, Inspector Tony Scarpa, who had earlier introduced himself as "Tony Scarpa, no relation to the mob boss, Scarfo." Scarpa, a short, balding man with a stocky build, looked and sounded like every Italian mob guy in New York and Philadelphia. His piercing, brown eyes and rapid speech made him seem a lot taller.

"It's a real pleasure meeting you two. Detective Frank tells me that you are looking into the Boy in the Box case. Ya know, a lot of people would have an ego problem. Ya know, someone comin' into their town, lookin' to solve a fifty-some-odd-year case. Not us." He shifted his stance and continued. "Ya know, this case has been picked apart by dozens of good cops, FBI, forensic people, you name it. At this point, it's all about the kid in that grave. We will do whatever you need to help you. Detective Frank asked for vacation time. No way; he is on the clock with us and is at your disposal full time. His load is heavy right now, but we can move a few things around. Ya know, you guys would do the same for us," Scarpa said without so much as inhaling once.

"Thanks, Inspector. Do you have any gut feelings about the case yourself?" Vic asked.

"Not really. I was never that involved with it. Only what I heard around here from some of the old timers. I never really looked at the case that closely. Shit, I wasn't even born when this happened. Can I ask why you picked this cold case when there are thousands around the country? I'm pretty sure New York has a good list, too."

"I just like a challenge, and I like kids. It tugged at my heart strings when I heard about this one," Vic said. He was not about to talk about Tia Carmen and his dream. Scarpa seemed the type to laugh right in his face, hearing that kind of thing.

"Inspector, we would like to see the evidence and reports. Are they still available?" Raquel asked.

"Yes ma'am. We brought it all into a room for you guys. You will have total access to everything we have on the case. Everything we have is in eight boxes. Unfortunately, the men on the case are all dead or mentally incapacitated, so, there isn't much first-hand knowledge. I suspect the perps are all gone, too...but ya never know, right? Detective Frank will bring you to the evidence room. If you need anything--anything at all--you just call me. Everyone in the building is at your service," Scarpa said.

"Inspector, if we can ever return the favor, just call us," Vic said.

"Look, Vic, the blanket that he was wrapped in when he was found in the box. It's so cheap and flimsy. I had a different idea about it. I thought it was handmade and nice. It's a piece of crap. It's inexpensive, cotton, flannel material," Raquel said as she looked at the blanket that had diamonds and blocks in green, white, rust, and brown colors.

Vic, Raquel, and Collin were walking around a large table that had the evidence found on and around the dead boy in 1957. The cardboard box that the boy was found in, measuring 15" x 19" x 35", was now folded and kept in a large, plastic evidence bag, just a regular box that carried a baby bassinet with a bold, red "FRAGILE" warning.

"Not much to find out about the box. We know where it came from, a J.C. Penney store near here. And the photo shows that the box was open, exposing the boy's body, rather than being taped or wrapped up somehow. The box may have already been at the scene. The killer could have just placed the body inside," Raquel said.

Also on the table along with boxes of files wrapped inside of plastic baggies were a child's tan scarf, a black shoe, size 1, a 7 1/8 blue derby hat, a small boy's flannel shirt, size 4, and a white handkerchief with an embroidered letter "G."

"Well, I guess we can get started with the files. Let's dig in. Collin, can you get us a large blackboard or something where we can start putting our notes? And maybe a peg board thing?" Vic asked.

"Just open that brown box on the wall behind you. There is a board with colored pens and a peg board on the opposite side," Collin said.

"Wow, fancy schmancy. So, no chalk screeching on blackboards around here," Vic said.

"I hate that sound. It goes right through me," Raquel said.

"Here is the box with all of the post-mortem photos," Collin said, lifting the heavy, cardboard box to show the weight.

"Maybe we should just get the macabre part of the job over with and start with that one. I think we will have the visual of the dead boy fresh in our minds while we read the reports," Raquel said.

"Good idea. Let's take a look before lunch," Vic said.

Collin carried the box of photos to an adjacent table. He opened the box slowly, and an eerie silence, a feeling of remorse and sadness, was palpable in the room.

The dead boy was frozen in time by the photographs. It was as if the child were right in the room with them.

The dark hair on Vic's arms and on the back of his neck stood at attention. His stomach quivered like it did when he was in grade school. Bad memories poured into his mind like a torrent.

Raquel could tell that Vic was in a sudden anxious state. She said nothing, pretending to be engrossed by the first few photos that Collin removed from the box.

"This poor kid. This poor, poor baby," Vic said.

"Look at this one. He was laid in the box with his hands folded and the blanket around him, not just thrown in. Looks like someone cared about him. Maybe an accidental death?" Collin said.

"Unlikely. This kid was pretty battered," Raquel said.

"But someone took the time to trim his nails and cut his hair," Vic said.

"Perhaps to hide or suppress evidence. What do you make of the water-soaked feet and hand? Look at that wrinkling effect. Only water does that, right?" Raquel asked.

"Maybe he was in a bathtub and one hand was out," Collin said.

"Or maybe he was dropped in a drum or a well of some sort and later removed," Raquel said.

"How long was he dead when he was found?" Vic asked.

"The report said as long as a few weeks. Don't forget it was February. Real cold, so decay was delayed," Raquel said.

"It was probably a woman who dropped off the body," Vic said.

"What? Why do you think that?" Collin asked.

"The way he was laid out. With a lot of care. Also, a man would have likely taken the time to bury the body," Vic said.

"Ground may have been frozen," Raquel said.

"A man would have found a way to hide the body. A few whacks with a pick, ten minutes of digging, and the body is gone. Whoever dropped this little boy in that lot wanted him to be found and given a decent burial," Vic said.

"At the risk of being caught?" Raquel asked.

" Fifty-seven years later, and no one has been apprehended," Vic said. *No wonder this boy can't rest,* Vic thought to himself.

"It's so wrong on so many levels," Raquel said, interrupting Vic's thoughts.

"Right. Let's start going over the detective reports. Then, I'd like to see where the body was found," Vic said.

CHAPTER 7

Collin Frank drove Vic and Raquel to the Fox Chase section of Philadelphia.

"It's called the Fox Chase section because, back in the 1700s, the rich people of the city would go fox hunting there. Lots of meadows and marshes back then. There was even a British troop raid that overtook Continental Army soldiers on Verree Road. Lots of great history and, of course, this murder. We're on Verree Road now. I don't think anyone nowadays thinks of the great patriots caught by the redcoats right here practically on this spot," Collin said.

"Are we near Susquehanna Road, where the body was found?" Raquel asked.

"Next right," Collin said.

"Totally different than the photographs we saw," Vic said.

"Oh, it's all been developed. In 1957, there were no single-family homes along Susquehanna Road. The only large buildings then housed the school for wayward girls, run by the Sisters of the Good Shepherd of the Catholic Church. The school was directly across from the field where the boy was found." Vic and Raquel both looked at each other with that oh-here-we-go-again look while Collin continued. "This is approximately where he was found." Collin parked the car and pointed to a row of three-story homes that all looked alike with two-car garages prominent on the lower part of the houses.

"Amazing development since then," Vic said.

"Yeah, it's a nice, white, middle-class neighborhood. No trouble really. Hard-working people. Back in the fifties, there was an empty, weed-overgrown lot here that some of the locals used as a garbage dump," Collin said.

"And someone decided to dump a battered little boy's body here," Raquel almost whispered as she gazed around trying to take it all in. "Totally disgusting."

"Where was the school for wayward girls?" Vic asked.

"See that development across the street? Good Shepherd was right up there. Now, it's all these retirement homes that were developed a few years ago. Really nice homes inside. My mom's sister lives here. State-of-the-art facility. I think the Church still runs it somehow," Collin said.

Two teenage girls were walking past the car when Vic, who was sitting in the back seat, tapped Raquel on the shoulder.

"Humor me, Ruiz. Jump out with me for a sec."

Vic approached the girls with Raquel next to him.

"Excuse me, ladies. We're from New York. I'm a writer. Have you girls ever heard of the Boy in the Box case? A little kid that was found dead around here someplace?"

"Oh, that's just a myth," the taller of the two said.

"No, no, it's real. I heard my parents mention it, and they said the murderer was never found," the other young lady said.

"Do they ever mention it in school?" Raquel asked.

"No, never. It's not a really big deal here," the shorter girl said.

"Okay, thanks, have a great day," Raquel said.

"Let's try again," Vic said.

A man and a college-aged boy were pruning a weeping cherry tree next to their home.

"S'cuse me, guys. We are writers from New York. Do you know of a young boy who was found dead in a box around here?" Vic asked.

The man answered, "Yes, that was many, many years ago. He was found right along here somewhere. Sad thing. I wasn't even born yet."

"Yeah, my grandparents talk about it sometimes. No one even knows who the kid was."

"Did your grandparents have any theories as to who the killer was?" Vic asked.

"My grandma said it was the carnival people or something like that."

"They used to have a touring carnival right around this area. Haven't had one here in decades," the older man said.

"Well, thanks for your time, guys," Vic said.

Vic and Raquel got back into the car.

"What amazes me is that life goes on. New homes, new stores, Dunkin' Donuts, no more lots. No one claimed the boy; no one was apprehended. It's like this kid was never even alive," Raquel said.

"Did you expect a plaque or a statue here?" Vic asked.

"It wasn't for lack of trying. Sergeant Cullinane, one of the detectives on the case, told me when I was a rookie that there was an enormous media campaign in Philadelphia and the Delaware Valley to bring constant attention to the general public. Information Wanted posters were circulated throughout the city by Philly PD, newspaper articles ran for weeks, radio and television news reports sought information, but nothing at all came up. Philadelphia Gas Works sent a notice with the boy's morgue photo in every mailed gas bill. Our guys were all over this thing. There is still a hint of embarrassment about this case if you want the god's honest truth."

"Who was the first officer on the scene?" Vic asked.

"His name is in the file. I don't recall it. Like I said, I'm not an expert on the case, but I did hear that he's dead. Anyhow, I was told that, when all the squad cars were lined up along this street and we were doing the limited forensics that was done back then, a few sisters from the Good Shepherd Home walked over and were praying the rosary for the boy. The whole community was shocked," Collin said.

"Any priests come by?" Vic asked.

"Not that I know of. Why?" Collin said.

"Just curious is all," Vic said and glanced at Raquel.

Raquel had seen that look on Vic's face before and knew where his mind was going. She made a mental note to bring it up when they were alone.

"Not much goes on here for us to see. Do we have time to visit the boy's grave? I understand from reading the website that the PPD raised money and had the boy's body exhumed and reinterred with a small monument," Raquel said.

"Sure, it's about a fifteen minute drive. He's buried at Ivy Hill cemetery over in the Mt. Airy section of the city. Yeah, some of the guys and the Vidocq Society set it up. Vidocq is all over this case. We will get to them at some point."

"Let's go over a few things while we drive over," Vic said.

"An autopsy was performed on the boy's body later on the day he was found. I took some notes from the report. The ME determined that the child died from "trauma to the head." He had numerous bruises and lacerations over much of his body. They were not even certain of his age because he was malnourished. Christ, you could see how thin he was in the morgue shots. His toenails and fingernails had been recently clipped, and he had been given a very crude haircut. Clippings of his hair were found on his neck and torso, so, the haircut had to be very fresh, maybe post-mortem. There were no signs that the boy had been recently sexually molested. There was, however, a brownish substance that clung to the walls of his esophagus, and an unknown, blue chemical or dye was found in both his eyes. No bones were fractured except for his skull," Raquel said.

Vic expelled the air from his lungs and covered his eyes with his right hand. He seemed upset to Raquel. Collin checked him out in the rear view mirror and wondered for a moment if he should pull the car over.

"What was it that was in his throat?" Vic asked.

"They never said. No definitive analysis was done," Raquel said.

"Forgive me, Collin, how fucked up is that? They have a substance, and they can't figure it out?"

"1957, Vic. They weren't all that sophisticated back then. They did the best they could with what they had," Collin said. He was trying not to sound defensive, but it came out that way.

"I'm sorry, buddy. I'm feeling a bit crappy. Let's head back. We can see the grave another day."

CHAPTER 8

Cleveland, Ohio-June, 1956

Father James Nelson and Sister Mary Magdalene of the Crown of Thorns had been having a secret affair for some time. Putting aside their vows of celibacy and the rules of their individual orders, Father Nelson and Sister Mary found the time and the places within the confines of the Marycrest Home for Wayward Girls to have their assignations. Marycrest was a sister school to the Good Shepherd Home in Philadelphia, where the Boy in the Box was found. It was run by the same order of Catholic nuns. Like Good Shepherd, Marycrest was an old, brick building, five stories high with a cross at its peak. The hallways had sparkling clean, green terrazzo floors. The sanitized smell of pine and bleach was reminiscent of a hospital. Nothing was out of order; nothing was out of place. Every room had a crucifix adorning one wall as did every hallway. Heavy, oak doors that led to what seemed like classrooms were kept closed at all times on the first floor. The second story housed a large chapel and administrative offices. The remainder of the building was made up of dormitory rooms. Sixteen girls per dorm, each a replica of the other. Two rows of eight beds facing each other with a five-foot path between them. Not much opportunity for privacy. The toilet had four stalls and six basins for washing. The shower, just off the toilet, was communal with six heads and no curtains at all. Very clean, very antiseptic, very depressing. There was a small cafeteria in the basement level of the building.

Her office, his office, the confessional, the boiler room, whatever was quiet and available. The two clerical lovers found their various meeting places incredibly stimulating. Sister Mary especially enjoyed giving Father oral sex in the confessional when the chapel was closed and dark.

The vestment-wearing lovers enjoyed the badness of having sex in various parts of the school. They would plot their fantasy locations: on the floor behind the altar, in the cafeteria on a table, and also in that "special" room in the basement where they kept the especially bad girls in solitary confinement.

Father James and Sister Mary Magdalene broke every rule imaginable except one; they did not use artificial birth control. After all, preventing birth was sinful. No condoms for this couple as that was against their religion. They kept to the rhythm method, tracking Sister Mary's menstrual cycle together. On the dangerous days, the confessional was fine for Father Nelson's needs.

Sister Mary and Father Nelson also discovered that they were both attracted to the girls at the school. At times, Sister Mary would wear the pale blue, simple uniform that the students wore, sending Father into a wild frenzy while satisfying her own fantasy.

Brutalizing the girls was equally a turn on, and the punishments were often meted out from Sister Mary while Father Nelson watched. Sometimes he would sit in a chair with his hand under his cassock, gently playing with himself. Other times, he would be inconspicuous in a partly open closet, flailing away.

Father Nelson and Sister Mary were in love with their sexual fantasies and perversions and with each other. If they were a lay couple, they would have made a striking pair. Father Nelson was tall with close-cropped, blond hair, blue eyes, and sharp, angular features. He had the body of an athlete and a full set of perfectly aligned, pearly white teeth. Sister Mary had the map of Ireland on her face. Even in the habit that encircled her face, Sister Mary was a stunner. Her huge eyes were captivating and changed colors depending on her surroundings. Blue, green, hazel; and, oftentimes, her eyes were each a different color, one green and one blue. Her full lips covered a beautiful, broad smile that lit up her round face. Sister Mary could have been a model had she not chosen to be married to Jesus Christ.

Sometime in early 1956, Father Nelson let things go a bit too far with one of the fifteen- year-old students. Unbeknownst to Sister Mary, Father began having sex with the teen. He groomed her for months until she believed that she was the most special girl he had ever met. He convinced her they would share a special love sent by Jesus that would remain their secret always. He went even further and convinced the unsuspecting adolescent that, once she could leave the school, he would leave the priesthood and they would be together forever. How nice of him.

In his passion for the young girl, Father Nelson decided that *coitus interruptus* was the best means of birth control. The rhythm method could not be employed in this situation due to its lack of spontaneity. He realized that, when she finally bought into his bullshit, he had to be ready. No tracking of menstrual history was possible. After a few months of his sexual abuse on the teen, the inevitable event occurred. She became pregnant.

All hell broke loose.

The girl pointed the blame on Father Nelson, who, of course, vehemently denied any wrongdoing. He was immediately supported by Sister Mary Magdalene of the Crown of Thorns as to his religiosity and integrity. The school and the archdiocese went into protection mode and circled the wagons of silence and denial around Marycrest. The girl in question was given counseling and moved to a home for unwed mothers. The home was as far away from Cleveland as possible, a similar home that was run by the

Sisters of the Good Shepherd in the Fox Chase section of Philadelphia near the Good Shepherd School for wayward girls.

CHAPTER 9

The Good Shepherd School was not the only show in town on Susquehanna Road. Once every two years, a traveling carnival leased an empty lot from the city of Philadelphia for the month of August in the Fox Chase section of the city. The last time the carnival was in town was the summer of 1956.

The Carnival was run by a *bon vivant* everyone knew as Sergio. Sergio's flowery, sing-song-sounding Italian accent was really Romany. The English name for the Romani is Gypsy.

His deep-set, dark eyes and wavy, jet-black hair speckled with gray made the middle-aged Sergio an instant hit with most of the ladies. Sergio was the cover name for Ferka Pitti, a Sinti Gypsy who fled Europe just before World War II got into full swing, when the Nazis were beginning to kill his people by the tens of thousands. Ferka Pitti's family were being systematically annihilated by the Germans who decided it was in their best interest to deport all Gypsies to concentration camps where they would be shot, hung, or gassed almost immediately upon arrival. Upwards of five hundred thousand Gypsies were murdered during the Holocaust, a word the Sinti called Porajmos, the Devouring.

Ferka Pitti's eight-year-old twin brothers, whom he adored and who idolized him, were selected to meet with and be experimented upon by the notorious, sadistic murderer, Dr. Josef Mengele at Sachsenhausen, a concentration death camp just north of Berlin. Ferka, then just seventeen, decided to take matters into his own hands. He tossed a homemade bomb into a transport truck carrying ten German soldiers, sending them all to a horrible, fiery death.

The retribution that was taken by the Germans upon the *Sinti* for this rebellious act made much of what the Nazis did during the Holocaust seem tame. A massacre followed the killing of the soldiers. Two hundred *Sinti* men, women, and children were slaughtered by rope, bayonet, and pistol. The men were forced to watch as their wives and children were killed first.

Ferka lived up to the Romany meaning of his name, "free." He avoided the awful bloodletting in his village after he toasted those soldiers. Ferka hid in the forest for days. He was aided by partisans and eventually made his way to the United States and the Hartford Circus where he learned his trade among other Gypsies.

Ferka became Sergio, and his carnival was one of the biggest and best in the country. It was arguably among the best events of the year in Northern Philadelphia. After all, the beloved Philadelphia Phillies finished twenty-two games behind the Brooklyn Dodgers for the National League Pennant. Seventy-one wins to eighty-three losses did not put too many asses in the seats at Connie Mack stadium. Sergio's Ferris Wheel was one of the main attractions at the moveable carnival with its multi-pastel-colored seats, which seemed to tip forward as the wheel approached the summit, sending screams of panic cascading down upon the carnival guests.

There was the kissing booth with the sexiest brunette who had the biggest, reddest lips ever seen in the state of Pennsylvania. Next to the booth, the coldest tap beer to wet the whistles of the adoring men who often used upwards of ten coupons from the twenty coupon book just to lay their chops upon the dark bombshell's lips. Hot toffee;, golden, lightly salted popcorn, the pinkest cotton candy, plump, juicy wieners, German pretzels with little salt diamonds, large, juicy candy apples, fresh coconut slices in water, chocolate and vanilla custard ice cream, and loads of other carnival delicacies made the aroma of the fair a gastronomic intoxication.

Dante's Inferno was the scary house-of-horrors, complete with several layers of hell and a live, hooded grim reaper beckoning the visitors to enter. At times, to add to the screaming of those inside the Inferno, the mysterious soul harvester would grab an unsuspecting guest with his seven-foot hook.

Pony rides for the kids, a convoy of Peterbilt trucks on a track, the Good Ole Boys flea market for the knickknack collectors, and a moving music truck that played the latest Rock n' Roll with scantily clad, sexy ladies and topless muscle men musicians made the fantasy of the carnival the place to be in Fox Chase.

What came along with Sergio and his carnival were the itinerant carnival workers, some of whom decided to stay in the community rather than continue with the gig in the next city on the schedule.

Sergio had rules for his workers: no fraternizing with the guests, keep your hands off the kids, don't look at the mommies, smile bright, say please and thank you, ma'am and sir, and try to take every last cent out of their pocketbooks, pockets, and wallets, and that included the kids.

Sergio was totally unaware of the actions of a married couple under his employ who had admitted in 1961 to permitting six of their ten children to die of malnutrition and neglect and disposing their bodies in various locations along the carnival route. The Dudleys took a liking to the Fox Chase section of Philadelphia and stayed for a brief time.

CHAPTER 10

By the time Vic and Raquel returned to their hotel room, it was obvious that he was in distress. His face was ashen and sweaty, and his breathing was rapid. Vic was having a panic attack.

"Oh, baby, you need to calm down. What's wrong?"

Raquel quickly got a cold, wet washcloth for Vic's forehead.

"What's wrong? Areyoukiddenmeorwhat??? Every time I think this thing is dead and buried, it rears its ugly head, and I'm right back where I started," Vic said.

"Tell me what set you off, baby."

"Being where the boy was found, just being around there, the vision of those nuns praying, and thinking that a priest may have been involved sent me over the side again. It just brings back horrible memories and thoughts, Raquel. I'll be okay."

"Yes, you will. But you need to understand that not all nuns and not all priests are bad. What happened to you was horrible, but there are some great people in the Church who do fantastic things to help others."

"Bullshit. You know as well as I do that every priest and every nun knows which of their colleagues are molesting kids. They just choose not to blow the whistle to protect their secure lives. So… bullshit."

"No, not bullshit. Fact! Sure, you are suffering, but look how far you have come. Your life is great, you have the best life has to offer, and a small set back is expected. Remember what the doctor said: post-traumatic stress disorder is a tough thing to overcome, but, by talking it out and living your life, it will diminish over time. You've been great for so long and without that medication. I'm so proud of you, Vic."

"Damn it. It comes from left field and, wham, I'm back in that creep's grasp. Maybe Deegan had the right idea. Kill the fuckers." Vic was starting to feel better and laughed at what he said.

"Good, your color is starting to come back. You had me scared for a minute, baby. Look, if you want to call this case off, I have no problem going back to the city and just going forward with our lives."

"Impossible. We are gonna do this with everything we have. This little boy needs justice, and his spirit needs to be freed. If I don't at least try to get this done, I will never be able to look in the mirror again. I'm telling you that he came to me. I don't know if it was my mind working tricks, Tia what's-her-name casting a spell on me, or what. That boy came to me."

"Okay, but here is a rule. No matter what happens, you mean more to me than anything else in the world. There is no problem if we turn around and go home at any point in this investigation. Agreed?"

"Sure, but it ain't gonna happen. I want to go to the grave site in the morning and get a feel for the place. I'll call Collin and tell him to pick us up at 9."

There was no hot sex at the hotel that night. Vic was still a bit jumpy, and Raquel thought it was best not to make any moves. She went to bed in her sweat pants and a floppy top and fell asleep quickly. Vic was reading reports from the homicide detectives who were on the scene when the boy was found on Susquehanna Road. He finally fell asleep around three in the morning.

"Hey, pal. Feeling better this morning?" Collin asked through the open car window.

"Yeah. Must have been a twenty-four-hour bug or something. All set to go."

"Good morning, Raquel. Let's head over to the cemetery."

"Morning, Collin. Have you had coffee? We are all set."

"You know us cops; my GPS has every Dunkin Donuts pre-programmed."

"Oh, no, no, not donuts; too many carbs for me. Let's just maybe get a couple of cups of coffee for the road, okay?" Raquel asked politely.

"Sure, no problem. Let me give you some more back-seat information about the burial. A few months after they found the boy and all the tests were done, ya know, autopsy, what have you, the department had a wake and a burial for him. Here are some pictures of the wake and ceremony," Collin said and handed the photos to Vic, who was in the back seat.

"We've seen a few of these. Look pretty glum," Vic said. He passed the photos to Raquel.

"These guys really bled for that boy. He was buried in the city's potter's field, and the investigation continued full force. As they came up dry and time went on like any case, it went cold. But these men always carried a torch. In 1998, they got Mt. Ivy Cemetery to donate a nice plot for the boy. You'll see; we're almost there."

"So, they exhumed the body in '98 I assume. Was any DNA testing done? They didn't have such a thing in 1957," Raquel said.

"Yes. There was very little left of the boy's remains. The FBI Philly Evidence Recovery Team helped PPD and was able to extract some DNA from the boy's arm bone. There were a few leads that called for a matchup. Like a woman who claimed to be the boy's mom. She was from another state, maybe Colorado, and she came forward claiming he was taken from her. No match," Collin said.

"I read that last night. There are a few other investigative holes I want to go over," Vic said.

"Here it is. Mt. Ivy. This is a non-sectarian, non-denominational cemetery. Perfect spot for him because there was no idea if he had been baptized or anything," Collin said.

The boy's grave is situated just beyond the stone-wall and archway entrance of the cemetery. The two-feet-high, dark gray, granite monument is directly in front of a family plot with old, stone headstones dating from the late 1800s. The boy's monument has a baby lamb at rest and the words,

"AMERICA'S UNKNOWN CHILD

DEDICATED NOVEMBER 11, 1998"

A few feet in front of the monument is a plain, light gray plaque that lay on top of the boy's potter's field grave for forty-one years. It reads,

"HEAVENLY FATHER

BLESS THIS UNKNOWN BOY

FEBRUARY 25, 1957"

A small fruit tree grows just behind the monument. Miniature American flags have been placed around the plot, and toy trucks and stuffed animals have been left by recent visitors. A light gray, granite bench is next to the grave, dedicated by the Vidocq Society on November 11, 1999.

Vic, Raquel, and Collin walked slowly from the car to the grave site. Raquel's eyes welled with tears, but she fought back the urge to wipe them.

"These officers really fell in love with this poor kid. Ya know, they even dressed his body in street clothes and distributed a photograph in the hopes that someone would recognize him. That had to be so tough to do," Vic said.

Raquel was watching Vic very closely to see if he would be able to deal with being at the grave. After the incident at the Susquehanna Road site, she was cautious and concerned, but she needn't had worried. Vic was back to being himself.

"I don't want to sound morbid, but I bring Carol and the kids here every November when they do a memorial service. I want my family to understand that no human being should ever be forgotten," Collin said.

"Not morbid at all, my friend. Okay, not much to learn here. Can we go back to the Round House and see some of that evidence again?" Vic said.

Raquel was staring at the six old headstones that were behind the boy's plot. It seemed that she was daydreaming for a second or two.

"Raquel? Ready?" Vic asked.

"Baby, Sarah Kulp, and next to her is her husband, Abraham B. Kulp, and maybe their son, John Kulp. All died over a hundred years ago. It's as if they are watching over the boy's final resting place. So very sad."

"Let's at least find out what this boy's name was so we can add it to the monument," Vic said.

"That would be nice," Raquel said.

CHAPTER 11

Vic and Raquel were going through the investigative reports with Collin Frank back at the Philadelphia Homicide office at the Round House. Vic also called his friend FBI Special Agent Sean Lewandowski, who helped with the John Deegan investigation. Lewandowski was moved to the Philadelphia office of the Bureau. He promised to stop by later in the day with copies of what the FBI had on the Boy in the Box case.

"Collin, there are more theories than there are about the Kennedy assassination in this file," Vic said.

"Yeah, no shit. It's taken on a life of its own. Every knucklehead in the state of Pennsylvania has what they think is the key to the killer."

Raquel was engrossed in one such report. "This one seems to be very plausible. It seems a woman was investigated in 2002. Claims that her wacko parents bought a little boy from his parents in 1954. She claims that her lovely parents beat the child and subjected him to torture, keeping him in their basement for almost three years. Listen to this: the investigators went to Cincinnati and met the woman at her psychiatrist's office. To keep her privacy intact, it was agreed they would refer to her simply as 'M.' The mother was a librarian, and the father was a school teacher. They lived in a Lower Merion. Where is that, Collin?"

"Upper class suburb of the city."

"So, she claims that the boy was mentally handicapped and couldn't even speak. They called him Jonathan. That's the name his birth parents gave him. The boy was never allowed to leave the basement and was malnourished. That confirms what we know from the autopsy report. The parents used Jonathan to sexually abuse him. Real nice people," Raquel said.

"So, what was the result of the investigation?" Vic asked.

"She said her mother called someone. She was ranting about the boy being dead, telling the person that he was more to blame than she was. M and her mother drove around for a while with the boy's body, looking for a place to drop the corpse. The mother beat the kid after he threw up in a makeshift tub of water. She testified that the mother cut his long hair and trimmed his nails so there would be no evidence. M said her mother wrapped the body in a blanket and placed it in the trunk of her car. Holy Christ, listen to this. A passing motorist stopped on Susquehanna Road when he saw a woman and a boy fumbling around in their car truck to see if they needed help." Raquel paused for a few seconds.

"And?" Vic asked.

Raquel was reading the report, wide-eyed. "Give me a second. The motorist did make a report after he read about the police finding the boy's body. This woman's statement matched the motorist's testimony, which was not publicized in the press. She stated that the motorist left after they ignored him and her mother then found the empty cardboard box in the lot."

"What does 'ignored them' mean?" Vic asked.

"Quite interesting. From what I read on the Internet, the press said that the motorist was checking to see if their car broke down. Here, the motorist said he just stopped and told them that they should not dump anything in the thicket. The woman's statement, this 'M,' verifies that."

"But the motorist said it was a woman and a boy," Collin said.

"Sure, a pre-teen girl who is flat-chested could easily be thought of as a boy. If her back was to him, who knows?" Raquel said.

"So, what was done with this? I have to think the homicide detectives thought, at this point, they found the killers," Vic said.

"Extensive investigation, blah, blah, blah. Every bit of her statement was thoroughly investigated. After six months, none of this woman's allegations could be found to have any merit. They even looked in the basement of the house for trace evidence."

"Do the math. That was forty-five years later. What trace evidence did they think would still be there?" Vic said.

"This final report states that the woman in Cincinnati, 'M', was deemed to be mentally ill and that she had access to the information on the case. Pretty vivid imagination, don't you think?"

"And you said that her psychiatrist was there?" Collin asked.

"Yes, and he was the one who called PPD. He stated that his patient had been telling him this story over many sessions since 1989. So, for thirteen years, he kept this story to himself."

"Doctor-patient confidentiality? Maybe he thought she was nuts, too," Vic said.

"Listen, I'm sure these investigators knew what they were doing and wanted to close this case. I wonder if this woman is still alive. Any record of a polygraph?"

"Doesn't say, but that would have been a good idea, don't you think?" Raquel said, as she looked at the reports.

"Monday morning quarterbacking always pisses me off. I hate to assume anything, but what would they have to gain to let this slip through their hands? Let's just say it's a non-starter for the moment, but I would love to meet that woman myself," Vic said.

The conference room door opened slowly, and there stood a smiling FBI special agent, Sean Lewandowski.

"Are you still with this stiff, Raquel? I thought, by now, you would have come to your senses," Sean said.

"He can never get rid of me! I left a good job for him," Raquel joked. She greeted him with a kiss on the cheek, and everyone in the room laughed.

Handshakes, hugs, and pleasantries followed as did a brief reminiscence of the John Deegan case.

"Why this case, Vic?" Sean asked.

"I read about the case, and I thought it would be a challenge, Sean. Besides, you know how I feel about kids."

"And, if you solve the case, your reputation soars. As if you need it."

"Areyoukiddenmeorwhat??? And, if I don't solve it, I'm a chump? Nah, I don't need the case. There is no financial windfall in it unless I write a stupid book, which will never happen. I just feel for this kid. Just call me a softy, I guess."

"How can the Bureau help?" Sean asked.

"Is this case on your radar screen, Sean?" Vic asked.

"Honestly, absolutely not. We have so much going on with counter-terrorism, narcotics, and a host of other federal crimes that a homicide from the fifties is long forgotten."

"Do you have a file on the case?"

"Sure, I brought a few reports that are from way back in the day. There were a couple of interstate connections, but everything was investigated and came up a dead end. You know we generally don't get involved with local homicide cases. In this case, the Bureau was asked by the chief of police to help in 1957. It became a national case. We also did help a bit with forensics, as you probably know, back in the nineties."

"I know, but I thought I would ask and get to see my big, Polish pal for old times' sake. Let's catch up one night. We are staying in town for a while. I understand that W.C. Fields' gravestone reads, "All things considered, I'd rather be here than Philadelphia," Vic said.

"Urban myth, Vic. It's not a bad place to be. I'll show you guys around one night."

"Sean, I have read about another case that occurred around that time that may somehow be linked to our boy," Raquel said.

"I've read up on the case, so, ask away," Sean said.

"Do you know anything about the abduction of a toddler from East Meadow, Long Island, that was never solved? A Steven Damman. Some people seem to think that he could have been the Boy in the Box."

"Yes, I do. The Damman boy was snatched outside a supermarket while his mother went into the store for groceries. It was Halloween of 1955--a nightmare for the family, I'm sure. He was with his baby sister, who was in her stroller. The sister was found just a few blocks away, but the boy and his bag of jelly beans were gone. There was a lot of conjecture that he may have been the boy found in Philly. The Damman boy was about three years old when kidnapped and had blond hair and blue eyes and a scar on his chin like your boy. Steven Damman also had a birthmark on his leg, but the Boy in the Box had too many bruises on his legs to make an identification. A police inspector from Long Island drove to Philly when your boy was found and determined it was not the Damman boy. Rumors kept swirling around for years that the Damman kid was the murdered boy found here. In 2003, a few years after DNA samples were taken from your boy, Damman's sister had her DNA samples submitted. There was no match. That was the end of the speculation, so, a dead end," Sean said.

"What a sick world we live in. Even back then," Vic said.

CHAPTER 12

Father James Nelson and Sister Mary Magdalene of the Crown of Thorns now worked at the home for wayward girls, in the Fox Chase section of Philadelphia. Their jobs were to find good homes for the newborns and offer moral and emotional support to the girls.

Only thing--they were no longer Father James and Sister Mary. Jim and Maggie Nelson took their jobs seriously as they truly wanted to help young women in trouble. Only thing--they also wanted to have sex with underage women. This was called pedophilia in 1957 just as it is today. Only thing--it was a word not used in daily parlance. Pedophilia was unheard of and well protected from the general public by the Catholic Church and every other organization that worked with children.

Jim and Maggie quickly befriended people who worked closely with children in Fox Chase. A local librarian, Mrs. Jameson, satisfied the couple's intellectual needs, and, along with her knowledge of local troubled teens, Lillian also had a direct line to the Nicoletti family who ran a for-profit foster home. Soon after meeting the librarian, it became clear to Jim and Maggie that she would be their best friend in Philadelphia. Mrs. Lillian Jameson called Jim and Maggie to meet her one evening for dinner. Fox Chase had a number of inexpensive, good German restaurants. On this particular evening, they planned to meet at 6 p.m. at the Old Brauhaus Restaurant and Beer Garden. Lillian Jameson didn't arrive until 6:45 and seemed out of sorts and nervous.

"So sorry to be late. I had a problem at home that really needed my attention," Lillian said.

"Is everything all right? You seem upset," Maggie said.

"Upset isn't the word. I'm furious. The one night I have a chance to get out of the house and away from that dullard of a man I'm married to, my daughter decides she needs to go study at a friend's house. Evidently, there is this chemistry test that is meaningful for god knows what reason," Lillian said.

"But, surely, you're happy with her choice to study rather than go for a joy ride or some other pre-teen nonsense," Jim said.

"She needs to understand that she must help me with that hideous child. There is just so much I can take of his moaning and bellowing. I have no idea what possessed me to take charge of this boy. There is a limit to my patience after all."

"And your husband?" Maggie asked.

"Useless. All he does is prepare his lesson plans and grade tests to the sound of some awful opera. He wants nothing to do with Jonathan or his own daughter for that matter," Lillian said.

"Did you speak to the Nicolettis? Will they take him back?" Jim asked.

"Well, they actually didn't have this boy living in their foster home. They referred me to the family who was looking to give him up. They brokered the deal without official paperwork and other such nonsense. Strictly a cash deal. I rue the day I decided to take this child in. It goes under the old adage, 'No good deed goes unpunished,'" Lillian said.

"Is there anything we can do?" Jim asked.

"Well, that's what I wanted to see you two about.

I'm at my wit's end and need to find a place for this...this creature," Lillian said.

"Lillian, you really don't paint a pretty picture of this boy. Nothing you have ever said to us leads us to think we could find a good home for him. Frankly, it's best for him and for you if you have him institutionalized. He needs constant care and attention, and you are just not equipped to do that," Jim said.

"He is a burden to you and your family, and I agree with Jim. It's best if you bring him to the state. They can care for him and offer whatever level of education he can absorb. His leaving may even strengthen your marriage," Maggie said.

"Let's just forget the marriage. It was doomed from the onset. We are still together only for our daughter, and the fact is, I will not be considered a divorcée in polite society. As far as the state goes, I'm afraid too many questions will be asked, and I'm in no position to answer them. Christ, I could lose my job! And then what?" Lillian said.

Lillian was becoming more red-faced and angry than when she had arrived.

"We'll come up with something. In the meantime, I'm starved. Let's look at the menu," Maggie said.

"I'll just have a sloe gin fizz. My appetite is gone. I would just like to drown this kid and bury my sorrows with him," Lillian said.

"Lillian, please!" Maggie said.

"Listen, Maggie, just don't fuck with me. You and your sidekick here are no babes in the woods either, sister."

Jim and Maggie quickly glanced at each other. They knew from their sexual escapades with her that Lillian was capable of harming the boy. They also already suspected Lillian was abusing the child from conversations they had had with her in the past.

Lillian Jameson would sometimes discuss how close she felt to the boy and how tender his skin was and things of this sort and how much she loved sleeping in the same bed after he was bathed. That type of talk had Jim and Maggie listening in earnest because, here again, an old adage comes into play. "It takes one to know one."

CHAPTER 13

Vic and Raquel were back in their hotel suite, reviewing the day they spent at PPD with Collin Frank and Sean Lewandowski. They had a light dinner and spoke only about the case, reviewing what they had learned so far.

"The more I read about this case, the more my head spins," Vic said. He continued. "Those detectives were good, dedicated men. They seemed to have done everything possible to find out who this boy was. Calling in the FBI shows they had no ego; they weren't worried about the Bureau making them look bad. Once they did that, they knew they would make the collar. They called in almost three hundred police academy recruits to comb the scene where the body was found. They found a child's scarf, a dead cat wrapped in a sweater, a handkerchief with the letter 'G' on it, and a boy's cap. Of course, they were going to find this kind of junk. People used this thicket as a garbage dump. Then, they checked hospital records, recruited people to look over photographs of children from orphanages, checked baby birth footprints for seven prior years. They assumed the dead child was born in a hospital in the area. That is all they could go on but, in retrospect, a weak assumption. They sent out four hundred thousand fliers and circulars, and a quarter of a million bills from the electric and gas utility had the boy's morgue photo. Can you imagine opening up your own gas bill and seeing a little boy's morgue shot? Bizarre, to say the very least."

"They didn't think that perhaps the child never went to school and was kept at home?" Raquel asked.

"Have I ever told you my puppy shit syndrome theory?" Vic asked.

"I think I would have remembered that one." Raquel was already laughing.

"You go out and buy a new puppy, cute little thing. Your puppy shits on the rug in your house. You try to train him, but he's not having any of it. So, what do you do? You can bring the puppy back to the store. You can yell at the puppy, put his nose in the crap, smack the puppy around. You can even shoot the puppy. But you can't get the puppy to clean it up."

"And that means?" Raquel asked.

"Like the crap on the rug, this case is all over the place. We have to put all the pieces together and clean it up ourselves. Get rid of all the theories and conjecture, and zero in on the few viable leads that we think will solve this case."

"Process of elimination?" Raquel asked.

"Kind of. I've been reading about this investigator from the medical examiner's office who started his own investigation on this case. What was his name again?" Vic said as he started rummaging through the notes and copies he had made from the Boy in the Box website.

"Here it is. Remington Bristow. From what I'm reading and from what we have heard in the past two days, I think he has already figured out who the Boy in the Box was," Vic said.

"What? That's crazy!"

"I'll go one step further. I think he knew who the killer was," Vic said.

"Are you losing it, baby?"

"This man embraced this case to the point where it totally consumed him. It came out later that Bristow had a daughter who was a sudden infant death syndrome victim. He never got over that and never got over seeing this dead boy in that box. He was an emotional mess, and his judgment was affected. I believe he left us enough information, though, for us to pick up the pieces and end the mystery."

"So, who do you think did it based on what we have already?"

"I have no idea...not just yet. Haven't you ever heard 'can't see the forest for the trees?' He just couldn't nail it down. He had it in his hands and let it slip away," Vic said.

"I say we get a good night's sleep and, in the morning, make an outline of the three or four things that Bristow had in his crosshairs. We attack those leads and go from there," Raquel said.

"I'm so drained from this after only a few days, it's not even funny. Bristow made it his life's work. He must have been a basket case. You're right. Let's sleep on it and start fresh tomorrow."

Vic had a difficult time falling asleep. Raquel's deep breathing was beginning to get on his frayed nerves, so, he left the bed and took his pillow to the small couch in the living room area of the expansive suite. He hit the remote and surfed the channels until his eyes became heavy. He stopped at the TMC network. *Casablanca* was coming to an end. Rick was walking in the puddles of water at the airport with Inspector Renault when he said, "Louie, this is the beginning of a beautiful friendship." The closing music came on, and Vic fell asleep. Vic was so drained and exhausted that the light and sound from the television had no effect on him.

Vic woke up as if in a stupor to Raquel shaking him. He was sitting at the edge of the couch with both his hands on his head. He was shivering and gasping for breath.

"Vic...Vic...baby? Are you okay?"

"Oh, god, Raquel. No, I'm not okay. This is total bullshit. The boy came to me again. I know it was a dream, but I felt him. I really did. He is so sad, that poor kid."

"Jesus, you are sweating like a pig."

"Can you get me some water? I feel as if my throat is closing."

Raquel reached over to the table, grabbed a bottle of Poland Spring, and quickly twisted off the cap.

"It's just a dream, baby. You are just wound up too tight over this thing. I want to stop. This isn't good for you," Raquel said.

Vic ignored her comment and stared at the half-drunk bottle of water.

But why did they do those things to me? Maybe these people needed a little boy in their life. But I hope they don't do what they did to me to another boy. That's not nice. I'm not in a happy place right now. It's not a sad place. It's just a place. Like where they kept me. In the dark.

I wish that someone could find out why I went to the place I am now and let me go to a nicer place. Maybe a playground with other kids. I want to smile.

I think those people called me Jonathan, but I'm not sure if that was my name or a bad word. They used to yell that word at me sometimes.

"That's what he said to me. He was standing a foot away from me, looking me right in the face. His eyes were like they were in the morgue shot, all fucked up. His head was all banged up, and his hair was chopped just like you see in those stills. Horrible... just horrible."

"We're going back to New York today and re-thinking this thing. I'm done," Raquel said.

CHAPTER 14

Raquel insisted that all plans for the investigation be put on hold. She called Collin Frank to tell him they had to return to New York and that she would call him in a day or two. Collin sensed that something was wrong but didn't ask any questions. After all, he was a cop and had that sixth sense that cops get after dealing with every human foible imaginable.

Vic was somewhere between sullen and angry. He didn't want to leave Philadelphia just then, but he wasn't going to have a huge argument with Raquel. They had only had a few big arguments, and nobody came out of them without pain. He knew from experience that, when she was adamant and dug in her heels, there was only one way to do things: her way. The way Raquel snatched the keys from the desk in the suite signaled to Vic that he had no choice in the matter and that she was driving.

Not a word was spoken until they reached that very malodorous part of the New Jersey Turnpike. The air was so pungent that Raquel's eyes started to tear.

"It's a *shem*, a real shem," Vic said.

"A shem? What's that?"

"My grandfather would call a man who let his woman boss him around a *schemanedu*, a Sicilian word for a man who lets his woman boss him around. It's not as bad as a *cornudu*, which is a man who knows his wife is fooling around on him and does nothing about it. But a schem is pretty bad. "

"Boss you around? Is that what you're thinking? I'm bossing you around? Look it, Vic..."

"Raquel, your Puerto Rican is showing. Your head is going like a bobble-head doll, and, when you say 'look it' like that, I know I'm in for a street fight."

"Really? My Puerto Rican? Maybe you should go back to your Irish wife and see how that works out again. You sound like a dago from the mountains when you talk like that, Gonnella. There is no way I'm risking your health and well-being for *any* case. I wish we never started this friggin' thing. These dreams of yours are creeping me out big time, Mister Schem. And what's that remark about a woman who's fooling around about?"

Vic remained quiet for a few minutes.

"That kid was as real as you are, baby. I can still see his face when I close my eyes," Vic said.

"Vic, I love you so much. I can't stand seeing you like this. I'm sorry I snapped at you. Yeah, that's my Puerto Rican, and I'm proud of it."

"I could see the bruises on his head, on his legs. His mouth was just open like in the photo, and it wasn't moving. I could hear him talking to me, though. He was so vivid, so real. He was holding his head where his skull was fractured. And that damn blue liquid in his eyes was glowing. "

"Baby, it's all in your mind. You are so intense, you know. That friggin' strong personality of yours is making this worse than it really is. That boy died in 1957. We weren't even born, so, why is it suddenly our responsibility to solve this case?"

"You don't understand, Raquel. You just don't get it. He is reaching out to me. I felt it in the cemetery, I felt it on Susquehanna Road, and it grabs me when I see the blanket his body was wrapped in and that fucking cardboard box. I can feel him."

"Don't get what? Your imagination is running wild. You live and breathe this case, you don't get enough sleep, you stare at the evidence and stills hour after hour like it's going to change things, and you wonder why you are getting nightmares. I don't know if they are even nightmares. Maybe psychotic apparitions are more like it."

"Okay, Doctor Ruiz. Do you take Oxford?" Vic made a feeble attempt at a joke.

"Vic Gonnella, I'm not kidding here. Nothing is more important to me than you. Forget that whole baby idea for now. If we do, we do. If not, then so be it. We can always adopt a child one day," Raquel said. Her eyes started to moisten. Although, this time, it wasn't from the chemical haze on the Jersey Turnpike.

"That's it! That is what we need to follow," Vic said, almost yelling.

"What, adopting a child?"

"Don't you see it? Do you remember reading about a foster home in the reports? That's where we have to focus our attention--somebody who had the boy, somebody who bought the boy, or that foster family with the Italian name. They are the key to this. I just know it. That's what the boy said to me. *Maybe these people needed a little boy in their life. But I hope they don't do what they did to me to any of the other boys.* Don't you see it? He's telling me there were other boys. These people have other kids they adopted out."

"We are not going back right now, Vic. No way, no how," Raquel said, her head bobbing again.

"We have to follow up on three key scenarios. One, that foster home. Two, that woman 'M' in Ohio, who said her mother bought and killed the boy. And, three, some carnival I read about. Those people, what's their names? The Dudleys. It's all about one of those three suspects. The rest are all bullshit."

"No, we are going home. You are going to rest, and, tomorrow, we see your doctor. He needs to know about this."

"No, we are not going back right now. Don't head to Manhattan. Take the GW Bridge to the Bronx," Vic said.

"The Bronx?"

"Yeah, the Bronx. I have to go see Tia Carmen."

"Tia Carmen? What for?"

"Just let's get there, okay?"

"Come on, Vic. We don't even have an appointment."

"Fuck that shit. She will see us. As a matter of fact, she's probably expecting us."

CHAPTER 15

It was only 10:30 in the morning when Raquel turned onto 180th Street in the Bronx.

The block that Tia Carmen lived on looked like a battle zone from the night before. Manny Sosa's bodega on the corner was burned to a crisp. What was referred to as Jewish lighting in this neighborhood in the 1960s was now a Dominican fireball. A few locals were rummaging through the charred remains of the small store, picking up a few scorched cans of Goya beans and smoke-damaged boxes of cereal and Pampers. A Waste Management truck was dropping off a large, metal dumpster into which the remains of the store would be shoveled. Standing outside the store with a camera around his neck, a clipboard in his hands, and a petrified look on his face was the white-bread insurance adjuster. His suit and tie along with the New Jersey license plates on his BMW announced that he was not of this world. Luckily for him, the fire inspectors were at the scene, attempting to determine if an accelerant had been used to ignite this fire. They had no shot. The fire was made to look like an electrical wire malfunction. The Dominican fire starters were as good as or better than anyone when it came to the total destruction of property.

A few doors down, a building superintendent was hosing down the sidewalk while three twelve-year-old boys watched. The caulk marks from the homicide squad and the victim's blood were making a macabre paste that would soon be flushed down the sewer, interrupting the breakfast of a swarm of ants and flies.

The carnage scene did not interfere with the *piragua* man, who had done a brisk business selling snow cones from his homemade cart the night before. Fires and murders were good for business. Fifty cents for a snow cone with gooey syrup. Two bucks for a shot of cheap rum. Two fifty for Hennessy.

Raquel wisely parked the car a half block away from the madness. She and Vic headed for Tia Carmen's building, which stood between the unrelated events. As they gingerly stepped over the steady stream, a familiar voice called out.

"*Mira,* poppie, how you been, my dude?" The wheelchair man was motoring toward Vic and Raquel from the burned bodega.

"What did you do, burn that store down?" Vic joked.

"No, poppie, he used to cash my government checks for me. Now, I have to go four blocks in my chariot."

"What happened over here?" Raquel asked. She pointed to the sidewalk where the caulk mark was rapidly disintegrating.

"That was really bad, mami. Raul Quinones was stabbed and died right on that spot. Two dudes from the Crips, I heard, but nobody saw nothing, nada. My back was facing them. By the time I turned my chair around, bam, they gone."

"Sure. My friend, we are going upstairs for a minute, so, watch my car, okay? Same deal," Vic said.

"It's not my business, poppie, but are you going to see Tia Carmen?"

"Matter of fact, we are," Vic said.

"She's not home. She be a fate worse than death. Been at Barnabas for two days."

"In the hospital? What's wrong?" Raquel asked.

"I don't know, but she not looking good at all, mami. Her color ain't right."

"How about her sister? Is she upstairs?"

"She just left a few minutes ago in a cab. Probably headed to Barnabas."

Vic gave the wheelchair man a five and took Raquel by the arm. They made a beeline to the car and to Barnabas Hospital on Third Avenue not very far from 180th Street.

"When I lived here, this place was called Saint Barnabas Hospital for the Incurable. See that high stone wall? That meant anyone who was in there never came out. I'm still afraid of this place," Vic said.

"It's just a hospital now. Pretty good trauma center," Raquel said.

"Naturally, this is a fucking battle zone. If you want to be an ER doctor, this is the place to learn."

"My cousin did his residency here. The gang bangers would threaten him if their boy died when he was working on them. I got him a pistol permit, which was a joke in itself," Raquel said.

Vic and Raquel worked their way up to the third floor, where Tia Carmen was being cared for in a semi-private room. The couple just walked in like they owned the place so no silly paper passes were needed. Just information. "Auffant?" was all Raquel asked the information rent-a-cop.

The second they walked into the room, Vic and Raquel could see that things with Tia Carmen were not good at all. Her color was indeed not good as the wheelchair man said. Tia's skin was a deep yellow jaundice. Idalis sat in a chair right next to Tia Carmen's bed with the curtain drawn on one side to give her roommate some privacy. Four older ladies from the neighborhood sat in chairs against the wall. They fingered their rosary beads, lips moving almost in sync.

Idalis softly smiled and nodded her head at Vic and Raquel. Tia Carmen motioned to Idalis to shoo the praying ladies from the room.

"They pray their rosaries. It helps and comforts them. That is a good thing. For me, there is nothing but energy, and my light is dim. No prayers. But it's okay, my time is growing near," Tia Carmen said.

Raquel sat on Tia Carmen's bed and held her hand. Vic stood behind his girl.

"Tia Carmen, what's wrong? Is this a sudden illness? You were fine a few days ago," Raquel said.

"I knew I was very sick for a few months. My pancreas. I have the cancer. It's my time, and this is what will take my energy away."

"Have you consulted another doctor? We know some great..." Raquel started to say.

"No doctor can change this, little one. They tell me this medicine will help me for a while, and, then, I can go home. My wish is that I die at my home here and my bones be buried in my home in Puerto Rico with my family where I belong."

"What can we do for you now, Tia Carmen?" Vic asked.

"You can tell me when you free the energy of that boy."

"That's why we came, Tia," Raquel said.

"Victor, remember, I said to you that the boy's time is short. His energy is somehow tied to mine. I don't know why, but, when my light goes out, so will his. Then, he will be done."

"He came to me twice, Tia Carmen. I don't know if it's a dream or real."

"It is very real, my son. His energy is here right now. He came in with you. His hope lies in your hands," Tia said. She smiled and gazed into a corner of the room.

"Tia, I'm worried about Vic. He has some issues that make these visits hard on him," Raquel said.

"I know, I know, little one, but this boy cannot hurt either of you in any way. Victor, when he comes, you listen and be gentle to his energy. All these years, his energy has been unsettled."

"What do you know that maybe you should be telling me, Tia Carmen?" Vic asked.

"If you think of the obvious, you will be thinking clearly. The boy's energy is bringing me to a place in my mind that has a family. A home, perhaps. A house with many children. I cannot see it too clearly. An old house. I see the hands of a woman on the boy. That is all I can see."

"A woman was his killer?" Vic asked.

"I did not say that. All I see in my mind's eye is a woman's hands. Now, you two must go. The pain medicine wants me to sleep. I will wait for you to return."

87

Raquel took Tia Carmen's hand in hers and gently kissed it.

The old woman looked into Raquel's eyes, smiled, and said, "Little one, that little boy needs you. I will wait for you."

CHAPTER 16

Vic and Raquel went to their Manhattan apartment, answered some mail, paid some bills, and returned to Philadelphia before dinner. It was clear to them from Tia Carmen's words and how she looked that time was of the essence.

Vic called Sean Lewandowski and Collin Frank to see if they were available for dinner around 7 that evening. They both were, so, Vic asked Collin to get a reservation where they could have a quiet table to discuss the case. Raquel and Vic agreed that Tia Carmen was off limits.

"People will think we have lost our minds," Vic said.

"I read where Remington Bristow brought in a psychic from New Jersey in 1960 who pretty much was in agreement with that woman from Ohio and what Tia said to us today."

"I didn't see that. What did she say?"

"It was really very strange. Bristow took some evidence, some metal staples from the actual box and some other items. Evidently, the psychic, a Florence Sternfeld, claimed to read images through various metal objects. Mrs. Sternfeld told him to look for a certain kind of house and a log cabin next to that house. Bristow searched Fox Chase for months until he found a property with a log cabin next to a home. And, guess what? The house was a foster home, and the kids would sleep in the log cabin during the summer."

"Crazy!" Vic said.

"It gets better. Now that I think about it, the whole case seems to be coming together. Bristow then brought the psychic to the Susquehanna Road site. Here is a woman who never left her small town in New Jersey, I think Palisades Park, if I remember. The psychic gets to the site, walks around a bit, and proceeds to take Bristow right to the foster home with the log cabin."

"Rod fucking Serling. Welcome to the Twilight Zone."

"Ya think? So, there's more. It took him months to find this house, and this Sternfeld lady brings him there within an hour after they get to Fox Chase.

"So, Bristow thinks he's got it nailed."

"So, now, there is a gap in what next transpires. He brings this information to the Philadelphia Police, and they refuse to follow up on the lead."

"That's some bullshit right there."

"Well, this is what I'm talking about. The minute people heard "psychic" and saw that Bristow was still hammering away at the case, they probably thought he was a whack job. Remember, this is 1960."

"Most people are still leery about this kind of psychic stuff, even today."

"This is why we can't bring up Tia Carmen. We will be accused of smoking angel dust."

"So, come on, what else did you read?"

Raquel opened a file on her laptop and started to scan her reports. She created a spreadsheet that included the key points of their investigation.

"Okay, the PPD refuses to investigate, and, a year later, the people who run the foster home get out of the foster-care business and move away. The place was shut down and put up for sale including the contents. Bristow goes to the auction and sees a bassinet that fits the description of one that would have come in the box the boy was found in."

"Stop! Get the fuck outta here, Raquel."

"I can't make this up, baby. Listen, Bristow finds the bassinet in the basement all covered in dust and unused for a long time. He sees plaid blankets similar to the one the boy was wrapped in. I imagine that he came to the conclusion that the blankets were used on the metal cots the kids would sleep on in the foster home."

"Identical blankets? There's the case."

"I don't know. I do remember seeing that they did testing on the blankets in 1957, when the detectives were looking for stores that sold that type of material, but nothing was determined except they were made in some far-away mills in Canada or somewhere."

"Slipshod detective work?"

"I'm not ready to condemn anyone. So, Bristow keeps bringing his theories to the PPD, and they keep refusing to do any more investigation on the case. I find it hard to believe, but I can only think that they thought Bristow was losing it. Bristow begs and pleads, and, then in 1984, do the math, twenty-seven years later, two PPD detectives interview the man who ran the foster home. Nothing comes out of the investigation. They find no incriminating evidence."

"I can't believe that."

"Now, Bristow takes it into his own hands and calls the guy, one Arthur Nicoletti, who owned the foster home."

"That's ballsy. I would have gone to see the guy."

"Who knows? Anyway, he asks Nicoletti, who still lived some-where in Pennsylvania, to take a polygraph, and guess what?"

"The guy refuses?"

"Indeed. Bristow went to his grave thinking that the boy's death was linked to the foster home. And get this: Bristow's theory was that the Nicoletti's stepdaughter, Anna Marie Nagle, was the boy's mother. And here is the kicker: the supposed mother was never married until the foster home guy's wife, Catherine Nicoletti, dies, and, then, Arthur marries his stepdaughter, Anna Marie. Shades of Woody Allen."

"Jesus Christ, I can hear the banjos playing in the back ground. Talk about white trash."

Raquel continued to scan her spreadsheet, pointing to her notes.

"There's more. Bristow finds out four years later, 1988, that is, that there was a doctor who saw the kids when they were sick. He discovers this from old police reports. One would assume that this was covered during the investigation, but there is no report that this doctor was interviewed by PPD. Bristow never even knew about this. Evidently, they didn't have this foster home on their radar screen, or else they felt it was nothing but a dead end."

"I'm getting more curious by the second."

"So, Bristow, who should have been a detective rather than a coroner's inspector, tracks down the doctor. He finds the doctor's wife. The doctor is dead, and his files were all destroyed. End of subject."

"So, no more Bristow? Did he give up?"

"He died five years after that. He always believed the foster family had something to do with the boy, but he could never prove it. No hard evidence, just some theories and hunches."

"But, from what we now know and what Tia Carmen has said, it was an old house with other kids. From six to as many as twenty-five kids at a time. The Nicolettis got the kids from the state and were paid by the head. The pieces of the puzzle seem to fit."

"And then came the conspiracy theorists and more loonies."

"What do you mean?"

"In 1998, *America's Most Wanted* did an episode on this case. People claiming to be the boy's parents came forward. Another guy maintained that the Nicolettis had Philadelphia cops as relatives and they were covering up the boy's murder. You name it, and the PPD has heard every theory except for that Lee Harvey Oswald and the CIA were in on the murder."

"Which makes people like us roll our eyes and walk away?"

"Precisely, so, if we tell Collin and Sean or anyone that some Spanish lady told us to solve this case and you are seeing the boy in your dreams, what do you think their reaction will be?"

"I agree. So, before we sit down to dinner tonight, let's recap what we have so far and what direction we think we should go."

"There goes your analytical personality. You want everything in a list so we can check off the boxes."

"Isn't that one of the reasons you love me so much?" Vic asked. He took his hand off the steering wheel and ran it up Raquel's thigh until he felt her warm spot.

"Eyes on the road, Gonnella. From the looks of things, I see you are feeling better." Raquel pointed to the slight bulge in Vic's pants.

"I am feeling a lot better. Want to stop at a cheap motel?"

"Ahhhh, no, let's get to dinner and see what happens tonight."

CHAPTER 17

The group met at the Capitol Grill on Chestnut Street. The restaurant was just a few minutes walk from Detective Collin Frank's office at the Round House and Vic and Raquel's hotel. The FBI office was a twenty minute drive for Special Agent Sean Lewandowski.

The Capitol Grill is a very classy place, replete with deep, dark-wood-paneled walls, partly covered by large oil paintings of William Penn, Benjamin Franklin, and other notaries from early Pennsylvanian history. Paintings of hunting scenes and stuffed animal heads screamed of testosterone. Regal, high back chairs surrounded elegantly set tables that were fussed over by attentive waiters in white shirts, black ties, and black vests. The three-piece-suited maître d' rolled out a table that featured the various cuts of aged steaks, live lobsters, and raw vegetables that could be cooked to order. The wine list was presented as if it were the Magna Carta. The prices of the food and wines fit the ambiance and presentation.

Vic was used to less fancy fare but thought it was a great reward for the hard work they were doing. The dinner with Special Agent Lewendowski and Detective Collin Frank was into its third hour before they got to the business at hand.

"It may be the wine talking, but I'm pretty sure we can narrow down the killer or killers of our boy to a few individuals," Vic said.

"What do you think, guys? We want to hear what you have come up with," Raquel said.

"I've spent the last two days immersed in this case. I've learned so much, but my head is spinning from all of the possibilities. I don't disagree that there are some things that may be overlooked. I'm really feeling the Dudleys, although they were cleared by the detectives on the case," Collin said.

"Who? The Dudleys?" Vic asked.

"Yes. They were itinerant carnival workers. The carnival passed through Fox Chase."

"Oh, yeah. I remember reading about them, too. What's your take?" Vic asked.

"This carnival that took place back then. It brought in a lot of unsavory types. I found out it was run by this Gypsy guy, Ferka Pitti, a.k.a. Sergio. Let's call him Sergio for now. Evidently, this guy was a real swordsman. Forgive me, Raquel, but he was banging everything he could. What he wasn't was a guy who would allow anyone to harm children. It seems he had a haunting past in which his two baby brothers were killed by the Germans in World War II. There was just no screwing around with kids around this Sergio. So, these white trash, lowlives, Kenneth and Irene Dudley, were in his employ for a few years. Irene had a litter of children who kept disappearing. One day, Sergio saw that a couple of the kids were missing, a little boy and a little girl. So, he brings the Dudleys into his wagon slash office and gives them the third degree. You know, how many kids do you have? Let me see them all. Where is that blond-haired boy and cute girl in the pigtails? Well, Sergio didn't like the way the couple got defensive and argumentative, and he proceeded to beat the living hell out of the husband and even smacked the screaming wife around a bit. He fires them; they call the cops, but nothing is ever filed or anything. Seems Sergio was well connected in town. One of the ladies who he was romancing had a brother in a high place in City Hall. Anyway, the

Dudleys stay in the Fox Chase area and work menial jobs for a while. I have a hunch that the boy was theirs and sold or given up."

"A hunch is not evidence, Collin," Vic said. Vic was starting to slur his speech a bit but was still sharp as a tack.

"No, no, let me finish. So, they leave Philadelphia and get with another traveling carnival. In 1961, they were both arrested in Virginia for being instrumental in the death of their seven-year-old daughter. She died of malnutrition, neglect, and exposure. And guess what. The little girl was thirty pounds and had a broken leg. Her body was found wrapped in a blanket under a tree. The mutt said she fell. The police in Virginia get them to admit that they let six of their ten kids die the same way. I did some more research. But, get this, the MO is frightening. They left a string of dead kids around the country. They were from South Carolina and moved with the carnivals like I said. In 1949, Dudley was arrested for burying his six-year-old son illegally near Syracuse, New York. The kid was buried in a blanket. Now, in 1958, their four-year-old boy was found dead near Lakeland, Florida, bound in canvas and a blanket. In 1959, their ten-year-old son and an eight-year-old son were bound together in, guess what, a canvas and a blanket. Found in Lake Pontchartrain, Louisiana. There's more. In 1960, a three-year-old daughter, wrapped in a blanket, was wedged in, hold on, a cardboard box.

Collin grabbed his glass of wine and took a big gulp.

"So, there is a pattern of behavior obviously. The blanket thing speaks volumes, and they were in or around Fox Chase at the time of our boy being found," Raquel said.

"Yes, they were. Now, Irene Dudley throws her husband under the bus. She states that Kenneth would beat the children brutally over the smallest thing, leaving them bruised and scarred. He forced his fingers down one of the daughter's throat because she was hollering. Remember those marks on our boy's head? A person would have to grab a kid by the head and hold on tight to do something like that. Maybe that is how he got those bruises on his head. The kid was crying or screaming, and he forced his fingers or something down the boy's throat. And the malnutrition? The wife stated that they had no money but the husband would eat while the kids went hungry. And they were often denied food as a punishment. Can you fucking imagine this shit?" Collin was so angry his face became a scarlet color.

"And they were cleared of killing our boy?" Sean asked.

"Yes! Cleared! I think there is more to this. I'm trying to find out just how they were not implicated in this case and brought back to Philadelphia. Four years after the Boy in the Box was found, these two people were found to have left kids all over the place, dead, beaten, and malnourished. And the kicker is they were all buried in blankets," Collin said.

"Has anyone ever checked to see if the blanket on our boy matched any of the other blankets found on the Dudley kids?" Vic asked.

"No idea. That would make it easier, wouldn't it?" Collin said.

"I think we need to do some more follow-up on the Dudleys. Do you think we can get DNA evidence on any living or even dead Dudley and see if it matches our boy?" Raquel asked.

"That's one way. But I want to find out why the PPD said they were not involved with killing our boy. I want to see the report and who did the investigation," Sean said.

"But what if they sold him? Maybe they were so desperate that they sold our boy to someone for food money. Who knows?" Vic said.

"That certainly has happened. But they let the other kids just die on them. The blanket thing is like the last bit of false caring that these two wing-nuts did for their kids," Raquel said.

"Look, I'm getting a bit sloshed on this great wine, but I have something to say." Vic raised his glass and, through half open eyes, started to make a statement."

"Okay, Vic, maybe it's time we call it a night and take a walk back to our hotel, get some air," Raquel said.

"Hold on, hold on. I want to say something. I'm a big, big Sherlock Holmes fan. He said something impressive that we have to keep in mind. Wanna hear it?"

"How can we say no?" Raquel asked. She smiled adoringly at her man.

"Old Sherlock said, 'It is a capital mistake to theorize before one has data. Insensibly, one begins to twist facts to suit theories instead of theories to suit facts,'" Vic said.

"Which means?" Collin asked.

"Which means...you want to know what that means? I'm not sure what the hell that means. I just remember Sherlock Holmes said that," Vic said.

Everyone laughed hard at Vic's comment. It was the laughter they all needed to break the tension of this long and trying discussion.

"What it means to me is that we need more information on these pockets of puss, the Dudleys," Raquel said.

"Holmes also said, 'The world is full of obvious things which nobody by any chance ever observes,'" Sean said. He raised his glass in a half salute to the ceiling.

"That is powerful. So, the answer is right in front of us," Collin said.

"It has been since 1957," Vic said.

CHAPTER 18

Vic grabbed the check, and the goodnights were said all around. The case was far from being solved by the four diners, but their plan was now a bit more focused. Whatever would be, Vic and Raquel would not be going back to New York in defeat. Their goal now was not apprehending the killer or killers. The boy needed to have a name. He was somebody, a human being with a soul and not just a piece of trash to be discarded in an empty box and found by strangers in an overgrown lot.

Raquel grabbed onto Vic and gently put her arm around his waist. He was not very steady on his feet from all of the wine he consumed. Raquel was strong enough to guide her man from the restaurant without him looking like a falling-down drunk. They walked slowly back to their hotel room with a great view of downtown Philadelphia awaiting them.

Raquel and Vic shared a shower together and Vic slowly fingered Raquel and sucked on her nipples deliciously, the cascading, warm water enhancing Raquel's pleasure. They continued their love-making session onto the lavish, king-sized bed. The foreplay lasted much longer than Raquel ever could remember until Vic fell asleep. To Raquel's disappointment, there was no penetration, but she understood the wine had had its effect on Vic.

After they had both fallen asleep, Raquel was awakened by a kick into her thigh that made her yell out an audible "Owww!" There were many times in their relationship that Vic had had a restless and fitful sleep. Raquel knew that, lately, Vic's dreams and nightmares were having a cruel effect on his psyche. She turned her groggy head and raised it off the pillow to read the alarm clock on the night table. It was 3:32 a.m.

Once the pain from Vic's knee jerk had subsided, Raquel looked away from the clock and turned her head on the pillow, facing Vic. She stared at him for more than just a few minutes. Raquel loved his face more than any man she had ever seen or knew and began gently to stroke his forehead and graying hair. Vic's face was bathed partially in the moonlight. She wanted so much to nurture and coddle him as his woman. Raquel felt sorry for the pressure that the Boy in the Box case was giving to Vic, and she blamed herself for taking on the task of finding the killer. She worried that the case would have an emotional effect on Vic and that he would revert to the sullen, depressed, and angry man she once knew. Raquel noticed that Vic's eyes were moving rapidly and that his body was still jerking as if he were fighting a phantom demon. Was the boy in his dreams tonight?

Raquel skated her hand softly down Vic's chest and down onto his inner left thigh, where she gently squeezed his flesh, feeling his tight muscles. He was strong yet soft at the same time, Raquel thought. This was one of her favorite parts of her lover, the most sensual part for her taste. Vic must have sensed her touch in the proximity of him. Raquel could feel the sheet move slightly with his instant erection. Raquel moved herself slowly and gently down the length of his body until she was in position. With both of her soft hands placed on either side of Vic's hips she took his erection into her mouth. Vic let out a slow moan that came from high in his chest. Raquel was now completely wet. She began to move her tongue slowly down the length of his shaft. This is when Vic totally came to life, touching her hair and gently pushed her head down farther until she swallowed him to the base. Raquel gagged slightly, and he eased up a bit.

Raquel was completely turned on by the sound of Vic's pleasure as she moved him in and out of her mouth, faster, faster, her tongue rimming the tip in a quick, circular motion. She knew his body well enough to sense when the pleasure would overcome him. Vic's back arched as he moaned louder. Raquel ran her tongue over his balls, slowly pulling one into her mouth. Vic grabbed himself and found her mouth. Raquel pushed him deep into the back of her throat. She felt his cum shooting into her, swallowing everything he gave, and, with the sound of his pleasure bathing the room, she herself came. Vic took his hands and gently brought her up to him. Holding her head to his chest, he ran his hands through her hair in an almost grateful gesture. Raquel could hear his heart beating fast at first then slowing, slowing as his breath became normal. Raquel felt her eyes close, her body once again giving way to much-needed sleep. There would be no more restless sleep for Vic this night.

Raquel's sleep that morning was not as restful. She began dreaming of her ex-husband, about whom she had never before dreamt. In the dream, they were at Orchard Beach in the Bronx, New York, in Section Nine on a blanket that looked familiar to her. She was lying facedown on the blanket as was her ex-husband. There was no sun, and the beach was empty except for six fat seagulls, standing around the blanket and staring at them. The more she studied the blanket, the more familiar it looked. Her ex kept asking her why they never talked about having a baby and why she wanted one now. She felt very uncomfortable with him next to her and asked him to leave. Raquel's mother appeared in the dream, telling her that Tia Carmen was not doing very well and that Raquel's son was missing. Her son? She had a son?

"I don't have a son, Mami. What are you talking about? I never had a son."

"You had better look, Raquel, I think he has been in there for too long. His lips will be blue, and his hands and feet will be shriveled up like an old man."

Raquel ran to the water, but there was no child. She frantically ran up and down the shoreline screaming for help and for Vic. She turned to where she had been sitting. A small boy was standing alone where her blanket was. Raquel ran from the water's edge toward the boy, but the sand became very thick. It was as if she were running in place, and she became exhausted. The boy picked up the blanket and walked toward her slowly.

"Who are you? What's your name?" Raquel asked.

"Why do you have my blanket?" The boy asked.

"Are you the Boy from the Box?"

"They put this blanket in there with me."

"Come closer, and give me your hand. I have to take you to see my friend."

"You need to hurry."

Raquel saw the boy clearly for the first time. He was very thin, bruises were all over his body, and his eyes were strange. His hand and feet seemed too large for his body.

"Oh, my god. It's you," Raquel said.

"I'm nobody right now," the little boy said. He began to walk toward the water.

"You think I'm dead," the boy said.

"Come back. Don't go into the water. Please come back," Raquel was shouting.

"Raquel, baby, you okay?" Vic was shaking Raquel awake.

"Oh, my god...Oh, my god," Raquel said just before bursting into tears and sobbing into Vic's chest.

"You're fine. I'm here. You just had a bad dream."

"It was the boy. He came to me. It was so real, Vic. He was so real. He spoke to me without moving his mouth just like he did with you. He took his blanket back and was going into the water. That poor boy! He was so badly beaten. My mother was there, too. She said I had a son who was in the water. So fucking strange."

"That's what dreams are, baby, strange."

"Yeah, but the water. The water is so important in this dream. Do you think he is trying to tell us something?"

"That's your mind working on you, Raquel, just as mine has. Let's get back to sleep, and we can go over this in a few hours."

"His murderer kept him in the tub and killed him in the bath water just like that lady in Cincinnati said."

"Okay, that's enough. Another theory that they determined was a dead end."

"Dead end, my ass. That's what he is telling me, and that's what I'm going to focus on."

"Sure. Right now, relax. Sleep for a while. Look who is calming who down."

"And I think he was sexually abused before he was killed in spite of the autopsy findings."

"We're going to see Collin at 11 a.m. at the Round House and go over the evidence again. We can talk about it then."

Raquel just stared at the ceiling, replaying the dream in her mind.

"Those motherfuckers."

CHAPTER 19

"This evidence has been picked apart for fifty-seven years. Every new detective, the Vidocq Society and their people, the FBI, writers, journalists, conspiracy theorists, and local busybodies have poured over this case with a fine-toothed comb. There have been more rumors and spooky stories about this case than you can even imagine," Collin Frank said.

"What do you mean spooky stories?" Vic asked.

"I have a story to tell that may make the hair on the back of your neck stand up."

The five boxes of evidence were laid out on the conference room table at PPD headquarters in a neat arrangement. Raquel was looking at a plastic bag that contained the blanket found on the boy. She was engrossed in the geometric patterns.

"This fellow wrote a book about this case. Real nice guy from California. Forgot his name for a second, but, for some reason, I remember his wife's name, Debbie Dombrow, one of those easy-to-recall names. Well, Dombrow is a psychic. I don't personally think that any of that stuff is real, but some people follow that supernatural stuff like it's factual. Whatever floats your boat," Collin said.

Vic and Raquel looked at each other and, then, quickly looked away.

"What about that psychic that Bristow brought into the case? Do you mean to tell me that there was just a coincidence that she brought him right to the foster home with the log cabin?" Vic asked.

"I've been taught to deal with facts not the paranormal. It makes great television, but come on. It would have to happen to me for me to believe it. But, anyway, the detective in charge of the case sent three of the boxes of evidence to this writer so he could better describe the items for his book. Our guy's feeling was that the case is so old and so cold that how could it hurt? Yeah, he broke the rules, but why not? Sometimes, you have to think outside of the box, right? If the book opens up a lead, who knows? The likelihood of the perp being alive was remote. Anyway, the guy promised to send the boxes back in a few weeks."

"So, what happened?" Raquel asked.

"One night as the writer and his wife were going to bed, they heard a small boy scream from a guest room just next to the bedroom their teenage daughters shared. Not just a regular scream, a long, hurting type of blood-curdling scream. The girls came running into their parents' room scared out of their wits. The sound came from a guest room where the three boxes were stored. Needless to say, the wife, the psychic, went nuts on him and made him take the boxes into the garage."

"I would have taken them to the nearest FedEx office," Vic said.

"Well, that's what Debbie Dombrow wanted him to do. According to the writer, his wife said something to the effect of, '... and get these fucking boxes out of my house.' They were pretty shaken up."

"Ya think?" Raquel asked.

"Well, according to what this writer told our guy, it was too late. There was now an unfriendly spirit in their house. Even after the boxes were sent back to Philadelphia, stuff in their house was flying off the walls and smashing into other stuff. The girls would be studying or listening to music with their friends, and, wham, a picture from a wall would come flying from another room, even around a corner, and barely miss their heads. Their clothes would be pulled off hangers and found crumpled in their closets. Noises were heard in unoccupied rooms. Books were found piled up on the kitchen table when none of the family was home. Water was splashing in the kitchen sink or the tub, and, when the family went in to investigate, they were found bone dry. Dombrow sensed who the spirit was and said something to her husband that stopped him cold. She said, 'Why you are wasting your time trying to solve this case? That spirit is not the boy. It's his killer, and she is an evil, hateful force who knows you are trying to solve this case.' The killer is that woman who bought the boy, just like that lady in Cincinnati reported. There was nothing wrong with her. She saw her mother smash the boy's head and kill him and then drop his body in that thicket in the cardboard box."

"So, the house was all of a sudden haunted?" Vic asked.

"Not for too long. The writer and his wife called in a group of parapsychologists, you know, like in Ghostbusters, and the spirit left immediately when they arrived, never to return."

"So, what does this prove other than there is no real evidence?" Raquel asked.

"It proves nothing. But, if you believe in any of this mumbo-jumbo, it leads back to that woman from Cincinnati. Her story pretty much jibes with Bristow's theory," Collin said.

"And I'm not sure I agree with the detectives who interviewed her, Collin," Vic said.

"They were pretty experienced, competent men, Vic," Collin said.

"Yeah, and they could have blown it. Let's not let our brother-hood toward other officers blind us to human error," Vic said.

"I think we need to pick apart that woman's, 'M's,' statements, and, if she is alive, go see her and get our own sense about her testimony," Raquel said.

"Okay, let's lay out the whole thing on her from beginning to end. I think you're right. If we determine it's a dead end, at least, our curiosity will be satisfied," Vic said.

"I'll get some more coffee," Collin said.

"Good idea, we may be a while," Raquel said.

CHAPTER 20

Cincinnati, Ohio---2014

"M" lived and worked twenty minutes by car from Greater Cincinnati Airport. Vic rented an SUV, and Raquel worked on getting their destination on the GPS system. They didn't have an appointment with "M," thinking that a surprise visit would be best.

"Here it is, 2160 Auburn Avenue. Who would have ever thought we would be a block from the William Howard Taft Historical Site?" Raquel said.

"I could have gone the rest of my life and not even known Taft was from Ohio," Vic said.

"There it is. United Chemical," Raquel said.

"Nice, fancy building. And she is a main player for this company. Very impressive."

"She has a PhD in chemistry and a list of achievements a page long, and she's still hard at it at sixty-eight years old."

"If what we read in the reports about her family life is true, it's amazing she didn't end up dead or in jail," Vic said.

Raquel took the lead at the reception/security desk in United Chemical's lobby.

"Hello, we are here to see Dr. Martha Jameson. Vic Gonnella and Raquel Ruiz."

"Do you have an appointment?" the uniformed guard asked.

"We don't. It's a personal matter," Raquel said.

"I will see if she is available. Please have a seat." The guard gave a look that a meeting wasn't going to happen.

After a few minutes, a striking, leggy blonde with a gorgeous smile appeared.

"Good morning. I understand that you would like to see Dr. Jameson. May I ask who you are and to what this is in reference?"

"We are from a private investigation firm in New York City. It's a personal matter that we would prefer to discuss only with Dr. Jameson. Is she in?" Raquel asked.

"Yes, she is in, but her schedule is very tight today. Perhaps, you can send a letter and ask for an appointment."

"We only need a short time. We have a few questions about her family. Now, please just tell her we are here, we are not leaving, and it's about her family in Philadelphia." Vic was his charming, smiling, and smooth self. The leggy Miss Ohio was defenseless.

"Give me a few minutes. I'll see what I can do."

Vic followed her runway chassé with his eyes until she swiped her employee card, opening the large, glass doors leading to the offices.

"Ah, hello…Valentino, I'm standing right here next to you," Raquel said.

"How did you expect for that tight ass to get us in? I had to put on the charm."

"And watch her ass for an hour?"

"She did have a great ass at that." Vic laughed. Raquel rolled her eyes and folded her arms. They would resume this discussion at another time.

The glass doors buzzed open, and Miss Ohio made her return appearance.

"Mr. Gonnella, Miss Ruiz, Dr. Jameson will see you for a few minutes before her next meeting. This way please."

Vic gave Raquel a self-satisfied, confident smirk before they were led to a room that could have held forty people. A large, in-laid, cherry wood conference table with plush, leather chairs was the focal point of the space. The room was equipped with state-of-the-art electronic equipment and what looked to be original and expensive oil paintings. Raquel recognized an original Marc Chagall among the artwork. Vic marveled at the individual speakers and microphones that were built into every seat position. Miss Ohio opened the conference door from the outside, and Dr. Martha Jameson appeared.

"Good morning. I'm Dr. Jameson. May I say that this is highly irregular? I can spare only a few minutes with you." Martha Jameson was a tallish, well-tailored woman with the air of authority and success. Her hair was pulled back in a tight bun and was mostly gray. She had the look of a person who is stressed out all the time. She looked every bit of her sixty-nine years. There didn't seem to be much of a personality, and Vic immediately knew that she would not succumb to the New York, Italian charm.

"Thank you for seeing us, Doctor. We apologize for the intrusion. I'm Vic Gonnella, and this is Raquel Ruiz. We are the principals of Centurion Associates, a private investigation company based in New York City. We wanted to discuss the history of the boy who was murdered in Philadelphia in 1957. We have had access to the entire record of this case and have read statements from you, which were given to the police."

"So, here we go again. I really don't want to discuss this and will refer you to my attorney, Mr. Gonnella. This is not my first trip to the rodeo on this case as I'm sure you already know."

"Forgive me, Doctor, here we go *again*?" Raquel said.

"Young lady, I have been in treatment for many, many years due to what happened in my life. I did not have a good life, but, what I have left, I intend to treasure. When my psychiatrist thought it best for me to tell my story, the investigators in their infinite wisdom thought I was mentally unstable. They also said I had access to the evidence and made up a story. Now, I do admit to having psychiatric challenges, but I do not wish to waste my time on this subject again."

"Dr. Jameson, we don't think you're any crazier than the rest of us. We just want to try to get the facts and find out what happened to that boy," Raquel said.

Martha Jameson stopped to process what she had just heard. After a pregnant pause, she sat in one of the lush chairs and demurely crossed her legs. She motioned for Vic and Raquel to sit.

"Please stop. Stop referring to him as "that boy." He had a name. His name was Jonathan. He was the most pathetic creature I have ever seen. I cannot tell you how this has affected my life."

"You seemed to have been very successful in your career Doctor," Raquel said.

"Miss Ruiz, a career is one thing; a life is another."

"I see. We have just a few questions to ask to help us tie the case together," Raquel said.

"To what end? My mother and father are long dead. Their memory is left only with me, a memory I would prefer to keep repressed. I am reticent to go through this again, and I do not want what I have built in my career to be adversely affected by dead, maniacal parents. In short, I don't want my name in the press. This is why the police agreed to refer to me as 'M.'"

"And your anonymity will remain intact, I swear to you," Vic said.

"I will hear a few questions. If, at any time, I feel uncomfortable, I will end the interview."

The conference door opened, and Miss Ohio appeared, smiling coyly at Vic.

"Dr. Jameson, your meeting is ready."

"Postpone it for thirty minutes, Justine. Thank you," Dr. Jameson said.

Justine gave a last, dimply smile to Vic. Raquel shifted in her seat.

"Thank you, Doctor. What can you tell us about the day your parents obtained the boy, sorry, Jonathan?"

"There was a group of homes in Fox Chase. I don't really know what they are called. Attached, semi-attached, row houses-something like that. It was where the economically challenged residents of the area resided. Itinerant farm workers, carnival people, laborers, and such. We, Mother and I, went to see the people in this house. I remember the man's face. I don't recall his name, but his face is still clear to me. A woman handed Jonathan to my mother. They seemed to know each other, and they exchanged a few words. Mother was flirty with the man who went back into the house. He told the woman to make sure she got the envelope.

Mother gave her an envelope, presumably with some money, and they said goodbye."

"They seemed to know each other?" Raquel asked.

"My mother was quite a flirtatious woman. It always embarrassed me. I think that she and that man knew each other in some way. There was a familiarity in their tone."

"Was Jonathan his son?"

"Evidently, he was."

"Did the man seem sad to be selling his son off?" Vic asked.

"Not at all. Matter of fact, he couldn't wait to open that damn envelope."

"What did the man sound like to you, Doctor?" Raquel asked.

"You know, that is an interesting question. Those buffoons never asked me that one. He sounded like a hillbilly."

"Southern drawl?" Raquel asked.

"No, a hillbilly. West Virginia, Kentucky, Arkansas."

"What is your memory of Jonathan living with you and your parents?" Vic asked.

"Jonathan was kept locked up in the basement. He rarely, if ever, came out. He didn't speak. It was more like a grunt when he tried to communicate. Think if you kept a puppy isolated in a dark basement with little food, no toys, no affection, urinating and defecating in a pot or on the floor. How would that poor animal develop? Very sadly."

"Did he cry out?" Raquel asked.

"Oh, my god. It sounded like an injured animal. And she would beat him."

"She would beat him? What about your father?" Vic asked.

"You see, my father was older than my mother. He was a school teacher and a quiet, pensive man. She was a librarian, and she also was quiet. Her personality changed after we ate dinner. She would take table scraps down to the basement. The look on her face changed just before she would go down those stairs. She was clearly a crazy person."

"You never told anyone?" Vic asked.

"That was impossible. I didn't want to be thrown in the foster home with those horrid people who ran it not far from where we lived."

"Do you mean the Nicolettis?"

"Yes. They were terrible people. My mother knew them. I think they brokered the deal between my mother and Jonathan's father. My mother would threaten me to bring me there if I looked sideways."

"Let's get back to your father," Vic said.

"He was more afraid of Mother than I was. He would hear Jonathan cry out and just shake his head and continue grading papers or reading."

"Never tried to comfort Jonathan or improve on his living condition?"

"He wouldn't dare."

"I have a delicate question to ask, Doctor. Forgive me, but what do you think your mother was doing at night with Jonathan?" Raquel asked. Raquel expected Dr. Jameson to repel at the question.

"She tortured him. Have you ever heard of little boys taking a piece of glass and burning ants and bugs with reflective sunlight or pulling the feathers from a bird one by one? She enjoyed seeing him suffer. It made her day."

"Was her masochism that of a sexual nature in your opinion?" Raquel asked.

"When I would see Jonathan from time to time, he had bruises all over his body. I was young and too shy to notice his private parts, and he always had diapers or pajamas. My mother's motivations haunt me."

"The night he died, can you give us a brief summary of what you remember?" Vic asked.

"My mother called to me to bring down a bar of brown soap and a brush to bathe Jonathan. She bathed him in a tub. Not a bathroom tub but one of those portable, metal tubs. Jonathan was especially agitated and was moving around while she was bathing him. Suddenly, he started wailing like an injured beast. Maybe the water was too hot or the soap got in his eyes; which, I don't know. Mother started beating him, first, with her hands, then, with the brush. I screamed out for her to stop. She turned to me, and, I must tell you, her face was contorted. She looked like a devil. I ran up the stairs in a panic. I heard a loud thump, and, then, Jonathan was quiet."

"And then?" Raquel asked.

"Mother called for me to come down with a blanket. I went into our storage closet and took the first blanket I could get my hands on. When I got down to the basement, Jonathan was still in the tub, slumped against a wall. He looked like he had fallen asleep, but there was some blood in the water. Mother told me Jonathan was dead, that he slipped in the tub and hit his head against the wall. "

"Where was your father?" Vic asked.

"He was up on the second floor in his room. They had separate rooms. He never came down the whole time. Mother was wringing her hands in panic. She kept saying that they would throw her in prison and take me away and that I had to help her."

"Did she try to revive Jonathan?" Raquel asked.

"No. She left him in the water while I ran upstairs for a nail file and scissors that Mother demanded."

"How long was he in the water?"

"A good long time, I would say. Maybe an hour or so. Mother trimmed all of his nails. His right arm was sort of bent around his head against the wall, and she trimmed those nails just like that. She washed him pretty well and then cut his hair very quickly. All the while, she was cursing him and the day she took him in. It was then that I noticed how so very thin he was when she was drying his limp body."

"Go on, please," Vic said.

"We took him in the blanket, and we placed him in the trunk of the car."

"Not in the cardboard box?" Raquel asked.

"No, that cardboard box was in that thicket already," Jameson said.

Vic shot her a glance, and Raquel immediately recognized her mistake.

"I'm sorry; I should not have interrupted you," Raquel said.

"When we arrived at this isolated place, Mother opened the trunk and I got out of the car to help her. My knees were shaking so much they were literally knocking together. I was hoping that Jonathan was still alive somehow, but, God forgive me, I was glad he was still dead." Martha Jameson showed the first bit of emotion since Vic and Raquel met. Tears welled up in her eyes, and her face began to twitch. She quickly regained her composure.

"Glad he was dead, Doctor?" Raquel asked.

"Yes, I knew his suffering would truly be over."

"Then?" Vic asked.

"As we were lifting Jonathan, who was wrapped in the blanket, from the car, a set of headlights came down the road. We kept Jonathan in the trunk. A man pulled up and said that we should not be dumping trash in the lot."

"Did he get out of the car?" Vic asked.

"No, we turned our backs to him, and he drove away. Mother saw the box and put Jonathan inside."

"Did she say anything to you at that point?"

"Not really. We drove home in silence, and she never mentioned it again. It was like it never happened."

"Is there anything else you can remember that will help us?" Raquel asked.

"There is one thing. Before Mother took him out of the tub, she went upstairs to use the kitchen phone. We only had one phone. I went to the bottom of the stairs to hear what she was saying.

Something to the effect of, 'He's your son, and he's dead, and you had better not make a fuss.'"

"Any idea who she was talking to?" Raquel asked.

"I can only guess it was the man who sold Jonathan to Mother."

"Doctor, was your mother ever cruel to you or any other child after that?" Vic asked.

"Mr. Gonnella, this concludes our discussion. I hope I have helped you somewhat. I reiterate my demand for anonymity."

CHAPTER 21

Collin Frank listened attentively to Vic and Raquel, taking notes as fast as he could. The cell phone connection to PPD from the rented car was clear.

"So, Martha Jameson thinks the detectives on the case were basically incompetent buffoons," Vic said.

"I'm not going to defend anyone, guys. All I know is that men in our squad who worked with some of those detectives back in the day thought they were very thorough and professional," reiterated Collin.

"Collin, she seemed very convincing. There is something strange about her, I'll grant you that, but something happened in that house. I don't know how she could make up some of the details," Vic said.

"Yes, and hold on a minute. First off, of course she is strange. If she lived with that mother of hers and her mother was indeed a child abuser and possibly a killer, how well adjusted do you think she is going to be? In spite of her brilliance, that woman is badly damaged," Raquel said.

"And is there a second thing?" Vic asked.

"I was getting to that. If Martha Jameson is psychotic or suffers from delusions of grandeur, of course, she could have made everything up. The cut hair and finger nails, the bruises, the head trauma, the malnourishment. That was all basically public information," Raquel said.

"Yes, but what about that motorist who scolded them for dumping garbage in the field?" Vic asked.

"What about him?" Raquel asked.

"Remember what the report read. The motorist stated that he hollered out of his window to stop a woman and a young boy from dumping trash. We know that the boy could have also been a young girl. The newspapers reported that he had asked them if they were having car trouble. Martha said he was pissed that they were dumping in the lot. How did she know that?" Vic said.

"You're right. Hmmmm. That is an interesting detail. Perhaps Martha somehow got to hear about the motorist's report or she simply guessed," Raquel said.

"More conjecture all around," Collin said.

"Follow me for a minute. When did she and her psychiatrist contact PPD?" Raquel said.

"My chart says February of 2002," Collin said.

"And she originally started telling her psychiatrist about this boy being murdered by her mother in 1989, some thirty-two years after the crime. In that time, she could have done all the research possible to put together a plausible story. Then, it took her another thirteen freakin' years to come forward. I'm not buying that all the way. Yes, she is very convincing, but, guys, she is very brilliant. That kind of mind is capable of anything," Raquel said.

"So, tell me why Martha told the detectives that her mother sexually abused her but ended our conversation and stormed out when I asked her if her mother was cruel to her? I didn't even use the abuse word," Vic said.

"Maybe she forgot her original answer to that question. That was her testimony eleven years ago," Collin said.

"Or maybe she is just sick of dealing with this melodrama and needs to let it go. Look, if her mother was molesting her and then bought the boy when Martha was around ten, molested him for three years or so, and then killed the boy, how many times should she be expected to rehash this shit?" Vic said.

"I'm just saying, I don't think this is a slam dunk. We have testimony, supposedly from an eye witness, who has some serious emotional damage, and we still don't have physical evidence," Raquel said.

"So, let's get some," Vic said.

"Vic, don't you think Rem Bristow and the PPD would have found that evidence?" Collin asked.

"What they didn't have in 1957 was DNA. Like us, DNA wasn't born yet. We need DNA evidence to link the boy to his birth parents," Vic said.

"We have one side of the equation, DNA from the boy. Now, what?" Collin said.

"The DNA of the man who sold the boy to Mrs. Jameson, Martha's mother, the quiet librarian, in 1954. You are so right, Vic," Raquel said.

"He's probably long dead. It would be a miracle if we could, first off, identify the guy and, then, get the family to exhume his body for samples," Collin said.

"No, no. First, we find out who he was, and, then, we find his male blood relatives. Other sons, grandsons, like that. If we get a match, we know Martha Jameson is the real deal," Raquel said. I remember working on a past case where I learned that the male chromosome markers are passed down identically from male to male in a family.

"Nice, and, if the guy's name is John Doe, we have a first and last name for the boy. Martha said it was Jonathan, and, then, we can make a supposition as to his murderer," Vic said.

"And, if there is no match?" Collin asked.

"We have several other suspects who are not yet out of the running," Vic said.

"Sounds like a plan. When are you guys getting back here?" Collin said.

"I'm not done with Dr. Martha just yet," Vic said.

"She will have the cops and her attorney on us in a minute. You saw how she walked out. That lady doesn't play," Raquel said.

"Collin, ask Sean for a favor. Let him run her down. I want to know more about her. Hobbies, residence, social life, family, summer place, men she slept with, women she slept with, you know the drill. I want to let a couple of days go by and run into her. Maybe we go with Raquel only on this encounter. I think I may have an angle, depending on how good an actress my lady is," Vic said.

CHAPTER 22

John Deegan was restless. Although he was finished taking on his self-imposed role of the avenger of abused children, he found retirement to be amazingly boring. Building his company into a multi-billion dollar enterprise kept his mind occupied for thirty years. At the end of his career, searching out and serving his form of justice to serial pedophiles was, in John Deegan's mind, a calling from God. It was also divine intervention that helped him to escape imprisonment or death, allowing him to live out his days on the Swiss side of Lago Lugano. He also credited God with imposing his deific will upon Detective Vic Gonnella. If not for Gonnella's gutsy judgment steered by his own difficult childhood as a victim of sexual abuse and Gonnella's determination always to do the right thing, Deegan knew his life would have been finished.

John and Gjuliana Deegan were very much in love. They were married not long after John faded into anonymity. John was trying his best to make up for lost time with Gjuliana, but some things could not be bought. Gjuliana regretted never having children, especially children with John, her only love. She also was missing her family back in New York. In sort of a self-imposed witness protection program, Gjuliana could never see her family again. If she tried, surely John Deegan's whereabouts would be compromised. There were tradeoffs when one was desperately in love with an internationally wanted criminal.

What would she do when her mother or father passed? How would she comfort the remaining parent? Her nieces and nephews, aunts and uncles, and cousins would soon forget her. More hurtful was the fact that she would never be able to have a place in their lives. To them, she would fast become a memory. Gjuliana's exile from her large, close-knit, Albanian family was far more difficult than she had anticipated.

John was bored, and his new wife was becoming depressed. Something needed to be done, or all of John's billions were useless pieces of paper and electronic transfer funds.

The last call to Vic Gonnella didn't leave John feeling warm and fuzzy. If anything, Vic was downright cold and on the cusp of nasty. Their conversation left John feeling empty and challenged. A challenge to a self-made billionaire, especially with the genius of a John Deegan, would not go unrequited.

John decided to work on his issues first, then, he would turn his attention to the love of his life, the former Gjuliana Bashkimi.

Vic and Raquel were heading back to their hotel when his cell phone rang. The phone had a 718 number that he didn't recognize.

"Hello, Vic Gonnella."

"Victor, it is me, Tia Carmen. Are you busy?" She sounded tired and weak.

"Ahhhh…Tia Carmen? I am never too busy for you." Vic hit the speaker button on his phone so Raquel could hear the call.

"I hope you don't mind my call. I am using a friend's phone. The hospital sent me home today. I am feeling better. I took blood. They are buying some time."

"Raquel and I are on the phone now, Tia. We are hoping for the best for you."

"Tia Carmen, I am praying to Our Lady of Guadalupe for you. I know you don't believe in that, but I do," Raquel said.

"My little one, all positive energy is good, but save your prayerful energy for more important things. How are you doing with the boy?"

"Tia Carmen, we have some leads, but that is all they really are. Nothing really new at this point, but we are working hard," Vic said.

"Has the boy come to you again?"

"Yes, he came to me, Tia Carmen. Very upsetting," Raquel said.

"Nothing to be afraid of, my little one. He is asking for help, and he will show you signs. His energy was with me at the hospital. He is gone from me for now. The boy showed me that you are close. I only called to tell you to stay with all of your ideas. It will soon be in front of your eyes."

Vic's phone clicked, indicating he had a call waiting. He ignored the interruption.

"Tia Carmen, what is the significance of the beach? The boy came to me on a beach."

"His energy will explain. I must go. I'm suddenly feeling tired. Thank you both for what you are doing."

Tia Carmen disconnected the call. Vic's phone rang immediately. The phone read, "UNKNOWN."

"Hello, Vic Gonnella," Vic said.

"Well, Detective, I hope that this call finds you in better spirits than the last time we spoke." John Deegan's familiar voice sounded like he was in the car.

Vic hit the speaker button again.

"Mr. Deegan, I thought that I made it clear that your calls were not especially welcome," Vic said.

"I got that, Vic. I am very perceptive to the point that our last call has left me feeling quite badly. My boredom is getting worse, but I am not in a vengeful place. My spirit is at peace, and I am looking for something to occupy my mind. Do you know of any good crossword puzzles I can work on?" John Deegan laughed at his innocuous joke.

"John, I am quite busy. Can you tell me why you are calling?"

"Busy? That's what I thought. Your office is well-trained. All they would say is that you are not available for a few days, which tells me you are away. Maybe on a case?"

"Yes, John, I'm on a case."

"And Raquel is with you, so, it must be an important one at that."

"If I were afraid of you, I would say you were stalking us," Vic said.

"No, no, not at all. I am simply calling to see if I can be of any service. You know, Vic, in a virtual world, we can work anywhere. I am not your average serial killer. I had a cause, I fulfilled my obligations to that cause, and, now, I want to be useful. You know I'm no dummy, Vic. Let me help somehow."

"I think you need to sit this one out, John," Vic said. Raquel looked at Vic and shrugged her shoulders in a why not gesture.

"Victor, from my sophisticated tracking devices here on the lake, I see you are in Cincinnati. I don't think you were visiting the Taft museum. What are you up to?"

"John, let's just say we are on a cold case. I will admit one thing. It was an abused boy from many years ago. There is your assignment. If you can figure it out, maybe we can use that great mind of yours. Let's see," Vic said.

"I'm back in the game. You just gave me enough to go on. I'll be back to you," John Deegan said. He hit the red button on his phone.

"Baby, why not? How can he hurt?"

"Raquel, the man is a killer. Never forget that. He is a trained and experienced killer. He is not our friend. Let's see if John Deegan, the genius, even calls us back. He is not good at failure. I doubt that he calls us anytime soon. Let him stay wherever the fuck he is."

"Two calls that we were not expecting. Tia and Deegan. Maybe we should put the two of them in a room and see what happens," Raquel said.

"Yeah, that would be some combination. A dying psychic and a maniacal killer. They would wind up ruling the planet."

CHAPTER 23

Collin Frank and Sean Lewandowski spent most of the next day doing what detectives and FBI agents do, snoop around, gathering information on an individual who is on their radar screens.

They found absolutely nothing that would indicate that Dr. Martha Jameson was nothing more than an outstanding, tax-paying, church-going, PhD of a boring woman. No police record whatsoever, no ex-boyfriend with tattoos and restraining order, not even a late charge on her Visa card. No prior marriages, no outstanding speeding violations, no nothing. In fact, there was never even a missed stop sign or a red light summons.

Sean had a stealth contact at Verizon Fios, Dr. Jameson's network provider. She did not even once rent a movie in the past seven years.

"This woman has led a life of a saint," Collin said. He was rubbing the strain out of his eyes from all the computer research he had done for most of the day.

"No one is this clean. She is either the perfect citizen or has the best cloaking devices known to criminal justice," Sean said.

"What about sex? No guy, no porn, no dildo?" Collin asked.

"Sex isn't a crime, Collin, not the last time I checked."

"According to my wife, it is. Nun a dis, nun a dat. I could swear she became a cloistered nun the day after we got married."

"I hear you. Johns Hopkins Medical School did research for twenty years. There is one food that prevents women from wanting to have sex. Know what it is?" Sean said.

"No idea."

"The wedding cake."

"Hahahahaha. I hear that. Anyway, this Jameson woman has no history at all. She does like to imbibe a bit but, even there, never to excess," Collin said.

"I guess she was so damaged as a child she decided to live a stellar existence when she broke free."

Sean and Collin reported their findings on Dr. Martha Jameson to Vic and Raquel. The only habit they could see from her credit card usage was that she charged food almost on a daily basis at one particular restaurant located halfway between her house and her office.

The next evening, Raquel "ran into" Martha Jameson as she was leaving Trovato's Ristorante, where she usually dined alone.

"Hello, Dr. Jameson. Do you remember me?"

"Of course, Miss Ruiz, what brings you here?"

Raquel was wearing a short, gray skirt and skin-tight leggings with gray boots. Two businessmen in pinstripe suits were entering the restaurant, and each made a double take at the shapely Raquel. One of the two made the mistake of saying a flirtatious "hello." Raquel starred him down with a you-have-no-shot look. Raquel turned her attention back to Jameson.

"I heard it was a good spot for a nice dinner. I needed to be alone to clear my head."

"Clear your head?"

"Well, to be honest, after meeting with you, some things from the past came back to mind, and I've been really, really upset." Raquel forced herself to tear up by thinking of how she felt at the boy's gravesite.

"Oh my, I am sorry. Come inside. I've eaten, but I will have a drink while you get something to eat."

The two women sat at Martha's favorite table toward the back of the restaurant in a quiet corner where she usually ate dinner while pouring over reports from work.

"Very nice place, Dr. Jameson."

"My favorite place in town. I'm here several times a week. The food is good, the place is clean, and I get some work done."

"I'm sorry to get so emotional. I must be honest again. I'm a detective. I found out that you came here often, and I wanted to run into you. I'm sorry to deceive you, Dr. Jameson."

"I figured that out, Miss Ruiz. Were the tears fake, too?"

"Oh, no, not at all. Look, I know that you saw some terrible things as a young woman. Seeing that boy abused by your mother and watching her dump his body must have been just horrible."

"I didn't just watch her. I helped her. I guess, in a way, I was an accessory after the fact. Luckily, I was still a child."

"You were forced to do what you did."

"I really had no choice in the matter."

"Well, when Vic asked you about your mother, you became agitated and abruptly left. Vic was also abused as a child. I know that pain very well."

"So, you know how difficult it is to talk about being molested."

"Absolutely. I know that you discussed your abuse with the Philadelphia detectives years ago. I was just surprised at your reaction now, why you wouldn't open up. "

"You know, there are times when I can discuss it, and, then, there are times when I want it buried-depends on my mood. Having people not believe my story upsets me greatly. Also, I don't want my colleagues to know my past. I am in a competitive field. I don't need people knowing my business and using this against me. I want my privacy protected at all costs."

"I understand and agree totally. How about now? Do you feel like discussing things with me?"

"You order something to eat. I'll have my second Martini, and we will see what happens."

The orders were placed, and the two women chatted about things in general. Women in the workplace, women in traditionally male-dominated roles, abused women. They switched to the familiar first name basis.

"Tell me, Raquel. You said Vic was abused. What were the circumstances? His parents?"

"His priest. I'm not sure which is worse to be honest."

"My goodness. A priest. So, he must feel abandoned by God Himself."

"That's exactly what happened to Vic. He still has his moments of rage."

"Abuse by a parent is no picnic, I can attest to that. I've been in therapy since my college days. Not so much rage as depression in my case. It lasted quite a long time. After a while you become numb to the physical attack. Mother stopped sexually abusing me when she bought Jonathan. I was getting too old to put up with that. I think that she realized I might tell a teacher or someone at school. She was very sick and very cunning. After Jonathan came, she never tried anything on me again. We never, ever discussed her touching me or killing that poor child. Never!"

"Did she have any other children whom she abused to your knowledge?"

"Pedophiles never act once, and they only sometimes get caught. Mother was very foxy. She had friends whom I definitely think were into that sick way of life. After a while, she was with them a lot. Mother often did not come home at night, going to work the next day from wherever she stayed."

"Another man perhaps?"

"Well, I think that was possible, but I believe there were children involved."

"How so, Martha?"

"This couple; I believe their names were Jim and Maggie Nelson. They seemed like they were up to no good. They came over to our house a few times. He made me feel very uncomfortable. Maggie seemed okay, but there was something strange about him. Like a deer in the headlights look if you know what I mean."

"How did he make you uncomfortable?"

"He would stare at me. He would stare at my breasts, my legs. He gave me the creeps."

"Anything else?"

"I told you my mother was a flirt. Well, around these two, she was in flirt overdrive, always saying suggestive things. I made myself scarce."

"And your father? Was he into this couple?"

"Hated them with a passion. I heard him saying to Mom one time that they were sick, fallen-away Catholics. Dad was a devout man, who spent much of his time working or reading scripture."

"Forgive me, Martha, but maybe your mom and the Nelsons were into a threesome thing?"

"I wouldn't doubt that for a second, but I believe there were children involved. She often drowned herself in perfume before going to see the Nelsons. And, another strange occurrence, Mother was always buying children's items and began speaking in baby talk. Mother behaved like a few different people. At work, she was the dutiful librarian, straight as an arrow. At home, she was a strange, sexual degenerate. With the Nelsons, she was playing the role of a sex goddess or a teenage girl. She was just awful." Martha took a long pull on her Martini.

Raquel shifted uneasily in her seat when Martha brought up the baby talk.

"How long did this go on?"

"Oh, for quite a number of years. The Nelsons were friends with these very strange people who ran a foster home not far from where we all lived. Mother took me to a back yard party there once. Maybe it was a Fourth of July or Memorial Day party; I don't remember the exact details. I guess I was fifteen or so. I was afraid of that place and the owners. I was thinking Mother was going to leave me there because I knew about what happened to Jonathan. My god, no wonder I've never had a normal life."

"Tell me a bit about the foster home. Do you remember anything about it?"

"Lots of children of different ages. Maybe fifteen in total. They were pretty tattered. They didn't look all that clean or healthy to me. There was this older man and his wife and a younger woman who ran the place. Perhaps, she was their daughter or an older adopted child. It was just a very sad place to me."

"Just a big, old house?" Raquel recalled seeing a photograph of the foster house in one of the PPD reports.

"A big, old house with a good-sized property. There was this log cabin in the yard. I thought it was very cute. I always wanted to stay in a log cabin from watching Davey Crocket and Daniel Boone on television when I was a little girl. When I looked inside and saw all these bunk beds with blankets, I quickly got away from there. Again, I was afraid I would be left there by Mother. It scared me to no end."

"So, let me get this straight. Your mother was friends with the Nelsons and the foster home owners. Did you ever see that man who sold Jonathan to your mother again?"

"Never, but I always had the feeling that Mother knew him somehow." Martha drained her martini.

CHAPTER 24

Vic and Raquel arrived in Philadelphia mid-morning the next day. They went directly to the Round House to meet with Collin and Sean and debrief them on their visit with Dr. Martha Jameson. There were so many possibilities and interconnections that Vic practically ran to the large, white display board in the main conference room.

Vic wrote the following bullet points in bold letters under the banner:

WHAT WE HAVE:

MARTHA JAMESON-MOTHER

NELSONS AND THE NICOLETTI CONNECTION

THE DUDLEYS-CARNIVAL PEOPLE

THE REST???

"I think we need to focus on the top three bullet points. Somewhere in there is the key to the boy's father, mother, and murderer. If we can find his parents, we can at least solve the mystery of who the boy was. That may lead us directly to the killer. Unless I'm wrong, does anyone have anything to offer?" Vic said.

"From what you both told us about Jameson, it sounds that she is very credible. My concern is pretty basic. How could the investigators who initially visited her discount what she said? Basically, they called her a nut job," Sean said.

"She is no nut job. Peculiar, maybe eccentric, definitely damaged, but not nearly crazy," Raquel said.

"Frankly, the detectives missed the mark. The case went cold not only because they had skimpy physical evidence but also because they did not follow up well on the Nicoletti connection. There is, in my opinion, a definite connection between the boy and that foster home. They needed to press Nicoletti more," Vic said.

"You think he did the murder," Sean said.

"I don't think he did it, but I think he was somehow involved," Vic said.

"What about all of the other theories, Vic?" Sean asked.

Vic paused and pointed at the bullet point that read "THE REST."

"There are so many theories that clouded judgment, took time, and sent the cops on wild goose chases. This happens all the time in homicide investigations. Unfortunately, this often makes an already tough case ice cold. The two young men who found the boy, did either of them kill him? Not very often does the killer call the police to say, "I found a body." And there was no physical evidence to link either of them. The one kid was an embarrassed, peeping Tom and the other, a Polish immigrant who was trapping small animals for pelts or food."

"Chasing a squirrel, Vic? I still don't get that," Collin said.

"Yeah, that's weird. The guy was out of his car to do something. Maybe he was spanking the monkey." Vic made the universal sign for male masturbation. Everyone laughed at his choice of words.

"No, seriously, this guy could have known more," Collin said.

"I seriously doubt that. He didn't have the profile of a murderer. A peeping Tom or just a young man full of testosterone, yes. Remember, this was 1957; a guy needed a vivid imagination to get off. There weren't many good girly magazines around, so, girls in uniforms did it for this guy," Sean said.

"There are a dozen other dead ends. That kidnapped kid from Long Island, that Martinez woman in Colorado who threw her three-year-old daughters into a trash can," Vic said.

"Hold it. What Martinez woman?" Sean asked.

"A woman killed her daughter in Colorado in 1960. She matched the description of the women who the motorist saw dumping our boy. There was no connection. But this drives home my point. A woman in Colorado was questioned by the PPD. That took time, effort, and money. After a while, a department throws its hands up. There are a lot of bad guys out there, and no PD has unlimited funds," Vic said.

"So, what you are saying is that Martha Jameson's mother and the Nicolettis are our best suspects. And what if we come up dry?" Sean said.

"Let's not play "What if?" right now. We need to dig deeper into this new Nelson lead. I never heard that name before. Martha Jameson gave it up to Raquel in a relaxed, trusting environment. Even she didn't connect the dots. Let's find out who these people are, see if they are still alive, and interrogate them.   We   may have come up with that proverbial loose end here," Vic said.

"Do you have a plan?" Sean asked.

"Yes, well, sort of, with the help of the FBI and PPD. We need as much information as possible on the Nicoletti family and the Nelson couple, records on the foster home and such. I'd like to see the names of kids who were brought there and their parents as well. It could be hundreds of kids. When did the Nicolettis start their foster home business, and when did they end it? Were there any other missing or murdered kids in the Philadelphia area after 1957? If you guys can help us run down these things, Raquel and I will jump right on them."

"No problem here," Sean said.

"You know I have orders to help any way I can," Collin said.

"Good, we are going back to our hotel to check in and follow up on some calls. I can't thank you guys enough," Vic said.

"Donuts. You know how cops love donuts. Bring a few dozen tomorrow," Collin said. Everyone laughed. Vic did the masturbation sign. They laughed even harder.

CHAPTER 25

Vic received an urgent telephone call from his New York office. The new NYPD Commissioner needed to see him as quickly as possible regarding urgent police business. Vic called One Police Plaza and was connected quickly to Commissioner Ernest Barrett. NYPD was investigating a murder of a teacher at a prestigious private high school in the Riverdale section of the Bronx. The teacher was killed and mutilated by a makeshift cross. Commissioner Barrett was concerned that the homicide might have been a copycat killing, reminiscent of the case that made Vic Gonnella a household name and a worldwide celebrity.

Vic promised to get back to New York the next day and arrive at NYPD HQ before noon. It was in his best interest to get on the best side of the new commissioner and bill him a hefty consultancy fee. Business was still business.

Raquel would stay in Philadelphia and continue to dig into the Boy in the Box case.

"Let's get some sleep, baby. You need to leave early, and I'm pretty exhausted, too," Raquel said.

"Okay, so, I guess that means no action again tonight?" Vic said.

"It will be here, all ready when you get back, you maniac. I want to follow up on the Nicoletti lead big time in the morning."

The couple showered together and played around a bit but not enough to get the engines started. Vic called it playing grab ass. Raquel laughed and ran from the bathroom, covering her delicious body in a huge bath towel. After they got into the king-sized bed, the only light in the room came from the red LED dots on the television and the alarm clock on the end table next to the bed.

Once in bed and cozy under the covers, Vic jokingly made low moans like a lion in heat sending Raquel into hysterics. She fell asleep with a smile on her face, and Vic lay awake for a few minutes. Raquel's deep breathing lulled him into a deep sleep.

Just before dawn, the dim LED lights began to flicker. The light gave off a glow, which illuminated the room. The low, disturbing moan of a child filled the room. Vic and Raquel both sat upright in the bed, and both saw the same apparition. It was the boy. This time, he was fully dressed. A week after his body was found, the detectives from PPD who were working on the case thought it would help someone recognize the boy if they dressed him in a white shirt and blue pants. They photographed his body in the makeshift attire and circulated the eerie picture around the Greater Philadelphia area. The boy was now standing in their room, wearing that outfit.

"Is this a dream?" Raquel asked, her voice hoarse and quivering.

"If it is, we are both in the same dream," Vic said.

The couple sat for what seemed like minutes as the boy looked from one to the other. The light in the room faded a bit, and the boy seemed to be shrouded in a fog-like aura.

"What do you want little one?" Raquel asked as she scooted a little closer to Vic.

The boy held the back of his head with his right hand and made a face like he was in pain. Vic felt like crying but bit down hard on his lower lip.

Suddenly, a low voice was heard. It was almost inaudible.

"Please find out who I am. My mommy and daddy didn't love me, but I love them. Please hurry."

The light flickered, and the image of the boy faded away as the sunlight began to peek through the drapes in the suite. The alarm clock made a clicking sound, and music began to play. The boy started to shake like he was dancing to the music, clicking both his thumbs in time. It was Elvis Presley.

"Well, honey, I love you too much

I need a your lovin' too much

Want the thrill of your touch

Gee, I can't a love you too much

You do all the livin' while I do all the givin'

'Cause I love you too much"

The light flashed wildly, and the boy seemed to evaporate into thin air. Vic and Raquel were frozen for a few seconds. They turned toward each other, their mouths open in astonishment. The music stopped, and the radio went silent.

"Holy shit," Vic said.

"Oh, my god. He was here. No bullshit, that little boy was here, Vic."

"If I told this story, no one would ever believe it. Fuck, I don't even believe it."

"Did you notice something?" Raquel said.

"Yeah, I noticed a freakin' ghost, that's what I noticed."

"When he spoke with you before, what did he sound like?"

"What do you mean?"

"When he spoke with me on the beach, he sounded different. He sounded like any little kid. His speech was a bit hesitant if anything."

"So?"

"This time, he sounded like a hillbilly. A really deep, southern accent."

"Yeah, but he was from Pennsylvania, right?" Vic said.

"He was found dead in Philadelphia. But we have no idea where he is from, where his parents are from. I don't know; what was that accent? Alabama? Mississippi? Georgia?"

"Anything south of New Jersey sounds the same to me."

"Nope. He had that deep, southern drawl."

"And that song-I know that song. Elvis all the way," Vic said.

"But not one of his big ones like "Hound Dog" or "Jail House," right?"

"Not a big fan. A bit before my time," Vic said.

"I'm going to look it up."

Raquel jumped from the bed and reached for her iPad. She Googled "YouTube Elvis Presley." In a second, there were hundreds of Elvis videos from which to choose. Vic stood behind her as she scanned down.

"There it is, 'Too Much,'" Raquel said.

Raquel clicked on "Play," and the video went to an annoying commercial for Shinola Watches. After five seconds, she clicked on "Skip Ad."

There was Elvis Presley, handsome as they come, pompadour up about four inches, his hair soaked with Vitalis, his backup singers standing very close behind him. It was an old, black-and-white television appearance. That was the song the boy was snapping to, for sure.

"Give me a second, baby," Raquel said.

She Googled the song "Too Much."

"Look at this. Bobbers.com. "Too Much" was on the charts from February third until February twenty-third. Three weeks at number one.

Vic and Raquel sat at the edge of their bed in silence, both trying to understand what had just happened. Raquel nervously bit her lower lip. Vic gave the thousand-yard stare at the alarm clock.

Vic's cell phone rang, making he and Raquel jump to their feet.

"Christ, it's Deegan," Vic said. He clicked the green button on the phone.

"Vic, sorry to call you so early. I hope I'm not disturbing you," John Deegan said.

"I'm too disturbed to notice if I'm being disturbed."

"I've read as much as I can on your case. It's very elementary, my dear boy. Find his father, and that will lead to the killer. You have an advantage over me at the moment, Vic. I'm reading the internet; you have access to the old investigative reports. The trail to his parents are in those reports somewhere. Make some assumptions. Expect that the killer and his parents are all dead. Actually, the killer could very well be his parents. Get to the relatives of some of the people around the case and grab their DNA samples. Compare that to the child's DNA profile, and, at the very least, you will know the boy's name. That may lead to the murderer." Deegan disconnected the call.

CHAPTER 26

Raquel studied the case evidence yet again. She poured over the boxes of faded material that was so old that it seemed like ancient history to her. Raquel looked at her notes carefully. They were becoming a confused jumble that made her want to scream out in disgust. Instead of shrieking, she stared at the muddle of papers for a few minutes and sorted out a plan in her mind. There had to be something in the reams of files and reports that would lead to who this child was. John Deegan was correct-they should look for who the boy was more than who killed him. Raquel knew in her soul that the reports would reveal that information.

On a long sheet of unlined paper, Raquel listed all of the names of the persons who were interviewed by the PPD from 1957 until recently. Next to the name, she notated a number from one to ten with ten being the greatest possibility of a relationship to the child. Six hours later, Raquel had only three individuals who made her eight-or-higher list.

The Nicolettis, the Jamesons and the Dudleys. This same list was established days ago as the key persons of interest. Raquel decided to view their files a bit more aggressively.

The meeting with Martha Jameson was fresh in her mind, and Martha's story was convincing. One question kept coming into Raquel's mind: why did no one believe her story? Martha was indeed strange, but how and why could she have concocted such a bizarre tale about her own family, about her own mother? Where and from whom did Martha say her mother got the boy again?

Raquel focused her efforts on the Jameson file, studying each and every report and notation. She came up with nothing compelling and the beginning of a tension headache. Then, a light switch went on in Raquel's brain.

Martha had said that she and her mother went to pick up the boy. Her mother took the child and passed an envelope to a man. Raquel needed to know who that man was.

Dr. Martha Jameson had given Raquel her card at the end of their meeting in Ohio. Raquel took that card from her wallet and called Martha's direct line.

"Hi, Martha; Raquel. How are you?"

"Just getting ready for one of my endless meetings. How are you, Raquel?"

"I'm okay. But just okay. I will explain another time. I have a quick question if you don't mind."

"From you, I don't mind at all."

"When you and your mom went to pick up the boy, sorry, Jonathan. When you went to get him, can you describe the man who was also there who sold him to your mother?"

"I can remember that he was short. He was very well dressed for the kind of house they lived in. Listen to what a snob I sound like. Well, at the risk of sounding snobby, the home was in a group of working-class row houses. The man was wearing a nice suit and tie with a big, gold tie clip like they used in those days."

"Bald? Skinny? Fat? Was anyone else there?" Raquel asked.

"We only went to the door, and they came out with Jonathan. He was normal sized, I guess. Not bald."

"Did he speak to your mom?"

"Of course. Like I said before, she was flirty and chatty, but he, at least on this meeting, was all business. They had a conversation about Jonathan and how he was slow and that he cried a lot. I would say it was a cordial conversation."

"I want to go over the man's accent once more, Martha. What did he actually sound like?"

"Wow, now you are taxing my memory again, but I do recall he sounded like he was from the south. I recall it because that kind of accent was very rare in Philadelphia. Most definitely a southern twang. Is it still called a twang, Raquel?" Martha said. She chuckled at her remark.

"Sort of like…Hey, y'all, how ya doin' daday?" Raquel did her best southern accent imitation.

"Perfect. Not bad for a New Yorker," Martha said.

"Thank you so much, Martha. Stay well. Looking forward to seeing you again one day."

"That would be delightful, Raquel."

Raquel frantically searched through the dead-end file in a huge three-hole binder that the old PPD detectives had amassed on the case. She recalled skimming over a short report about a woman who called back in February of 1957. This new information wouldn't necessarily help track the killer, but it might at least lead them to the family, which could then give the boy his proper name.

She found it. The document was nearly brown from age, and a circle on the bottom of the page was once the resting place for a coffee cup. The report, taken by Detective Joe McMillan, indicated that a woman called a week after the boy's body was found. A Mrs. Helen Ring was a landlord. She and her husband had rented out a house to tenants who left in the middle of the night, leaving the place a mess. She thought it strange that the tenants moved out so quickly and so soon after the news of the boy was made public. Mrs. Ring noted that the adults had several children, including a toddler. She noted that they were from Georgia or Tennessee. Their name was Jordan. The man's name was Bruce. She didn't know if the woman who lived there was the man's wife, nor did she know her first name.

Tennessee? Raquel frantically searched the report for a notation or follow up report. There was none. She was making the connection to the Elvis song the boy had sung to her and Vic... Graceland in Memphis, Tennessee!

Raquel was puzzled and pissed off at the same time. How could the detectives and everyone else who has either been a professional or amateur sleuth on the Boy in the Box case have ignored this lead? What annoyed her most was how she had not asked the right questions to begin with. The fine art of obtaining information starts at asking the easy questions first. Expecting the killer to reveal him or herself without digging deeply into the case was an unreasonable expectation.

Who Bruce Jordan was and where he ran to was the next link in the chain. Raquel was determined to find this family and their children. She would ask the easy questions first. Once she found them, perhaps the case would unfold. If the Jordans were indeed a dead end, Raquel had two more fat files from which she could possibly extract the boy's family members.

Vic called Raquel to check in. After all the "I loves you"s and "I miss you"s, and a few sexy, lover moans, Vic got to business.

"I'll be at least two or three days here, honey. There is a lot going on at HQ, and we are not the only security firm in town. I'll be damned if I let anyone else get next to this commissioner. I promised myself the new guy in that seat would be my new best friend," Vic said.

"Decent guy?" Raquel asked.

"No idea yet. Seems to be overwhelmed a bit, but that's to be expected. Any stub of the toe, and the New York press will eat him for lunch. He has a major political football with the stop-and-frisk thing. Let's face it, the last guy abused it to no end. Every foot cop had a quota. All HQ wanted were numbers to show how stop and frisk and lower crime rates were like hand in glove."

"No wonder the black and Hispanic communities were revolting. Talk about abuse of power!"

"The old boss…he was decent to me, but he started becoming a maniac with his power. You are so right, honey. I think, in the end, it started getting the best of him. Who said 'power corrupts and absolute power corrupts absolutely?'"

"It was John Dalberg Acton, and he actually said, "Power tends to corrupt, and absolute power corrupts absolutely. Great men are almost always bad men," Raquel said.

"Excuse me, Miss Columbia University, I find smart girls to be very sexy, you know," Vic said.

"Just make sure it's this smart girl, Romeo," Raquel joked.

"So, what's going on in the City of Brotherly Love?"

"I have an idea that I'm working on. I've got it covered. I'm hoping I don't get another visit tonight from the boy. It still scares me a little, honey."

"Raquel, I want to say something without pissing you off," Vic said.

"Somehow, I feel an argument coming on."

"No, honey, please listen for a second. This boy cannot harm you in any way. I'm not so sure I buy the whole energy thing just yet, but let me hear myself think this through. If he is truly a spirit or energy force stuck where he is, then, the boy is looking for our help. Perhaps, the boy appeared to Remington Bristow, and the poor guy had no idea how to handle seeing the boy. It sounds like people were not taking Bristow seriously after a while. Maybe his emotions got the better of him and…"

"What are you trying to say, Vic, that I'm overly emotional?" Raquel asked.

"Honey, stop. Not at all. Please follow me. Bristow was unable to use the boy to help solve the case. Bristow got too close, and his imagination was all over the place. The more the boy comes to us, the more we are learning. Don't be afraid of this child. Welcome him."

"Honey, I hear what you're saying. I'm not at all afraid of him hurting me, but seeing him is unnatural and upsetting. If he comes, he comes, but I'm not lighting candles and setting up a Ouija board."

CHAPTER 27

Raquel set her mind on the Jordan family.

The best place to start was in the Philadelphia Department of Records, where any and all records from the 1950s were kept, mostly on microfilm. The Jordans were renters and not property owners, so, there were no tax records for that family. As it turned out, there were a few Jordans in the Philadelphia area, which made the search a bit more tedious. But there was no record of a Bruce Jordan, the name that Mrs. Ring had given.

Raquel cross-referenced to the Federal Census of 1940. Still no Bruce. Social Security death records had thousands of Jordans, but no Bruce. United States draft records, nothing. Department of Motor Vehicle records didn't go back that far in Philadelphia's record keeping. It seemed that the Jordan family suddenly left their apartment in February 1957 and went deep cover.

Raquel's neck was throbbing, her eyes began itching, and her butt was sore after being hunched over the computer screen for so many fruitless hours. The frustration of looking for a needle in a haystack was beginning to piss Raquel off, and that was never a good thing.

Raquel took a deep breath and thought of that Sherlock Holmes quotation Vic mentioned about looking toward the obvious. If the Jordans had any children at all in Philadelphia, there was likely a birth record. That would narrow the search down considerably.

Raquel left the PC and took a short walk over to the Philadelphia Records Department office. In general, records personnel are civil servant workers who are simply marking time until they can pension out. They are miserable creatures who hand over forms to be filled out without even looking up at the people they are supposed to be serving. Philadelphia Records personnel were no exception. However, this was not Raquel's first day at the rodeo. Raquel's ethnic good looks, her gold, private investigator's badge, and her determination made the records people look up from the counter at her. After all, she was one of them, a minority, a woman, and she carried an underlying attitude to trump their swagger. Books and microfilm from the 1950s were quickly brought forward into the stark, gray room made available with coffee for Detective Ruiz. Now, all Raquel had to do was find this dude.

Raquel was determined to read every Jordan birth certificate until the name Bruce came up. It had to be done, and, as it turned out, the task wasn't all that difficult.

After looking at three other birth records, Raquel found a record for Robert Jordan, born September twelfth, 1954. Son of Major Bruce Jordan. Major was his first name, not a military rank.

"Son of a bitch!" Raquel said aloud.

Without looking closer at the birth certificate, Raquel asked one of the clerks for a copy of the record.

Within a minute, the copy was printed from the microfilm.

"Here you are, sweetie. Your COB on one Robert Jordon, son of Major Bruce Jordan and Miss Lillian Jameson," The clerk said.

Raquel nearly fell on the floor.

"What did you say? Miss Lillian what?"

"Jameson, like the whiskey, honey. Although I prefer Hennessey, baby," The clerk said.

Raquel practically tore the copy from the woman's hand.

"Holy shit!" Raquel said.

"Son of a bitch, holy shit-now, throw a "motherfucker" in there, and I know you from the hood," the clerk said.

Raquel and the woman shared a belly laugh as Raquel put her arms around the ample woman and hugged her tightly.

Raquel was beginning to think differently about the ability of the Philadelphia PD. How could they have passed over Mrs. Ring's call so early into the investigation? How could anyone miss this report or call it a dead end until it was thoroughly investigated?   Raquel picked up her cell phone to call Detective Collin Frank. She wanted to tell him about the Jameson lead and ask for help tracking down the Jordans. Just as she was searching for his number, something told her to do this herself. Could there be something within the PPD that didn't want to solve this case? Sure, the brass seemed very much willing to help her and Vic, but why was there no accountability? No follow up?

Raquel called Vic instead.

After she explained all of the details that put Bruce Jordan and a Jameson woman together, Raquel got into the real reason for her call.

"Baby, I can't believe these guys were so minor league. You mentioned about looking at the obvious. If this lead were followed back in February of 1957, they would have collared the perp within ten days. Could there have been a reason this was so conveniently overlooked?" Raquel said.

"I'm not a fan of conspiracy theories, but I think you need to go with your gut on this," Vic said.

"That's all I have to do! Make Collin feel that he is part of a bunch of criminal cops from the fifties. He is such a good guy and a great help so far."

"Just keep it quiet about your Jameson information, and send him on an errand."

"An errand?" Raquel said.

"Yes. You said you had some ideas about those carnival people. What were their names again?"

"Dudley."

"Yeah, the manor-born Dudley family. Look, let him check out the DNA link between those maniacs and our boy," Vic said.

Raquel took the short walk over to PPD. It had started to rain. More than a few drops caused her blouse to cling to her figure. A few glances were enough to make her feel self-conscious as she made her way to Collin's workstation. Raquel held the blouse a few inches from her body hoping that the humidity would dry it quickly and reduce the nipple marks. By the time Raquel reached Collin, her face was reddened by embarrassment.

Collin's desk was empty except for the PPD Homicide Department daily activity sheet. The names of the freshly killed and the assigned officer ran halfway down the page. Another busy night of killings in the City of Brotherly Love.

"Miss it?" Raquel said.

Collin looked up from the report. He took a quick glance at his friend's girlfriend's wet blouse and quickly diverted his eyes back to the page. He seemed embarrassed more that he was looking at the assignment sheet than he was for catching a glimpse.

"Yeah, I do. I really do," Collin said.

"Collin, listen to me. You are not an indentured servant to this case. If it's not doing it for you, opt out. No harm, no foul."

"Raquel, I guess I miss the street action more than I thought. I'm looking at the cases and saying to myself, 'This one would have been mine.'"

"Instead of chasing the Fox Chase boy from fifty-seven years ago. I get it," Raquel said.

"I can't give up on, Vic. I don't want to piss him off."

"He will not be pissed off, trust me on that."

"And then I blow my retirement job?" Collin kept looking up quickly and glancing down at the paper in front of him.

"I have one more assignment for you. Wanna try?"

Collin nodded like a little boy, never looking up at his friend's girlfriend. Raquel's blouse was practically dry, her nipples back to normal.

"I need you to track down the Dudleys, you know, that fine family from the carnival. We want to match our boy's DNA to the mother and father."

"They are most likely dead, but I will do my best," Collin said.

"Dead or not, you can try to track down any surviving children of these mutts. They have the penance of carrying the Dudley DNA."

"I will get the samples you need. After all, how tough is it to get spit on a Q-tip?" Collin said.

"Collin, you can look up now, my blouse is dry. And thank you for being a gentleman."

Collin's fair complexion went red.

"And when you finish with the Dudleys, I will ask Vic to speak with your supervisor."

"Raquel, you know how it is. Once you get that smell of the blood on the street, it's like an addiction. I need to be back in that game, or I will get cold. I really hope you understand."

"Let's not talk about that again. Of course, Vic and I both understand that allure. Half the time, we both wish we never left the department. The other half, we are thrilled we did."

CHAPTER 28

Vic and Raquel decided to meet in Memphis and take the Boy in the Box case to the next level. Finding the boy's family was their sole agenda for the moment. Vic flew from JFK Airport, Raquel from Philadelphia International. They coordinated times the best they could, and Vic drew the short straw, having to wait for his lady for an hour and fifteen minutes.

Vic spent his time reading all of the Elvis Presley signs and brochures about Graceland, the home of the King of Rock n' Roll. Posters for several BBQ restaurants all claiming to be the best in Memphis, St. Jude Hospital, made famous by the great personality of Danny Thomas, and a brochure for the Lorraine Hotel Civil Rights Museum were also among Vic's reading material. He collected the material at the first information desk he passed. He had no idea that St. Jude Hospital was in Memphis and even less of an idea that it was the gravesite of the famous Lebanese comedian.

He completely forgot that Dr. Martin Luther King Jr. was assassinated by James Earl Ray in Memphis. Perhaps, he never even knew that either, Vic thought.

The small airport, the slower pace of Memphis, which had cute, happy, smiling, blonde-haired and blue eyed, short-skirted ladies, and the other local attractions appealed to Vic. Especially after coming fresh from the snake pit of the New York City office of the police commissioner. Being embroiled in the politics of a new commissioner and an overly ambitious new mayor made Vic's head spin, but all he wanted out of NYPD now was a few healthy consultation fees. He knew that, within the NYPD, nothing of value came easy. Vic and company would certainly give a pound of flesh for any work that came their way from the commissioner's office.

Raquel's plane arrived on time, and she texted Vic,

"I may attack you right on the escalator." He wrote back, "Stay on the plane, and I'll do you

right in your seat."

Clearly, these two were missing each other like crazy. This kind of teasing kept their relationship exciting and fresh.

Raquel threw her arms around Vic's neck and sighed into his chest. Vic made a sound from deep in his throat that turned Raquel on like lighting a roman candle firework rocket.

"Mmmmmm. Lady, do I miss you. You smell so good, honey."

"Pheromones, Vic. I'm as horny as I've ever been for you. Do we need to go right to work?"

"Absolutely not. I was figgerin' on goin' down to the Central Bar-beee-que, gettin' a mess of wet and dry ribs, some corn bread 'n beans, and then shootin' over to see the king. Then, we can go ahead and check in at the Motel 6 yonder on Route 66," Vic said in his best fake southerners twang.

Raquel laughed so hard several TSA agents looked out from a Delta Airline gate to see what the commotion was all about.

"You are nuts, do you know that? That's another reason I love you, Gonnella."

"Yes 'em, Miss Raquel. I'm pretty keen on y'all."

"I could go for some pork, but what king are you talking about?" Raquel said.

"Lord, have mercy! Graceland, darlin', the home of the one and only, Elvis Aaron Presley. Right cheer in Memphis."

"Oh, my god, right! I'm not a big fan, but how many times will we get to this place again? Like never! So, let's go, but not until after we check in and we spend some time together under the sheets, Gonnella. And if you think I'm taking my panties off for you in some Motel 6..."

"Fear not, my love. We are staying at the Peabody Downtown, the most famous hotel in all of Memphis. I ordered a suite for us, replete with cold champagne, strawberries dipped in chocolate, and extra towels." Vic said. His accent was now like Sean Connery in *Goldfinger*, lisp and all.

"Extra towels?"

"So I can cover your mouth when you are screaming to God and your momma."

Raquel started laughing again. The TSA agents stared a bit longer this time.

Vic went to National Car Rental and picked up the prearranged Chrysler 300. No waiting as advertised. In a few minutes, they were heading to the Peabody.

"Honey, all kidding aside, let's review our plans for the case," Raquel said.

"Sure, but I'm not leaving here until I see Elvis and the MLK assassination site and eat the hot sauce at Central BBQ."

"Right...King was killed in Memphis. I'd like to see that place, too," Raquel said.

"That's here, too. Holy crap, who ever knew that Memphis was so happening? I bet they have no good dance clubs though," Raquel said.

"Are you nuts? This city is seventy-five percent black and..."

"Don't say it. Don't say all blacks can dance. Just don't say it," Raquel said.

"Raquel, please! I was just about to comment that the black population in Memphis are sophisticated music lovers and demand excellence in their dance clubs."

"You are a freak, Mister Gonnella," Raquel said.

"And I understand there may be as many as four Puerto Ricans in all of

Memphis, but they pass off as Mexicans," Vic said.

"GONNELLA!!!" Raquel screamed.

"Okay, so tell me about this family we want to get the DNA from," Vic said.

CHAPTER 29

Vic and Raquel were on the case to find the Jordan family and attempt to get some DNA samples. This DNA would determine the boy's parental lineage and, at the very least, add his name to his gravestone. Was he Jonathan Jordan? They would know if all of the pieces of the puzzle fit together nicely. Vic knew from experience that nothing comes easy in investigative work. He thought that Raquel was wearing rose-colored glasses and excited to be near what she thought to be the resolution of this case.

Back in the Bronx, things were rapidly deteriorating for Tia Carmen. On this trip to St. Barnabas Hospital, she was taken by a New York City EMT. Her blood pressure was so low that the doctors feared the worst and soon. The usual suspects, the ladies with their rosary beads and miraculous medals, were hard at prayer in Tia Carmen's room and in the stark, sterile hallway of the hospital's new building. Being in the new wing was especially important to patients who remember the hospital from back in the day. The old building, surrounded by a twenty-five-foot stone wall, was well known as a place to die. Sick people entered at the front gate and were taken to the funeral home from the morgue door near a loading dock. Being in the new building at least gave some people a glimmer of hope.

Tia Carmen was a realist. She knew her days were short. She spoke in a weak voice to her sister.

"Idalis, my sister, I must speak to Raquel and Victor. Would you please call them?" Tia Carmen said.

Dutifully, Idalis sprung the cell phone from her straw pocketbook and searched for the name. In less than a minute, Raquel was on her cell phone from their room at the Peabody Hotel. She put the call on speaker so Vic could hear the conversation.

"Raquel, my little one, how are you doing with the case?" Tia Carmen said.

"Tia, you don't sound very well."

"I will be total energy soon, my little one. I have life only because I fight for it. I want to see this boy's spirit go free. Then, my job here is finished."

"Victor and I are in Memphis, Tennessee. We have a strong indication that the boy's brother is living here. Not positive, but it's the best lead we have, Tia Carmen. If we can test the man's DNA and it matches the boy, we will at least know who he belonged to."

"Have you found the man?"

"No, Tia Carmen, but we are trying to find him. We are hoping he will cooperate."

"Raquel, he will give you what you need. He has a young son, a college boy, who will help you. Move quickly, my little one. As my flame flickers, so will the boy's."

Tia Carmen handed the phone to her sister. Idalis pressed end. Raquel heard the call disconnect.

"How does she know that? We have no idea what to expect, and she is lying in a hospital bed in the Bronx and orchestrating this whole thing," Vic said.

"Let's get going. There are so many Jordans here that I don't know where to start. We need to find a Robert Jordan. There are several."

Vic used the hotel phone while Raquel used her cell. The frustration of not finding a connection quickly reminded them how difficult the task of finding a needle in a haystack was. The Robert Jordan lead came up with two black men and a disconnected tape recording. They decided to start calling every Jordan listed on the Internet White Pages directory. After much of the same results, they came upon a soft lead, one Grace Jordan.

"Miss Jordan, my name is Raquel Ruiz. I am a special investigator looking for a Robert Jordan who lives in or around Memphis. He is not in any trouble. We are investigating a cold case murder from back in Philadelphia in 1957. We believe the victim may be related to Robert. Do you know of a Robert Jordan?"

"This is total bullshit, and Bobby will not cooperate. He doesn't live here, and you are not the first person to call us. Just leave us alone," Grace Jordan said.

"You've been contacted by others?" Raquel asked.

"Yes, some group from Philadelphia and a writer, looking to tie this murder on our family. They asked for us to provide DNA samples. This ain't never going to happen, lady. We give our DNA to the government, and god only knows what they will use it for. Now, just leave us be. Bobby knows nothing about this anyway. If you call again, I will call the police." Grace Jordan hung up.

Raquel was speechless for a few seconds.

"Vic, holy shit, we are not the first ones at the rodeo."

Raquel and Vic were now off to the races. Their first call was back to Collin Frank.

"Collin, what do you know about anyone from Philadelphia calling people in Memphis for DNA samples?" Vic asked.

"First I'm hearing about this. How did you get that intel?" Collin said.

"Some lady we called freaked out on us. Said she was asked by a writer and a group from Philly. Any speculation?" Vic said.

"One of two things I would guess. Two books were written. Maybe one of the writers was on the lead or the Vidocq Society," Collin said.

"Those Vidocq guys don't share very well it seems," Vic said.

"Ex-cops and FBI. What do you expect?"

"Okay, we are going to press forward here, and, when I get back, I need you to get me a sit-down with these Vidocq boys."

"No problem, Vic. You sound pretty pissed."

"I am pretty pissed, Collin. So is the Puerto Rican, and no one wants to get on her bad side-trust me."

CHAPTER 30

Vic and Raquel made dozens of calls, including one to a Bobby Jordan at Parsley Road in Memphis. There was no answer, no tape-recorded message, and nothing that would make a connection to the Bobby Jordan they were searching for. Raquel had a brainstorm that seemed too obvious and easy to both detectives: Facebook.

Punching in Bobby Jordan displayed a seemingly endless amount of hits. Adding Memphis to the search narrowed things down, and just a few faces came up. Eliminating the few black men and a few young guys, Raquel honed in on a Bobby that hadn't used his page in over eighteen months, when he had posted about a friend of his who passed on from a long illness. This Bobby Jordan seemed to fit the age profile. Through a scraggily, mostly gray beard, this Bobby looked to be in his sixties. Short, thin, and with a friendly face, Bobby Jordan liked motorcycles, beer, and, most importantly for his age connection, he was a Vietnam veteran. In his profile photo, there was a young man in his early twenties with a broad, friendly smile. He wore a University of Memphis Tigers, blue and gray team hat. Bobby was smiling widely through his unkempt hair and beard. Raquel paid the five bucks to leave a non-friend inbox message. If he hadn't used the site in eighteen months, the likelihood of a response to her message was a stretch.

No name was attached to the photo, so, Raquel scrolled down to Bobby Jordan's friends. There was the uncooperative and nasty Grace Jordan with her children and husband, a Ruth Jordan, who had hung up on her during her Jordan calls, and a Phillip Logan Jordan. Raquel clicked on Phillip, and there he was, the same young man in the photo with Bobby.

"Honey, this may be something. This kid, Phillip Logan Jordan, may be Bobby's son. If Bobby is dead or otherwise uncooperative, maybe he could be a DNA link," Raquel said, calling Vic away from the room's desk where he was making calls.

"Hmmm, what now?" Vic said.

"I'll leave a message, and look! There is a University of Memphis e-mail address. PhilLJ@memphisu.edu. He's a journalism major. He may like the story. I'll send an e mail now."

Raquel spoke aloud as she wrote the e-mail.

"Dear Phillip, My name is Raquel Ruiz. I'm investigating an issue that may involve your father when he was a young boy in Philadelphia. Don't worry; he is not in any trouble. I would appreciate an e-mail or a call to my cell, the number for which can be found on the bottom of this message. Hoping to hear from you. RR"

"That was concise. I want to run both of these guys' records with PPD and the FBI in the meantime," Vic said. Vic immediately used his cell phone to call Sean Lewandowski.

"Good idea. Hopefully, we will hear…."

Raquel's cell phone pinged with an incoming e-mail. It was from Phillip Logan Jordan.

"At work. Be free at five. I will call you. Phil."

"Oh, my god, Vic, pay dirt! That was fast. He's calling me after work. Now, we are getting somewhere!" Raquel said.

"Honey, don't get all crazy about this lead. It could be a dead end. Let's not stop and sit around waiting for pie in the sky, okay?" Vic said.

"Listen to me, Vic. Don't get all preachy with me, okay? I'm feeling this, so, don't piss on the fire. Didn't Tia Carmen say a young man was going to help us? And, besides, what else do we have to go on at the moment?"

"Don't get all ghetto on me, Raquel. I'm just trying to keep things real. If this is a dead end, then, what? And the Tia Carmen thing is getting a bit tiring."

"Then, what? How the fuck do I know? Then, we call the rest of these Jordan fuckers up until I'm swiping the inside of their cheeks for DNA samples, that's what," Raquel said. Her big, dark eyes were flashing wildly.

"All I'm saying is we should keep calling for now. Let's see what happens later."

"Fine, give me that freakin' list," Raquel said.

By 5 o'clock, Raquel and Vic were barely speaking to each other. More calls were made with nothing except a few hang-ups and several "have a blessed day" dead ends.

At 5:10, Raquel started to bite the nails on her right hand and pace around the suite. At 5:20, she started saying things in Spanish.

"*Pendejo…Estas gentes son unos idiotas. Cabrón!*"

Vic thought that discretion was the better part of valor and said nothing. Every minute that went by, Raquel's anticipatory anxiety was mounting. Vic feared that she was about to turn on him with a torrent of anger and frustration.

Then, the phone rang. It was Phillip Logan Jordan. Raquel's anxiety was swept away in an instant.

"Hi, Phillip. Thanks for calling. This is Raquel Ruiz. Do you mind if I put you on speaker so my partner, Vic Gonnella, can be in on our conversation?

"Sure, of course, but please call me Phil, okay?"

"Sure, Phil. To cut to the chase, we are here in Memphis and hoping to meet up with Bobby Jordan. Is he your father?" Raquel asked.

"Yes, he is. And a great dad, I may add."

"Excellent. We are trying to solve the case of a little boy who was found dead in a field in Philadelphia in 1957. Did your dad ever live in that city?" Raquel was full of questions.

"Dead? Well, yes, he did. The family moved to Memphis after they lived there. They were from the south to begin with."

"Hi, Phil, this is Vic Gonnella, do you know what your grand-father's name was by any chance?"

"Sure do, Major. Why do you ask?"

Vic and Raquel looked at each other and spontaneously gave the thumbs up sign.

"Well, that's the family that we have been searching for. See, we think the little boy that was killed may be your dad's brother. We are here to try to find out if that is the case," Raquel said.

"You guys sound like you're from New York. You came all that way to Memphis to see my family?"

"Yes, we did," Vic said.

"So, what do you need from Bobby?"

"Frankly, from Bobby or from you. A DNA sample, an easy swipe of the inside of your cheek with a cotton swab," Raquel said.

"Well, not from me. You see, there is a good chance that Bobby is not my biological father, even though he is the best dad ever."

"Okay, then we need Bobby's help. We've tried to reach him without success. Can you help with that?" Raquel asked.

"Sure, why not? Let me speak with Dad tonight. He works crazy hours at the University. I will reach him and see what he says. I'll call you back with his answer, okay?"

"Thanks so much, Phil. Maybe we can meet up with you and him tonight or tomorrow," Vic said.

"Cool. Call you in a bit," Philip said.

Raquel's anxiety clock was reset.

"Okay, Mister Negative-About-Everything," Raquel said to Vic as she flashed him a sexy smile.

"I am so happy to be wrong," Vic said.

CHAPTER 31

Both Bobby and Phillip Logan Jordan had clean police records. Not even a single point on their driver's licenses. There was nothing to indicate any criminality or indiscretion whatsoever. Law enforcement hates when that happens. They have no leverage to work on. No good-cop/bad-cop routine. Good, clean citizens are the bane of their existence.

At 8:45, Phillip Jordan called Raquel's cell phone. She and Vic were at the Central BBQ deciding whether to have the half wet and half dry ribs, chicken, or the combo and which level hot sauce they should try.

"Hi, Raquel, it's Phil. How are you guys doing?"

"Great, Phil. We were just thinking about you."

"Well, I spoke with Dad, and he said he would be happy to talk with you guys. He doesn't understand the story very well, but I'm sure you can explain it better than I can."

"That's great, Phil. When and where can we meet him?"

"He doesn't get off work until around 6:30 tomorrow night, so, that's best. And he said why not come right over to his place. Oh, and, by the way, he never knew of any brother."

"That's perfect. So, we should come to your dad's at 6:30?" Raquel said.

"That would be fine. I can be there as well."

"Phil, do you have time for us before that? We really would like to meet you. How about lunch?"

"I would normally say yes as I'm not working tomorrow, but I promised to spend some time with my girlfriend."

"Well, bring her along! What's your favorite place? We want to try a good restaurant. Kind of up to here with BBQ," Raquel said.

"The best restaurant in Memphis for my money is Flight, but it's real expensive for us. It's a special occasion type of place."

"Phil, we are inviting you guys; don't worry about the cost. It's on us. It's a special event when we meet new friends."

"I'll check with Lauren and text you, okay?"

"Perfect. Can we say 12:30?"

"Great, where are you guys staying?"

"The Peabody," Raquel said.

"Nice place. Flight is only a few blocks away. You can walk," Phil said.

"Good, we can have a chance to sleep in a bit. See you at Flight.

Raquel gave a high five to Vic, who was in awe of the way she handled herself.

"Now, let's finish this mess a barb que and have a few pops and get back to the hotel and get jiggy under the sheets," Vic said in his imitation southern accent.

They went through a whole roll of paper towels trying to keep the sauces off of their hands and faces. Their mood turned from a bit quiet to jubilant. Raquel started dancing in her chair to the country and western tunes playing at Central. A couple of local guys sent over beers to Vic and Raquel. They seemed to like the show she was putting on, as did Vic.

When Vic and Raquel finally left Central BBQ, the locals who sent over the beers had a surprise. Vic picked up their tab. Slick move for a Yankee, they thought. All in good fun.

Back at the Peabody, the party continued. Vic put his favorite Sinatra songs on his iPhone, and the couple danced intimately until Vic was aroused and unable to continue.

They made love for what seemed like a few hours and fell asleep in each other's arms.

After some time, the iPhone suddenly went on again to Sinatra singing "The Summer Wind."

Vic heard it first and shot up into a seated position on the bed. There he was. The boy was standing at the foot of their bed. Vic nudged Raquel, who was already awakened by the music. She sat up as well and had a quizzical look on her face.

The boy was smiling and clapping his hands to the music. He seemed happy for the first time in all the past apparitions. He was trying to say something, but the words were choppy and muddled with his excitement. When Sinatra sang the final words, "I lost you, I lost you to the summer wind," the boy faded away.

"Jesus Christ Almighty, Raquel, he's trying to tell us something. He's trying to tell us we are on the right track," Vic said.

"Absolutely, honey. I have to call Tia Carmen first thing in the morning."

"Raquel, it IS first thing in the morning. It's 8:30.

They both laughed as they leaned over and gave each other a kiss. They both moaned and smiled simultaneously.

"I feel as if we just went to sleep. Hand me my cell please."

Vic was already reaching for it when Raquel asked. She pressed the speed dial number for Idalis, and the phone was ringing instantly.

"Hello, my little one. I was expecting you to be calling me," Tia Carmen said. Her voice was much stronger, and her tone was happy.

"Tia Carmen, you sound good. Are you still in the hospital?" Raquel said.

"No, my dear. The doctors released me last night. I took a turn for the better," she said.

"I'm so happy, Tia Carmen. I have news to tell you."

"Little one, I know the news. The boy came to me. You and Victor are on the right road. I want you to know that my improvement is only temporary. Work fast," Tia Carmen said.

As usual, there was no small talk with the old woman. She disconnected the call.

"Their energy is more connected than ever," Raquel said.

"Who? What energy?" Vic asked.

"Don't you see it? It's not only that Tia Carmen has visions of the boy. Their energy is connected. If she dies, he is gone. If he feels happy, she gets better. They are totally connected, Vic. When he came to me at the beach and said to me, 'You think I'm dead,' he was trying to tell me his energy has not yet left this place. In a sense, he is still alive."

"His body is gone, but his energy is still here. Is that what your theory is?" Vic questioned.

"That's not a theory, my love. That is fact."

CHAPTER 32

Flight is the kind of restaurant you would expect to find in New York, San Francisco, or Los Angeles, certainly not anywhere in the state of Tennessee. Rich mahogany and cherry wood furniture, billowing window treatments, fine artwork, and subtle mood lighting enhances a romantic flavor that exudes an expensive dining experience. The leggy hostess seems to be strolling on the catwalk in Milan rather than escorting patrons to their table, almost to the point of distraction. And Vic was easily distracted.

"Well, Romeo, why don't you take a picture with your cell phone so you can refer to it later?" Raquel quipped.

Vic laughed. "What do you want from me? She's a supermodel."

"And I'm just a twerpy Columbia grad with an overbite?"

"You are gorgeous, my love. And you know I'm only window shopping," Vic said. He laughed out loud at his witty statement.

"Hmmm, maybe I'll start checking out the muscle men at the bar," Raquel said. She couldn't help but laugh herself.

They ordered a bottle of Pellegrino water and waited for their guests to arrive.

"Honey, my palms are sweaty. I'm actually nervous about meeting Phil. This means so much on so many levels," Raquel said.

"I'm excited, too, but I wouldn't say nervous," Vic said.

"I wonder what they look like."

"Turn around; they are on their way."

The supermodel, a six-footer, was chasséing to their table, followed by Phil and his girlfriend, Lauren. They looked like college students. Phil needed a shave, and Lauren was wearing a pair of jeans with ready-made holes in them. They made a handsome couple.

Vic and Raquel stood and made their introductions to the younger couple.

"Great choice, Phil. I can't wait to see the menu," Vic said. He was breaking the ice and not getting to the business at hand right away.

"They serve flights of different meats and pastas, so, you get a tasting of various foods. You'll see. Venison, bison, quail with different sauces and great vegetables, and the deserts are amazing," Phil said.

Phil was a handsome young man with a good, friendly face. Lauren was very pretty with sparkling, blue eyes and a perfect smile.

"So, how long are you two a couple?" Raquel asked.

"About two years. We met at school. We both have different majors but met at a mixer," Lauren said.

"I'm journalism; she's accounting. Going for her CPA license soon," Phil said.

"Yes, I saw that you were a journalism major on Facebook. It was amazing that I found you. In our business, we have access to people data from every agency in the United States, but Facebook seemed to be the way to go," Raquel said.

"How did you guys meet?" Phil asked.

"We were both attached to the NYPD and were working on a homicide investigation. It was love at first sight for me," Vic said.

"I thought he was just another senior officer with a keen eye for good investigative talent. Little did I know, he had drafted me for my looks," Raquel said. Both couples laughed at her quip.

There was a lot of small talk and debate over what to order. Vic ordered a wine that was to everyone's liking. They ordered lunch and awaited the appetizers.

"I'm amazed that you guys found us. My dad said it might be one of those Internet scams, but I could tell by your voice that you were sincere. Can you tell us more about the dead boy?" Phil said.

"Sad case to say the least. This four-ish-year-old boy was found dead in an empty lot back in 1957 in Philadelphia. He was killed by a blow to his head. No one has ever found out who he was or who killed him," Raquel said.

"Oh, my god, that is so sad," Lauren said.

"And you think he was my dad's brother?" Phil asked.

"It's a theory that we are working on. There has been a lot of conjecture going back fifty-seven years, but this seems to have some legs to it," Vic said.

"We think that a woman may have killed the boy. She may have done it in a fit of rage, although there are a lot of things that point to her abusing him for a while," Raquel said.

"She may have bought the child from his natural mother and father," Vic said.

"So, if you think the boy was my dad's brother, the man who sold him could have been my grandfather?" Phil said.

"Yes. Do you remember him?" Raquel asked.

"I do. Major Jordan. A real character! I remember he was always dressed in a suit. He always wore a diamond tie clip. Back then, those tie clips were popular, I guess. Anyway, there was always talk in the family that he had a few girlfriends. What we would call a player today," Phil said.

"Do you remember your grandmother?" Raquel asked.

"No. I don't think they stayed together very long. She wasn't in the picture when I was young, although my dad has some pictures of her on his wall."

"How about any aunts or uncles?" Vic asked.

"Not really, no. They may have stayed in Philadelphia or maybe the south if there were any."

"So, Dad and his family moved to Memphis? Do you know when they moved?" Raquel asked.

"My dad would know that. He can fill you in on the family history. I told you on the phone that he may not be my real father. I have two brothers who look alike. I look nothing like them, and my mom was, from what I can gather, a sleep-around."

"Is she around?" Raquel asked.

"Last I knew, she was still alive but wanted nothing to do with us. She left my dad when we were little for another guy and never looked back. Dad raised us all by himself. He's an amazing guy.

He is like a mechanical genius. He had worked at the University for many years and can fix anything. He also invents stuff. Never made a whole lot of money, but we made do."

The GPS advised them to make a left, and their destination would be on their right in eight hundred feet. In the driveway of Bobby Jordan's small ranch home sat a Harley Davidson and an old Ford F100 that had seen better days. Before they could get out of the car, Bobby and Phil Logan Jordan came bounding out of the house to greet them.

"Wow, good old southern hospitality," Vic said.

"Aww, he looks like such a nice man," Raquel said.

"We shall see."

Just as in his Facebook profile, Bobby Jordan had the look of Willie Nelson without the bandana. His look was weathered, but his smile was refreshing and honest. Bobby was short and very thin. Phil was beaming.

"Hi, guys. I'd like you to meet my dad, Bobby Jordan," Phil said.

Bobby kissed Raquel on her cheek and shook Vic's hand with both of his.

"Welcome to my home. Hope you guys didn't have a hard time finding us," Bobby said.

"GPS may be the best invention since the telephone, Bobby. Turn-by-turn perfect," Vic said.

"Phil tells me you guys are staying at the Peabody. The best in Memphis."

"And really nice. Very comfortable." Raquel continued with the small talk.

"Well, let's all go inside and chat," Bobby said.

The inside of the home was much like the outside. A nice, lived-in home would be a perfect description. The first thing that Vic and Raquel noticed was a full wall of family photographs on the hallway leading to the kitchen. The living room was hard to the right of the entrance door and quite small. A dining room abutted the living room and was filled with computers that were dismantled. The dining room table was a workbench for the hardware. Vic made room on a faded sofa by moving some magazines. Raquel sat in an upright kitchen chair next to the couch. Bobby sat in his well-worn easy chair. Phil stood next to his dad.

"So, you guys are on a mission, I hear," Bobby said.

"We are on a case that has become a mission, I guess," Vic said.

"Phil told me about this poor little boy. We read up on the case online. I'm not so sure I can help you, and I'm not sure this boy is related to me, but I'm happy to be of any assistance that I can. Why shouldn't this boy be able to rest in peace? I saw a lot of horrible things in Vietnam, and I learned from that experience that we are all in this world together."

"Tell us about your mom and dad, Bobby. Did they ever discuss another child around you? Do you have any memory of a baby boy who lived with you?" Raquel asked.

"Absolutely not, but I was a baby when we left Philadelphia. I don't even have a recollection of the place where we lived, although there is a photo of me and another child in my crib. Here, let me get it off the wall."

Bobby sprang up from his chair with a youthful enthusiasm. He took several framed photographs off the wall.

"See here, this is me. I don't know, maybe two years old, maybe a bit younger. I think this child is a cousin or neighbor. Never did find out who it was," Bobby said

"This was taken in Philadelphia?" Vic asked.

"Far as I know. Here is a photo of my daddy, Major Bruce Jordan, and my grandma is the big woman leaning on the front of the Buick. I don't remember this other woman at all. I think she may have been his second wife. He was married a few times, I understand. He had a way with the ladies. And he was always in debt. Gambling, I believe," Bobby said. He laughed a bit and looked shyly at Raquel.

"And this one?" Vic pointed to a third photograph.

"That's me at about ten years old. Taken at school here in Memphis."

Vic took the photo from Bobby and handed it to Raquel. Vic had a quizzical look on his face. Raquel looked at the photo and smiled at Bobby, missing Vic's cue.

"You were so cute, Bobby. Do you have any pictures of your other sons? Phil said you have other boys," Raquel said.

"I sure do. I'm proud of all of my boys."

Bobby was up at the wall again in a flash and took down another pair of photos.

"This is Dwayne, and this here is Greg. They are a bit older now, but this was taken when they were in high school."

"They are much darker than Phil. And taller," Vic said.

"Phil took after my side. Their mom is Italian, and they got that Mediterranean blood going on, I guess," Bobby said.

"Like you, Dwayne and Greg both have that right ear sticking out a bit," Vic said.

Raquel looked at Vic as if she were embarrassed by his question to Bobby.

"Well, that's why we are looking for a DNA sample, Bobby. That may be all the proof we need, or perhaps there is no match," Vic said.

"I'm all ready. Let's do it," Bobby said. He rubbed his hands together to prepare for the task at hand.

Raquel opened her pocketbook and took out a large, folded manila envelope. In it was a DNA sample kit that their laboratory advised them to use. In the sample kit were two pairs of clear surgical gloves, a box of large Q-Tips, and several sterile envelopes.

"Bobby, I can do it for you, or you can do it yourself. All you need to do is put these gloves on and wipe the inside of your cheek with the Q-Tip for thirty seconds. Then place it in this envelope, and we can then immediately seal it. I'd like two samples from you," Raquel said.

"I can do it. Man, this reminds me of CSI on the TV," Bobby said.

"Do you want my samples, too? I may be a match to the boy as well," Phil said.

"Good idea. Why not?" Raquel said.

The samples were all taken and the envelopes sealed according to the lab's instructions. Raquel placed the four sanitary envelopes into the larger manila one.

"Well, that's that. We can't thank you enough, Bobby and Phil. We should have the results in about ten days," Vic said.

"Happy to help, and happy to meet new friends. Maybe you guys can put me up if I ever get to New York on my hog," Bobby said.

"It would be our pleasure," Raquel said.

"One more thing, Bobby. I have an envelope here with five hundred dollars. It's my way of saying thanks," Vic said.

"Oh, I could never take that money, Vic. I'm doing this to help you guys," Bobby said.

In his New York style, Vic put the envelope on the crowded-with-magazines coffee table.

"I'm leaving this here. You guys decide how to split it up," Vic said.

"Well, I can't say it won't come in handy," Bobby said.

CHAPTER 33

Directly across from the Peabody Hotel on Union Avenue in downtown Memphis, Vic and Raquel found a FedEx office that was still open when they returned from their visit to the Jordans. The four envelopes were coded and put into next-day-priority envelopes to Collin Frank at the Philadelphia Police Department and to the private DNA lab in New York City. The clerk assured them the envelopes would arrive before 10 o'clock the next morning. Another thing that Vic and Raquel didn't know about Memphis is that the FedEx corporate office was just a few blocks from the Peabody. The store clerk proudly told the two northerners that their service was the best in the delivery business. This was reassuring to the detectives. After all, their case was dependent on these sample results being delivered to their destinations on time.

They needed a quick snack and decided to walk a few blocks to the Downtown Central BBQ. The food is heavy and addictive, but why not? This was their last night in Memphis on this trip and likely forever.

"Look, Raquel, the Lorraine Motel where Dr. King was killed," Vic said. The motel and museum were directly across from Central BBQ on Mulberry Street.

"We can kill two birds with one stone: see the Museum, and get BBQ. We'll have more time for Graceland tomorrow. But, oh, the museum is closed. Look at the sign, honey. 'Closed at 5 p.m.,'" Raquel said.

"I really just wanted to see the place where he was shot and the sniper's vantage point. I've always been intrigued by this case. It changed the course of American history in some ways."

"Let's ask the guard if he can let us walk around," Vic said.

The guard turned out to be a history major at the University of Tennessee and was delighted to point out some of the details that Vic had wanted to see.

"On April 4th, 1968, Dr. King was rooming with Ralph Abernathy in room 306 right there on the second level. He stepped out of that room and was shot by James Earl Ray from that window right over there at 422 South Main Street," the guard said.

"The balcony seems so much lower than I imagined, and what I can remember from the photographs. And that distance is nothing for a man with a rifle," Vic said.

"It's only two hundred and seven feet. King was a sitting duck, to use a common term. Look at the tiles on the ground here. They signify the trajectory of the fatal bullet fired into Dr. King."

The balcony had a large, white and red memorial wreath attached to the balcony directly in front of room 306. Under the short balcony, the museum has two period vehicles on display, a white Cadillac Coupe de Ville and a Buick with classic rear fins from that era.

"The cars are enormous by today's standards," Vic said. He was really taken in by the whole scene and seemed to be in deep thought.

"Did Dr. King die on this balcony?" Raquel asked.

"No ma'am. He passed at the hospital a few hours after the shooting," the guard said.

"In spite of what Jessie Jackson said," Vic said.

"I see you are well informed, sir. Reverend Jackson stated that Dr. King died in his arms. In fact, Jackson was on the balcony earlier but not on the balcony until after they took Dr. King to the hospital by ambulance."

"Jackson was playing to the media. Not a nice man," Vic said.

"Well, sir, this IS the Civil Rights Museum, and Reverend Jackson played a major role in the movement. I can't comment on Reverend Jackson's character."

"And some conspiracy theorists think that Ray was not even the assassin," Vic said.

"The facts say otherwise, sir. Clearly, James Earl Ray killed Dr. King that day."

Vic and Raquel thanked the guard for his time and information and strolled slowly over to the Central BBQ on the corner of the street. Vic stopped and turned back toward the Lorraine and its iconic yellow and red motel sign. He drew a deep breath.

"Honey, there were a dozen people, in and around this place when this great man was gunned down right here, and there are still theories and conjecture about the facts. Look at the case of our boy with so much time and foggy information. This is just what makes detective work so amazing and so frustrating at the same time. We think we know who killed the boy, but we are not totally sure. We think we have a good lead on the case, but what if we're wrong? My stomach is in knots right now. There is so much unknown. We may never know the truth. It's like the Deegan case. Will I ever really know the total circumstances that surrounded that case?" Vic said.

Raquel was concerned that the stress could be getting to Vic again.

"C'mon, I'm hankerin' for the brisket tonight and those pork and beans and some collards…just some good ,ole, down-home soul food," Raquel said. She used the best southern accent a Puerto Rican New Yorker could muster.

Just as they were about to enter the Central, Raquel's cell rang. It was Phil Logan Jordan.

"Hey, Phil, we decided to get some Central tonight. You around?" Raquel said. She was doing her best to lighten things up for Vic.

"Wish I could, Raquel. Got some reading to catch up on. I just called to say thanks for the way you guys treated my dad. He thought you guys were great."

"Aww, he is a wonderful man. You are a good son, Phil."

"Well, that's why I'm calling. I want you to know that whether or not that DNA test comes back that I'm his natural son or not, he will always be my dad and I love him with all my heart."

"Phil, we don't have to take your test. If it's bothering you, we can just trash your sample or just not talk about it again," Raquel said.

"I wanna know, Raquel. Please be honest with me, okay?"

"I promise. Goodnight, Phil."

"Say hi to Vic, and get some of those sweet potato fries for me."

"Honey, I think we need some of that cold beer inside," Raquel said.

CHAPTER 34

"'Ola, poppie,' ola, mami chula,¿ cómo estás? I haven't seen you in a while! Are you here to see Tia Carmen again?" The wheelchair guy gave his best, nearly toothless smile at Vic and Raquel as they exited the car. Vic found a choice parking spot in front of the tenement building.

"Look at you, heffe. How are you feeling?" Vic said.

"Not so good these days. The doctor wants to take a few more inches off my stump and maybe a finger. Little by little they are chopping away at me, poppie."

"That's not good. You need to take better care of yourself. Eat the right foods, and get that diabetes under control," Raquel said.

"It's too late for me, mami. I just go day to day and let my friend Jesus take care of the rest."

"How has Tia Carmen been?"

"One day, she looked really bad, the next day, like she could run to Brooklyn. Today, she walked to the store with Idalis. Everyone is praying so hard for her."

"Okay, same deal. Watch our car, and you get the twenty when we come out," Vic said.

"See, I told you so. Jesus sent you to me today."

Vic and Raquel moved quickly to Tia Carmen's apartment. The aroma of Spanish cooking permeated the hallways. The steel front door was held open by a small book that was lodged into the door jam. Several people, all with very serious, almost morbid-looking faces, were waiting to speak with Tia Carmen. Raquel slowly led the way into the apartment, followed by her wide-eyed partner.

A frail-looking Tia Carmen was speaking softly in Spanish to a young woman, who was clearly distressed. The woman's eyes were swollen from crying, and her mouth was trembling. Raquel whispered the translation of Tia Carmen's words to Vic.

"Your momma is here with you. She wants you to know that your brother's death, while sudden, is not the end of his energy. He will soon be with her, but he first needs to calm his energy. The drugs took him, it's true, but he will be at peace. Your momma wants you to watch your two babies closely so they do not follow this path. You will have another baby, another girl, who will bring you much happiness," Tia Carmen said.

"And my papa? Is he with my momma?" The young woman asked.

"Your momma is saying that you should not be concerned about your papa. His energy, like his life, has been wasted. His energy is gone. She wants you to be strong. Now, she is fading. She has left us for now," Tia Carmen said.

Exhausted, Tia Carmen slumped in her chair. Idalis took the sobbing young woman gently by her elbow and walked her toward the door.

Three of the ever-present praying women busied themselves saying Ave Marias and twirling their rosaries in their hands. Two women were arranging platters of homemade food and cleaning dishes.

Tia Carmen looked up from her chair and smiled warmly at Raquel.

"My little one, you have come to see me again. How happy you make me," Tia Carmen said.

"Yes, Tia Carmen, but you are working so hard when perhaps you should be resting," Raquel said.

"What I do is not work, little one. What I do is my purpose. I will do this with my last breath."

"Victor and I are awaiting some news on the boy. We came back to see you and to take care of some business until the news arrives. We are hoping some tests that have been taken will give us the answers that we need."

"And what if you are disappointed?" Tia Carmen said.

Raquel was nonplussed. She looked at Vic for some support. He too had no idea how to react to Tia Carmen's comment.

"People are sometimes not what they appear to be. You must know this and keep on your path. Oftentimes, there are things that occur in life that you may not fully understand. Know that your vitality is strong and you must keep working to keep your energy positive."

"I don't understand, Tia Carmen. I need you to be clearer," Raquel said.

"You will understand in due time."

"Tia, please explain something. Is your energy tied to the boy? Is his energy tied to you?" Raquel said.

"We are all part of the same energy. Some are dependent on others. Some repel others. My life energy is wavering, and, for now, the boy's energy is dependent on mine. Why, I do not know. Perhaps, I will know soon, when my next journey begins."

Tia Carmen closed her eyes as if she had fallen asleep. Idalis said that it was time for everyone to leave Tia Carmen until another time.

Vic went to the kitchen and put a handful of bills into the yellow Café Bustello can. He and Raquel somberly left the apartment with the others and filed down the dark stairwell and out onto the street. Their eyes needed to adjust to the bright sunlight for a few seconds. As they approached their car, they saw that the man in the wheelchair had fallen asleep on the job. His begging cup was held by three mangled fingers in his badly scared right hand. The other two digits were gone. Vic placed a twenty dollar bill in the cup and looked at Raquel who was near tears. They stood in the street, oblivious to the passing people, cars, busses, and loud Latin music coming from the surrounding stores and apartment windows.

"Honey, what's wrong?" Vic asked.

"Everything is wrong. This whole case is wrong. We may never see this through, honey. Tia is telling us that we will be frustrated, I don't know, disenchanted. I'm not sure how much longer I, no, how much longer *we* can deal with this. And this whole energy idea. I'm not sure I'm buying into the whole thing anymore. And look at this poor man, slumped in his chair. And look at this fucking place. And we are surrounded by sadness. And..."

"Raquel, honey, stop. Do you remember when we were at Graceland and we walked around Elvis' home? The place where he lived and died?" Vic said.

"Yes."

"And do you remember the room where he played the piano and sang for his friends the day he died?"

"Yes, I do."

"Do you remember what you said to me when we were standing, looking into that room?"

"No, I don't"

"You said, 'Honey, I can feel Elvis' presence. I bet you his spirit is still here.' Remember?"

"Now, I do, yes!"

"Well, that is the energy that Tia Carmen is talking about. And I, for one, am not giving up, not for all the money in the world. We are not giving up on that little boy."

"You are right! You are always right, honey!" Raquel threw her arms around Vic and gave him the biggest squeeze and kiss. "Thanks, honey!"

"Mmmm, thank you!"

CHAPTER 35

When Vic and Raquel got to their New York City office later that morning, the look on the office and investigation personnel faces told a story. Both Vic and Raquel were not looking very well. Tired, drained, anemic, shot, and stressed were some of the whispers that were mentioned. It was obvious to everyone that whatever case they were on was leaving an emotional and physical mark on them, but they also knew how determined their bosses were.

Vic called the New York DNA lab to make sure the Jordan samples were received and in process. They were. Vic was assured that the test would be completed as quickly as possible. That would be a minimum of five working days. The news was not so positive with the PPD. The samples were not there according to a new man on the "case." Sergeant Robert Kutcher had not seen any FedEx package from Memphis. Vic decided to play it safe and use his tracking number to see where the samples were. FedEx has an amazing system to track every envelope and package anywhere on the planet. Within a few minutes, Vic was informed that the envelope had indeed arrived at PPD that morning. The signature was e-mailed to Vic and, within minutes, he had the time and signature. He called Sergeant. Kutcher back immediately. He was unavailable, out in the field. Vic left a message for him and then went about doing other things in his office. After all, there were few days of down time on the case. Vic called a few hours later and left yet another message. Not known for his patience, Vic was starting to get antsy for the lab results, so, next, he called Collin

Frank. Collin was also out in the field, and his cell phone mailbox was full.

"Raquel, I'm getting pissed at PPD. No return call all day? Aretheykiddinmeorwhat?" Vic said.

"Relax, honey, we can't do much until the samples are run, and we need to be a bit patient."

"Fuck that! I have a mind to drive down to Philly and strangle someone."

"Give it till the morning, and let's see. I'm sure it will all be fine."

The next morning, Vic was on the phone with Kutcher at 8 sharp. He knew that the Sergeant was on the 8-12 shift. He was not at his desk. Vic left a message. He immediately called Collin's cell. Still full. He called PPD HQ for Collin's office. "Out in the field," he was told. Vic started calling Kutcher every hour on the hour without a return call. No call back. At one point, Vic was told that Kutcher had left for the day.

Finally, Collin returned Vic's calls.

"Hey, pal. What the fuck? I call this Kutcher a dozen times and no return call. Someone needs to teach him about professional courtesy. All I want to know is if my samples are being processed."

"Let me make a few calls. I'll get back to you when I find out what's up," Collin said.

"What's up? Tell this prick I'll be down there in two hours and I'll show him what the fuck is up."

"Calm down, pal. These things take time."

"To tell me if the samples were received and are being processed takes time? C'mon, my friend. All I need is a simple answer. Is that so much to ask?" Vic said.

"Okay, I hear you. I'm on it."

Vic finally got a call from Kutcher three hours later. Kutcher didn't sound like he wanted to answer the call. It sounded to Vic like he was being disturbed."

"You called?" Kutcher asked.

"Only about six hundred times, Sergeant," Vic said. He was steaming mad.

"Look, Mr. Gonnella, we have a lot of cases that are taking precedent over your case right now. I'll have to check around to see where that package is."

"I sent the signature to you yesterday. Seems pretty simple to me. Find out who signed for the envelope, and ask where it is. You don't need to be a great detective to figure that out now, do you?"

"Listen, pal, I don't appreciate the sarcasm. We had three DOAs yesterday. I'm up to my elbows in blood. I can't drop everything to look for this right now. Besides, the signature and the printed name are illegible. No one knows who signed," Kutcher said.

"No wonder you motherfuckers haven't solved this case for fifty-seven years."

Kutcher slammed his receiver down, disconnecting the call.

"Son-of-a- bitch bastard," Vic said aloud.

Raquel heard the commotion from her office and walked over to Vic's office. Vic explained the conversation verbatim.

"Honey, what have you told me a hundred times? You know, what your grandfather always said," Raquel said.

Vic held his head with both hands, seated on the edge of his chair behind his desk. Raquel waited for a response.

"When you lose your temper, you lose the argument," Vic said.

"And you attacked this guy that way?"

"He pulled it out of me, honey."

"And now you have an enemy instead of a friend. Not very smart."

Vic's secretary buzzed in. "Vic, Collin Frank on four."

"Oh, boy. Now, you've done it," Raquel said.

Vic composed himself for a few seconds before he picked up the phone.

"Okay, pal. Call me an asshole," Vic said.

"Vic, what's up with you?" Collin said.

"I just got the lecture from Raquel. The guy was playing bad cop with me. I'm wrong. But what the fuck? I want those samples run."

"We can't find them, Vic. Shit happens. Don't tell me NYPD never lost anything on you."

"Okay. What now?" Vic said.

"Now, I have to see what's going on at my end. Try to relax a bit. They will show up."

"Jesus Christ, Collin. They will show up? Our entire case is in that envelope. Can't you see why I'm so hot. or was all that kiss ass when I came up to PPD the first day just theatre?"

"Vic, you sound like you're losing it. Step back for a day. Let me speak with Raquel."

"Oh, so now I'm being treated like a petulant child. You want to talk to my mommie? Here she is!"

Vic handed the receiver to Raquel.

"Collin, I know these things happen, but we are fighting time," Raquel said.

"Fifty-seven years, and you guys are fighting time?" Collin said.

"I can't explain what I mean just yet, but, in time, I will tell you the whole story. Let's just say we need a favor here, Collin."

"Okay. I'll see what I can do, but please try to calm him down. You know, attract more bees with honey," Collin said.

Collin and Raquel said their good byes. Raquel noticed something in Collin's voice that she hadn't heard before. She decided to keep that feeling to herself for the time being.

"Vic, try to remember what it was like when you were on the job. Kutcher has people to answer to, his CO, his deputy commissioner, his commissioner, whatever! They have to answer to a mayor, the press, and the families of murdered people. No one has an easy job, honey. You need to cool off."

"They suck!" Vic said.

"Life sucks, and then you die. Let's get some things done here and leave them alone for a day or so. It will all fall into place, you'll see."

"Let's go to Sam's Place. I'm missing garlic. Massimo will make me a nice dish of linguine, white clam, and I'll feel like a human being for a change."

CHAPTER 36

Not one to sit on his laurels, Vic decided to continue working the investigation. He decided to call the California author of the Boy in the box book, Jim Hoffmann. The call lasted for ninety minutes. What Vic came away with was more information than he had expected. Hoffmann was certain that Martha Jameson was the daughter of the woman who murdered the boy. He also agreed with the theory that the boy was sold to her through the Nicolettis and that Mr. Nicoletti was indeed friends with Martha's mother. He believed that Nicoletti brokered the sale of the boy. Hoffmann's clairvoyant wife, Debbie Dombrow, also put a price tag on the sale. Twelve hundred dollars, a pretty sum in the early 1950s.

So, why didn't the PPD believe her story? Hoffmann recommended that Vic call Joe McMillan, the coroner's investigator, who had met with Martha Jameson along with two detectives from the PPD. Vic could hear it straight from the horse's mouth. Hoffmann went one step better. He provided Vic with the eighty-eight year old McMillan's private telephone number.

Vic called McMillan immediately. The old man was surprisingly sharp and bright and recalled every detail of the case as if he were still on the case. McMillan was living in Philadelphia in an assisted living home.

Midway through their cordial and frank discussion and after Vic listened to the man's maladies, Vic probed hard for answers.

"So, tell me, Joe. When you met with Martha, did she seem a bit off to you?" Vic asked.

"A bit strange, yes, but certainly not off, not crazy, if that's what you are getting at," Joe said.

"Did you believe her story? Did her mother kill the boy in your opinion?"

"Let's just say that the three of us walked away from her believing her story fully. She had every detail down pat. She was very convincing."

"So, why was she ultimately discounted?"

"When we returned from Cincinnati, which was where we met with her and her psychiatrist, we started an investigation on her and the family. As you know, her parents were both deceased by this time. We found a man who used to walk the family dog when he was a young teenager. He had keys to the house, and he said he never saw a boy there when he went to pick up the dog. Never saw the boy outside with the family. No one else who we interrogated ever saw a boy. It seemed that Martha took frequent walks with her father. Everyone thought she was a boy by the way she looked and dressed. But no boy," Joe said.

"And, based on his testimony, you all felt she made up the whole story? That sounds a bit funny to me."

"Well, we all were convinced that she could have gotten the details of the case from the newspapers and such. We decided she was not the real deal."

"Did it occur to you at the time that perhaps the boy was kept in the basement, maybe locked up?"

"I don't recall if that came up."

"Are you familiar with the Ariel Castro case in Cleveland, Ohio, in 2013, Joe?" Vic said.

"Hmmm. Refresh my memory please."

"This Castro guy, a real knucklehead, kidnapped three women and held them prisoner for over ten years in his home in a residential neighborhood. One of the women even had a baby as a result of being raped by Castro. None of the neighbors ever saw or heard the women or the six-year-old child she had. They were shocked when the women finally escaped," Vic said.

"I seem to remember that case in the news. Whatever happened to them?"

"The women are trying to go on with their lives. Fortunately for society, Castro hung himself while in prison."

"Hmmm. That is quite interesting. So, what you are saying is that our boy could have been held inside the house without anyone ever noticing. Makes sense now."

"Yes, including the dog walker. But, Joe, hindsight is always twenty/twenty."

"That's very kind of you to say, sir."

"Joe, did Martha respond to you after the investigation?"

"Yes, she was quite upset with us. She told us she would not speak of it again and that she had to go on with her life. She had a big job with a drug company in Indiana, and she was afraid to lose her position. She even worked for that company overseas for a while. I seem to recall in England somewhere," Joe said.

"Did she admit to you that her mother sexually abused her as well as the boy?"

"Oh, yes. She hated that woman. That also led us to believe that she was making up the whole story to get at her mother."

"So, many years after the death of her mother, she made up this elaborate story, making her out to be a murderer?"

"Yes. There was no physical evidence that led us to prove what she was saying was factual. The case stayed open."

"We believe we are on the right track to prove who the boy was," Vic said.

"Such as?"

"We have DNA samples taken from who we believe was the brother of the dead boy."

"Interesting. What have the samples told you?"

"Nothing yet. We are waiting for test results."

"So, at the moment, you've proven nothing. You still don't have physical evidence. You have one of many theories."

"At this very moment, you are correct, Joe. But, in a few days, today's science will determine if we are right or wrong."

"I wish you well, sir. It would be nice to have a name for the boy, but excuse me if I'm skeptical. I've looked into so many theories that I'm ready to add this one to that long list," Joe said.

"Can I call on you again, Joe?"

"I insist that you do. I'm waiting for a break since we buried and then reburied that child. I was there when he was exhumed. Well, not at the gravesite but in the coroner's lab. I was still working then."

"Really? What was the condition of the remains?" Vic asked.

"Skeletal."

"Did you see the boy's body before he was buried the first time?"

"Of course, many times and for a long time. We didn't bury him right away. We were waiting for a break in the case and actually dressed the child up in street clothes in the hope that someone would recognize him. We finally had to bury him in the city cemetery. Very sad indeed."

"What do you think of the detectives on the case?"

"I worked with these men on many cases. They were very competent, very thorough. They were all enormously upset with this homicide. Some of the guys had children themselves, as did I."

CHAPTER 37

Vic and Raquel were having a great time at Sam's Place. Right off Lexington Avenue on East 39th, Sam's was one of those small Italian restaurants that serves fabulous food, good wine, and warm service, but they don't hit you on top of the head when the check arrives.

The owner, Massimo, worked at the famous Ristorante Tre Scalini at the Piazza Novonna in Rome, Italy. Massimo is charming beyond words; Raquel especially enjoyed his entertaining stories. Max, as his friends called him, was on stage when a patron showed he enjoyed his banter. Raquel and Vic were in real need of a good Italian meal and a diversion.   Vic and Max would share stories about Rome and the Italian culture, even though Max, like many owners of Italian Restaurants in New York City, was born in Albania. His heart may have been Albanian, but his showmanship was pure Italian.

"Max, tell us again about the first time you met Sophia Loren in Rome while you were a waiter," Vic said.

First, Max had to make a toast to his favorite couple. He poured three glasses of Amarone, and they all clicked glasses. Now with the formalities completed, Max began to tell his story. It wasn't so much the story that captivated Raquel and Vic as it was Max's Italian mannerisms and facial expressions that brought the story to life.

"Well, anyway, I wasn't a waiter then. I was only a busboy learning the trade. My Italian was, how can I say, povere, poor at best. Miss Loren was doing a movie with Carlo Ponte, her husband and director, in the piazza, and she decided to have lunch with us. She and Ponte were having an argument over one thing or another, so, she was dining alone. The owner took her order, and the place was wild with excitement. The paparazzi were beside themselves with their silly cameras and calling her name for their attention. She was removed from the entire scene and paid them no attention. When her spaghetti with Bolognese sauce arrived, she motioned to me for some grated formaggio, you know, the parmigiano, although I found out from her years later that she preferred locatelli cheese on her pasta. Allora, I took the small bowl of cheese quickly to her table and started to sprinkle the spoonful of parmigiano on her pasta. I don't know if it was her eyes or her ample cleavage, but, the next thing I know, my boss is screaming at me, calling me words I never had heard. The cheese was all on Miss Loren's, well, her tits. Madonna Mio. I was fired on the spot. Miss Loren was laughing like crazy. She scolded the owner for his scolding me and said, 'Young man, you make me feel like I'm at home in Napoli. My sister Anna Maria and I did this all the time to each other when my momma wasn't looking. My cousins, too. Here, sit with me while I eat my lunch.'"

Now, Sam's Place has about twelve small tables. Not only did Raquel and Vic applaud the story, but so did every patron in the place.

"So, did you lose your job?" Raquel asked.

"I was promoted to waiter that day," Max said to yet another round of applause.

Just as The Max was warming up, Vic's cell phone rang. He saw the familiar number come onto the screen. Knowing that the cell reception in Sam's place was not good, Vic signaled to Raquel to join him outside the restaurant.

"Hello, my friend. How are you?" John Deegan asked.

"Hello, John, I was having a quiet dinner with my girlfriend when you called. What's on your mind?"

"The case of course. I have a sixth sense that you are running into some trouble."

"What makes you think that?"

"Well, your answer for one thing, but, if I'm right, the Philadelphia police are not being entirely forthcoming with you, Victor."

"At the moment, I'd be lying if I said you were wrong, Deegan. How do you sense this?"

"Never mind about my genius. As I see it, there is one of two things going on. Or perhaps both if we're lucky," John Deegan said.

"If WE'RE lucky? So now, you are part of our team?"

"Of course I am, Victor. You need that guy who is far away from the forest to show you the trees."

"Okay, I'll bite. Let's hear your theory, smart guy."

"They are either embarrassed that the famous, brash, New York former detective, may solve a case that they have no idea how to solve….or," Deegan said and then suddenly went silent.

"Or? Or what, Deegan?" Vic said. His tone verged on annoyance.

"Or they are covering something, something that would embarrass them even more," John Deegan said.

"And what, may I ask, great wizard, could that be?"

"That's the tricky part, Victor. Say good night to your beautiful lady. Oh, and, by the way, you could never have a quiet dinner at Sam's Place. Max is too much a bon vivant.

Deegan ended the call. Vic was left with his mouth agape on the sidewalk on Lexington and 39th Street.

CHAPTER 38

The next morning, Vic and Raquel were still discussing Deegan's call. After having discussed Deegan late into the night until they fell into a restless sleep, Vic and Raquel awakened, still pondering Deegan's insightfulness. "I still can't figure out how he knew we were at Sam's. Was it just a guess?" Raquel said.

"There are thousands of restaurants in this city. A guess? I doubt it."

"There are a few explanations and only one or two fit. Deegan has someone that is close to him here, someone who has regular access to him. They spotted us at Sam's and called him. No lucky guess there," Raquel said.

"Or?"

"Or Sam is related to Deegan's wife, Gjuliana, and he called her and told her we were having dinner at his place. You know all Albanians in New York are related, right?"

"Or?"

"Or what, Vic? We've been over this all night," Raquel said. Her voice was a bit edgy.

"Or Deegan is here."

"Shut up! Here like in New York? He wouldn't dare. And face life imprisonment? No way!"

"Follow me, honey. Deegan said he was bored. How long can a guy like him stare out at the lake in Switzerland? He's a born New Yorker. Loves the action of this place, and he is itchy to help us solve this case. Deegan enjoys the psychological game of cat and mouse."

"So, how did he get back into this country?"

"For him, that's the easy part. He was trained to disguise himself, and, with his dough, he could buy any identification he needed. Christ, he can do the forgeries himself for that matter."

"How do you account for how he knows you are pissed at PPD?"

"The man is a genius. Phone tap, long-range audio surveillance. Who the fuck knows what Deegan is capable of?" Vic said.

"Jesus, he could be anywhere! He could be outside of this building disguised as a cabbie, waiting for us to go to the office. Would you turn him in if you found him?" Raquel said.

"Nope. Unless he kills someone, the world is his to do whatever makes him content. After all, the man made us famous, and we are playing in his game."

"I don't see us getting together with him to have coffee and chat."

"If he wants that, we will have no choice in the matter. Let's wait and see if he surfaces again. Right now, I need to call Collin and see what the hell is going on at the house of fools in Philadelphia."

Vic called Collin Frank from the apartment phone and put the speaker on so Raquel could join in the conversation.

On one ring, Collin picked up the call.

"Homicide, Frank," Collin said.

Hey, pal. No call, no text, no fax, no e-mail? Long time no talk," Vic said.

"I was just thinking about you. How's it going?" Collin said.

"You tell me. Any news on your end? Did the samples show up?"

"Not yet. This place is like Dodge City. Another two DOAs last night. I'm up to my ass right about now."

"Collin, I am thinking about going back to Memphis, getting new samples, and personally delivering them to your illustrious Sergeant Kutcher. Maybe, I can get some action then. I don't think that guy can find his own ass with both of his hands," Vic said.

"Collin, hi, it's Raquel. What do you think we should do?"

"Hi, beautiful. I think you should sit tight for now. I'll work on Kutcher. He's pretty pissed off and insulted but not a bad guy. I'll take him out for a beer when our shifts are over. He likes his beer," Collin said.

"In the meantime, we are heading back to the City of Brotherly Drive-bys either tonight or tomorrow. If I have to, I'll kiss his ass myself. Maybe, I came on a bit too strong," Vic said.

"You think? Vic, you all but cursed the guy's mom," Raquel said.

"Okay, so, I'll bring a bouquet of flowers," Vic said. He was still in denial about his faux pas.

"Let me know when you get here. Just so you know, Sean is in Los Angeles on special assignment for a while. He's out of pocket but is reachable," Collin said.

"Collin, if I embarrassed you, I apologize. It's just that…"

"Vic, I am a bit embarrassed, but I have to be honest with you. Fifty-seven years is an eternity. I know you guys want to solve this case, but we really aren't as intent on solving it as you guys are. There are whispers around here that you are after the publicity, wanting to do a television show, a movie, all kinds of shit. Believe me, we are up to here in street blood. Our commissioner is on the hot seat for what's going on here right now not about some dead kid from the fifties."

"That doesn't sound like you, Collin. I know we are intent on solving this case, but it has absolutely nothing to do with publicity or any of that shit. That's not even a consideration," Raquel said.

So, when are you two going to tell me the real reason you are on this case? I feel like you are afraid to tell me or there is some mistrust in me. I have to be honest with you guys at this point," Collin said.

"Because, if we told you, we feel you may think we are bat-shit crazy and maybe we should be remanded to an institution. It's really a personal reason, Collin," Vic said.

"Sorry, guys, one and one are not adding up to two for me," Collin said.

Collin, listen to me. We will talk it over and see you tomorrow. Maybe, you're right. Maybe, you need to hear our reason," Raquel said.

"Gotta go, guys. See you when you get here."

When the call was ended, Vic looked as if he wanted to start a street fight. His face was getting that reddish hue to it. Vic was now grinding his teeth.

"Now, I don't trust him, honey. He sounds like he couldn't give a rat's ass about this case just like the rest of those jerkoffs in the Round House," Vic said.

"I'm getting that, too, Vic. Let's get down there and feel the pulse. We have some damage control to do at PPD. Let's just try to remember what it was like to be on the job. You know that life can suck at times," Raquel said.

"I guess so, honey. Let's take a nice shower together and see where things go from there," Vic said.

"Mmmm, I was thinking the exact same thing."

CHAPTER 39

With two large containers of steaming hot coffee in hand, Vic and Raquel left at 7 o'clock the next morning for Philadelphia. Raquel noticed that Vic had a death grip on the car's steering wheel as they made their way across town and into the Lincoln tunnel.

"Ease up, cowboy. You look like you're going into battle," Raquel said. She caressed Vic's right hand gently until he untightened the strangle hold.

"Oh, boy. You're right. I'm so wound up."

"And you have no excuse. Last night was a session like we haven't had in a while. I'm as relaxed as can be. Must be a testosterone thing."

"Yeah, that was something. Maybe, we can do round two tonight. What do you say?"

"All depends," Raquel said. She lowered her voice to sound like Kathleen Turner in Body Heat.

"All depends on what?"

"On you. If you freak out today, the store may be closed for business.

They both laughed and said nothing to each other until they reached Newark on the New Jersey Turnpike.

"The stench is not so bad today. Maybe, there's a westerly wind," Vic said.

"Are you planning on soothing the ruffled feathers at PPD?"

"I will be my charming self for a change. I have to remember that these guys are cops and not business people. They have a lot to cope with. I was way out of line."

"So, do we tell Collin about our reasons for taking on the case?" Raquel asked.

"Not sure. Let's play things by ear. I'm leaning toward yes, but we run the risk of him thinking we are wacked out. Don't you agree?"

"I'm torn. I would like to take him into our confidence, but there was that tone in his voice that was way out of character. Like you said, let's play it by ear."

Vic serenaded Raquel with a few songs from a CD. Sinatra, Live from the Sands. After Frank was finished, Vic popped in an Elvis CD that they had purchased at Graceland. Vic and Raquel sang together until they reached the Round House.

Collin Frank was waiting for them in front of the building. The three of them walked together to Collin's office in the homicide unit.

"Good news, guys. They found the envelope. Some asshole had it in his drawer and went on leave. Can you imagine?" Collin said.

"Great! Now, can I grovel to Kutcher?" Vic asked.

"No need for that. He felt bad about how the whole thing went down. I'll call him in, and you'll see that he's a decent sort."

"What's the next step?" Raquel asked.

"Kutcher will explain. Here he comes," Collin said.

Sergeant Kutcher was a short guy with a buzz cut and a friendly, smiling, round face that was welcoming to Vic and Raquel. He had a noticeable limp.

"Sergeant Kutcher, I'm so sorry for being a jerk to you. I should have known better than that. I apologize," Vic said. Vic quickly killed any eight hundred pound gorilla before it entered the room.

"Forget it, Vic. I should have handled things differently myself. Guess I'm dealing with too much stress these days. It's behind us," Kutcher said.

"Hurt your leg, Sergeant?" Raquel asked.

"Well, in a matter of speaking, yes. It's the result of being shot on the job a few years ago. The limp is permanent. I could have taken full disability, but I like what I do, and my wife would drive me crazy if I were at home, so, here I am."

"Now, I really feel like an asshole. I didn't know I was talking to a real hero," Vic said.

"More like the asshole than the hero. We were serving a warrant on a perp, and I didn't frisk him good enough. Stupid blunder. He shot me, we killed him, and I came up a bit lame. Could have been a lot worse. I have four kids."

"One for the good guys," Collin said.

"I'd say. Glad you are still on this side of the grass. So, I'm grateful that the envelope was found. It makes things a bit easier," Vic said.

"There is a problem though. The sample we have of the boys DNA is mitochondrial. That's the maternal side of the victim. They ran the test that way when the boy was exhumed. You have samples from the father's side. We can't make a match obviously," Kutcher said.

"Oh, shit. My bad! I never even knew about that. Now, what?" Vic said.

"There is a lab at the University of Texas that may be able to do it. They have new technology that is within the ninetieth percentile for accuracy. I'm sending the samples to them. That should take a few days at least," Kutcher said.

"I'll take ninety percent all day," Vic said.

Vic invited Kutcher and Collin to meet them for lunch later in the day. Both had pressing work ahead and declined. Collin said he would meet with Vic and Raquel for dinner around 7.

The rest of the day was uneventful with the exception of Vic beating himself up for his rookie mistake.

Vic started to slide into a depression. Raquel feared that he would go low enough to act out as he and most people who have been sexually abused as children are known to do. Generally, Vic would become morose; his personality would become nasty, even violent, in his thoughts and words. Raquel decided that they would see the sights in Philadelphia: the Liberty Bell, Independence National Historical Park, the Rocky Statue, the Reading Terminal Market, and, of course, John's Roast Pork or Geno's Steaks, or both, for the best cheese steak sandwich in the city. Raquel knew that Vic, being a foodie, would welcome the diversions. Food and sex were his top two things in the world. She would take care of the second thing later that night.

Raquel's prescription to keep Vic busy for the day worked like magic. He was in good spirits throughout the day and barely mentioned the case. Although Vic and Raquel were stuffed from testing the Philly heese steaks, Geno's beat out John's Roast Pork in their opinion. They kept the 7 o'clock dinner date with Collin.

Vic ordered a nice bottle of Stag's Leap Artemis while Collin ate a great Italian meal at Vetri on Spruce Street. Food wasn't on the agenda for the couple as, now, they wanted to get down to brass tacks.

"What do you think, Collin? Is the bridge repaired with Sergeant Kutcher?" Vic asked.

"Absolutely. Like I said, he's a good guy. It's all forgotten."

"Can you push him on getting those samples done quickly at the University of Texas?" Raquel asked.

"What is this enormous rush with you guys? You heard him say it would take a few days. You know these tests sometimes take up to two weeks. It's not like bringing your car in for inspection," Collin said with a casualness that Vic and Raquel didn't like. They both also noticed an edginess to his voice.

"Is there something else bothering you, Collin? You seem a bit, I don't know, maybe less committed to the case," Vic said.

"Honestly, I want to know the real reason you guys are on this case. You're both so pushy. Is this just a New York thing or what?"

"Yes, we are pushy. We don't want to give you every detail, but we have been involved with someone in New York who wants to see the case solved and doesn't have much time left to live. That's all we're prepared to say at this point," Vic said.

"And get that publicity and movie shit out of your mind, Collin. I will swear to you, right here, my hand to God, that it has nothing to do with any of that whatsoever," Raquel said.

"All we want to do is put a name on that kid's tombstone. Don't you think he deserves that at least?" Vic said.

"And if you fail? Is it the end of the world for you two? Will life go on?" Collin said. By now, Collin was feeling no pain after a few cocktails and some wine.

Vic and Raquel looked at each other, searching one another's face for a viable comeback.

"Collin, some things are important for deep personal reasons. We want to start a family soon, and we feel that we owe this kid a better sendoff than he had gotten so far," Vic said.

"What? That's bizarre!" Collin said.

"Listen to me, Collin. Maybe, it's bizarre to you, but it's important to us. When we first started with you, I thought you would go through a wall for us. I'm not getting that feeling from you right now. What the fuck is with you?" Raquel said.

"Honey, please," Vic said.

"Honey, please, bullshit. I'm just calling it as I see it. Collin, when you wanted off the case, I could tell you were missing the action of the job. We had no problem with that. But where is the support right now? Is there something you need to tell us?" Raquel said.

Raquel's voice carried a bit, and a few diners looked over at their table to see if a full-blown argument was about to take place.

"It's just that there are things that can happen that may disappoint you both and…and I, I don't know, maybe, I'm just over protective of you, my friends. That's all," Collin said.

"We are big boys and girls on this side of the table. Both of our lives have had big things happen that knocked us down. Do we look to you like we are made of ricotta cheese?" Vic said.

"Not at all. Okay, let me see what I can do to move things along a bit faster," Collin said.

"We appreciate that, Collin, we really and truly do. If we are wrong about our theory, we will need to decide if we want to continue on the case or let it go," Vic said.

Raquel wasn't buying it. She didn't believe Collin for a second. Call it her female intuition or her maternal instincts, but Raquel was now thinking ill of Collin and the entire PPD.

CHAPTER 40

Back at their hotel suite, Raquel was showing her Latina side but not in the bedroom.

"I'm telling you, Vic. Something smells like rotten fish. And, like all rotten fish, it stinks from the head. All of a sudden, Collin is like, "You guys are gonna' fail. I want to protect you from being disappointed." Bullshit! This maricón must think we are stupid. What happened to his loyalty to you? What happened to his commitment to the case? Jesus Christ, you offered him a retirement job and everything. What turned him around?"

"I'm not sure, but he is pretty tough to figure out at the moment. He doesn't want to tie himself to us or the case right now. I had to laugh a little though. You know, the role reversal. We were like playing good cop/bad cop at the restaurant. This time, you were the prick. Honestly, you did get a little loud, Raquel."

"Loud? I'll show you loud. The next time this fucking guy pulls this shit, I will drill him another asshole. Pendejo! And did you notice anything about that fuck Kutcher? All smiles, but he has eyes like a shark. Deadly," Raquel said.

"Want to know what's bothering me the most?" Vic said.

"What, the fact that this whole losing-the-envelope thing was a crock of shit? You know they never lost that envelope, don't you?"

233

"Yes, I tend to agree with that, but what is really disturbing is that our boy, John Deegan, is a step ahead of us as usual. He all but told us this was going to happen," Vic said.

"Maybe, you should call him and ask him to tell you how he knows all this," Raquel said.

"Won't work. Deegan loves to play the game. It's like a game of chess to him. It keeps him sharp, playing us like pieces on a board. He wants us to figure things out for ourselves."

"So, if you're right, he already has the end game figured out in his mind."

"Exactly. Maybe not letter perfect but pretty damn close, I bet. He will just keep feeding us tidbits as we go along," Vic said.

"Then, I want him to know what's at stake. If Tia Carmen dies and the boy's energy leaves, it's too late for us."

"You can't really believe that, honey. You will have your baby with or without Tia Carmen's intervention. C'mon now, this stuff only goes so far with me. What will be will be with you and me and our own family."

"I gave my word to her, Vic, and I intend to keep it. I've been around Tia Carmen my entire life, and it's the only thing I really believe in. Please stay with me on this."

"Until the last dog dies, my love."

CHAPTER 41

Realizing that they would need to wait for some time to get the DNA sample results, Vic and Raquel decided to return to New York once again. This time, Vic called ahead and scheduled a staff meeting at Centurion Investigation for 10 o'clock. Vic and Raquel needed to tend to business and return to some form of normalcy in their lives. They both sorely needed a change from the mind pounding they were taking on the case.

Four of the firm's field managers would make a presentation to brief Vic and Raquel on the various investigatory jobs that were in the queue.

"Who wants to lead off?" Vic asked.

"I don't mind," John Sheehan said. John was a retired, twenty-year NYPD detective who had worked Bronx Homicide for a while with Vic. Sheehan was well liked at One Police Plaza and still very connected to the department. He was so highly thought of by NYPD brass that he was asked to work the personal protection for Pope John Paul II when His Holiness visited New York and celebrated mass at Yankee Stadium. He often told stories of this assignment, calling it the defining moment in his police career and his spiritual life. A tough cop with a good, honest attitude, John was the office leader on the top cases.

"The surveillance on the Hunts Point Market case is just about wrapped up. It's what we thought all along. The Gambinos have made some major inroads into the market. Nothing at all misses their hands. They are shaking down a few of the major fruit and meat purveyors. Nothing comes in or out of the market without a heavy mob tax. Even the diesel and gasoline is theirs. Not like the old days when stuff fell off trucks or like the hijacking we saw in the sixties and seventies. It's much more sophisticated today. The mob has become very good at tapping into the real cost of commodities and adding their vigorish. We are about ready to take this to Bob Johnson over at the DA's office in the Bronx," Sheehan said

"No wonder the cost of living is murder in this city," Vic said.

"Indeed. Our calculation so far is just under thirty percent to the mob's side. We have them cold," Sheehan said.

"Fantastic work. What do you have for proof?" Vic said.

"Video, audio, tampered books and records, and a mole. The guy will need witness protection without a doubt. Matter of fact, he is already in hiding. I think the wise guys are already on to the investigation. They are lying very low at the moment," Sheehan said.

"Our boys safe?" Raquel asked.

"As best as we can determine. We've moved some of guys out already. No sense in taking chances and waiting for a message from the bad guys," Sheehan said.

"Good move. Anything else, John?" Vic said.

"Some small stuff in comparison. That Newark politician is still doing his thing at the docks in Elizabeth. His coke habit is up to a thousand a day. He's ready to implode. We are working with the DEA on this one. Good profit margin for us," Sheehan said.

"Sal?" Vic said.

Sal Angrisani had left the U.S. Marshall Service after twenty-two years to join Centurion. A street guy with a history of working in the New York City construction trades, Angrisani was a two-fisted, no-nonsense investigator with friends on both sides of law enforcement. He grew up with the good and the bad guys. Sal was comfortable with mafia-made men as well as city, state, and federal police authorities. His reputation was that he took money from the bad guys to turn his head when they needed him to do so. Right now, he needed all the help he could get from both sides.

"We are working very well with Homeland Security on the case at JFK. They have a leak at the airport, and we discovered who the perp is. Not even an Arab like we first thought. You would never guess the guy we have fingered is a former jeweler who is running an Al-Qaeda cell in Queens. The guy is setting up these maniacs for something big. What it is, we are not sure of yet, but it's big. Looks like he is getting some of these diaper heads through the airport and into safe houses. It may have something to do with a big event in the metro area. Sporting event, concert, something that will scare the living shit out of the entire country. We have a short leash on him. The HS guys hired us on the QT," Angrisani said.

"Moneymaker?" Vic asked.

"We are billing out at half a mill so far, and the meter is ticking. Looks like forty-five percent, give or take."

Raquel's secretary interrupted the meeting.

"Raquel, I'm sorry, I have a call from an Idalis. She said it's urgent, of a personal nature."

"Oh, my god, Tia Carmen," Raquel said. Raquel's face went ashen. She left the conference room immediately. Vic called for a ten-minute recess.

"Idalis? Is everything all right?" Raquel asked. Raquel's heart was in her mouth, waiting to hear the worst news.

"Yes, Raquel, everyone is fine here. Tia Carmen would like to see you as soon as possible."

"What a relief. You've never called me at the office before, and I was thinking...well. We will finish up here at the office and come right over. Are you home?"

"Yes, we are. And there is so much food here. Plan to eat lunch with us please."

Vic walked into Raquel's office, thinking he would find her crying and in a heap.

"Honey?" Vic said.

"She's fine. She needs to see us ASAP. I have no idea why. We are having lunch there. Can we speed up the meeting?"

The last two field managers went through their more mundane investigations quickly. A prominent lawyer's wife was having him followed. An oil company had some drivers under surveillance. A huge retail chain was concerned about back-door discounts. Things like this, Vic called their "bread and butter clients." Nothing glamorous, but every twenty dollar bill that came into the office was important.

The ride up to the Bronx was quick. From the FDR Drive to the Bruckner Boulevard overpass to the Sheridan Expressway took all of ten minutes.

"You know what I think? I think the Bronx is beautiful. Look at how calm everything looks right now," Raquel said.

"On a perfect day like this, everywhere is beautiful. Just see what happens to this place at night. This is the calm before the nightly storm," Vic said.

"I know. I haven't been off the job that long. I'm just saying how great this place could be."

"There is some improvement over the past twenty years or so. Remember when all these buildings were vacant with those silly boarded-up windows with painted-on flowers and curtains? Don't see that anymore. Anyway, the Bronx would be fabulous except for the people," Vic said.

"That was awful. I started accepting those fake windows as a way of life."

"Just goes to show you we can get used to anything at any point in our lives."

They pulled up to Tia Carmen's apartment house. The street was fairly empty, and the sun was blazing down on that side of the street. The wheelchair man was asleep in his chair under a store awning. He looked worse than ever. His skin was a jaundiced color, and his ample underbelly was exposed, hanging down onto what should have been his lap. A piragua lady, her head covered with a red and white kerchief, sat next to him with her ice cart, covered by a faded white sheet, waiting for her next sale. It was reminiscent of a scene from any third-world country.

"What were you saying about the beautiful Bronx honey?" Vic said.

"That's just like you. The glass is always half empty," Raquel joked.

"Just keeping it real is all."

The aroma of cooked food wafted throughout the hallway as Vic and Raquel made their way to Tia Carmen's apartment. A teenage couple was making out on the stairway. Raquel stared at the girl as if to say, "This will lead to trouble," until she noticed the baby bump. Trouble had already found her.

The good women attending to Tia Carmen were in the same positions as Vic and Raquel's last visit. Three were praying, and two were fussing in the small kitchen. Platters of food covered in aluminum foil awaited anyone who needed a home-cooked meal.

Vic and Raquel made their way to Tia Carmen.

"Ah, finally. My little one, you are well?" Tia Carmen said.

Yes, Tia, we are well. You are looking good, too," Raquel said.

"And, Victor, you are as handsome as ever."

"Tia Carmen, I think you need the doctors to check on your eyesight," Vic said.

"Never mind. I can see much better than anyone. I called to tell you a few things. The boy came to me last night. He woke me with his terrible crying. Almost like an injured animal. Instead of his usual sad face, he looked like he was terrified. He did not try to speak or to signal. Just wailing and crying. I could do nothing to comfort him. His energy is ebbing away as is mine. Our time here is very short."

"Tia, why do you think he was crying so?" Raquel asked.

"Great disappointment, perhaps, or fear of the unknown. I wish I knew for sure," Tia Carmen said.

"I think I understand. I share his pain," Raquel said.

"How is your investigation going, little one?"

"To be honest, Tia Carmen, we have confronted a few road-blocks that we don't have answers for just yet. We need some more days to prove some aspects of the case," Raquel said.

"We wish we had better news for you," Vic said.

"I see large, slimy serpents around you both. The serpents have large, split tongues. You cannot trust these creatures. They will destroy everything around them with their venom. Be warned, my little one, and you as well, Victor."

Vic and Raquel glanced at each other with a look that spoke volumes.

"Can you tell me more?" Raquel said.

"As my time draws nearer, my visions are not so clear. This is all I can tell you at the moment. I'm going to the hospital to-morrow for more blood. Perhaps, that will help make the visions better," Tia Carmen's eyes were heavy.

"Please have some lunch with us. There is so much food. I will make you each a plate," Idalis said. She rattled off something to the women, who scurried around the food with plates and utensils.

"I am sorry I cannot be of more help to you, my little one. I am sleepy; my energy has been sapped from the boy."

"Okay, Tia, rest, and we will see you soon," Raquel said.

"Oh, and one more thing. A man came here last night. He said he was a friend of you and Victor. He was dressed in fine cloth-ing. A most beautiful, blue suit and tie. He was older than you but younger than me. His eyes were piercing blue and very clear, but his energy was pained. He has done some very awful things in his life, and much was done to harm him. I believe that he and I to-gether have helped to gather what is good about him and strengthen his energy. There is a nurturing side to this man that has been unnoticed because of his past. He wanted to know if I needed anything."

"Did he say his name, Tia?" Vic asked.

"He did. His name is John. He left so much money."

CHAPTER 42

"Son of a bitch! Areyoukiddenmeorwhat?" Vic said.

The car was gone. No matter how old you are or how rich you are, there is still that flip of the stomach when you get to where your car is parked…and it's gone.

"Holy shit. I can't believe this! Broad daylight!" Raquel said.

"So much for the NYPD stickers and police parking permit. And so much for your beautiful Bronx," Vic said.

"Mira, Poppie, Mami! What are you two doing here? Where is your car?" It was the wheelchair man, motoring his chair over to the two former NYPD cops who were now standing in the black, asphalt-covered street where their car was supposed to be.

"We got here a little while ago. You were sleeping over there," Vic said.

"That is so messed up. You should have woke me. I always watched that car for you."

"Did you see who took it, my friend?" Vic said.

"I had no idea it was here. That was some beautiful machine. I feel terrible," the wheelchair man said.

"Raquel, go back upstairs, and call it in. I'll ask around a bit. Either way, we are taking a gypsy cab back to Manhattan."

Raquel called Borough Command, and a car arrived on the scene in minutes. By now, the Mercedes was in a chop shop or on the way to the docks in a container truck. It was destined for the blowtorch or a new home overseas. Nobody from the hood would be joyriding a vehicle like that owned by two former cops.

Instead of the gypsy cab, the patrolmen insisted on delivering Vic and Raquel back to their office in their squad car. Not a word about the case was mentioned while they were in transit.

Vic called his assistant into his office. Raquel sat quietly on the black, leather sofa, her legs crossed, her arms folded over in front of her chest, and her lips pursed.

"Arlene, please call my insurance company and report that our car was stolen. They will e-mail the paperwork to you. Then, call Pamela at Benzel-Bush Mercedes in Englewood. Tell her I need new wheels by tomorrow morning. Something like I had. No, this time, make it a tank with fifty caliber guns," Vic said. He laughed at his own joke. After all, it was just a car. Nobody was hurt.

"One more thing, Arlene. Shut that door on your way out, and hold any calls please," Raquel said.

"I don't know where to start. My head is spinning. The fact that these fuckers at PPD are lying to us or that Deegan is definitely here in New York is blowing my mind," Raquel said.

"First of all, don't jump to conclusions on the PPD. Let's give Collin a few days and see what he comes up with. As far as Deegan is concerned, I may have to rethink not calling him. Maybe it's time for a sit down with him," Vic said.

"He probably robbed the fucking car. Or hired someone to do it just for shits and giggles."

"That never dawned on me, but I wouldn't put it past that friggin' maniac."

"Do you think he will see us?" Raquel asked.

"I have no idea. Let's go have a drink and think about whether we should even call him. The last forty-eight hours has been loads of fun, hasn't it?"

CHAPTER 43

And drink, they did. Vic always wanted to go to the Peacock Alley at the Waldorf Astoria Hotel on Park Avenue. That's where he and Raquel decided to park themselves at a table for two facing the heavy lobby traffic for a while, take in the scenery, drink, relax, and discuss the events that were making the case troublesome. They had already had a few cocktails when the interesting part of their conversation began.

"What the hell are two Bronx ex-cops doing sitting in this place? There are so many real pubs and bars within walking distance of our office, but you want to sit among the rich and famous. What's that about?" Raquel said.

"Rich and famous? Fuck, we ARE rich and famous. Look at that blonde over there. She's been staring at me for twenty minutes. Probably knows my face from the Deegan case. She's all but sent her phone number over," Vic said.

"You are really pissing me off, Gonnella. What if I said that big guy over there has been looking at me and trying to lick his eyebrows to impress me? How would you feel?"

"Where? What guy? He can lick his eyebrows? I gotta shake his hand!" Vic said. He feigned looking around the bar and stood up from the table.

"Don't try to joke your way out of this. You have had a roving eye for some time. That charming flirting game of yours will lead to other shit, and I will cut your ass like some fish."

"Oh, stop it, you've had too much to drink."

"I haven't had too much to forget you fawning over that leggy blonde at Martha Jameson's office. You had to do all you could not to start beating your meat over her, and she was only all right."

"That was just to get what we needed out of her."

"Bullshit, you wanted to get a lot more, and you know it. What, I'm not good enough for you, so, you need a backup plan?" Raquel said. She flicked the swizzle stick from her Mojito at Vick's face.

"Very Puerto Rican, Raquel. I'm just lucky we're not eating steak. Jesus Christ, what's got into you?"

"I don't know, but I can tell you what's not getting into me for a while."

"Are you really pissed about Justine?" Vic said.

"Justine? Justine? You remember her name, you bastard?" Raquel said. Her voice carried into the vast, ornate Waldorf lobby. There was a momentary pause in the noise level of the room.

"Honey, you are getting carried away. Lower your voice please; it's embarrassing," Vic said.

Raquel leaned into Vic at the table as if she wanted to whisper a secret. Vic leaned in toward her. Raquel shouted her reply.

"Go, and be with your precious Justine." Raquel sat back in her chair and took a big pull on her drink.

"I'm sorry. I'm just good at remembering names. Part of the job. You know that. And besides, yeah, she was attractive, but you have my heart, honey. You know that," Vic said. Vic reached for Raquel's hand, but she was not having any of that.

"Listen to me. Is this part of your psychosexual problem from being abused? Do you need more action? Do you have a sex addiction? Tell me so we can address the issues and salvage our relationship."

"Salvage our relationship? You ARE drunk, woman. That is the furthest thing from my mind and from the truth. Of course, I notice other women. It's only natural. That's as far as it goes with me," Vic said. He motioned for the waiter to bring the check.

"No, no check. I want another drink, and we are not leaving here until we talk this out and talk about Deegan."

"There really isn't anything to talk about. I get your message loud and clear. I'll be more sensitive in the future."

"And what happens if we ever have this baby? I lose my shape, and you are all over the Justines of the world. I can tell you now, that ain't going to cut it, Gonnella. I won't live like that. Not for you or anyone else. Been there, done that, as they say."

"I promise that will never happen. I love you, Raquel, more than I've ever loved anyone or anything."

"My mother always said, 'Actions speak louder than words.' We'll see if Casanova Gonnella rears his ugly head again."

"I'm not going to pull my eyes out of their sockets and walk around with my head down, Raquel. I'm a man, and I will walk on eggshells because you think I'm out on the make. That's not me."

"Okay. I get it. Let's talk Deegan. You gonna call him," Raquel said.

"Argument over? We are good?"

"Yes, we are good. Sorry I yelled at you."

"I've been thinking about this Deegan call. I don't think I should call. Let me tell you why. The guy is a serial killer. For whatever reason, he is free. He still murdered a lot of people. For me to call him, to work with him is not in our best interest. If we work with him now, if I ask for his help, we may never be able to shake this man. I don't think it's a good idea."

"But what if he calls you with information?"

"I can listen, but I can't ask. For all we know, he is sitting at the bar disguised as a banker, a woman, he can be anywhere at any time. Now that we know he is here in New York, we must assume that he is around us, watching."

"Should we be concerned for our safety?"

"I don't think so, no. He wants to keep playing his mind game. It's what makes him who he is. I must tell you, if I'm wrong, if he makes a move on either of us, I'll drop him where he breathes."

CHAPTER 44

A few days went by. Vic and Raquel busied themselves overseeing other cases and meeting with a few NYPD brass just to keep relationships fresh. In their world, as in most of life, things get stale really fast. Out of sight, out of mind, as the old saying goes. A lunch here, a call, an e-mail, drinks, dinner, whatever works to keep your name in front of the people who matter.

Vic decided to call Collin as he had not heard from him or anyone else at PPD. The case was indeed fifty-seven years cold, and it could fall back into the frozen tundra very quickly.

"Hey, pal. How are things?" Vic said.

"Just about to call you. Been real busy with the latest mutts acting badly with knives and guns," Collin said.

"Anything new on our case?"

"Well, yes, in a matter of speaking. I have some shitty news to tell you. Hold on, let me close my door."

Vic gave a thumbs down signal to Raquel who was sitting in front of his desk at the office. From the sound of Collin's voice, he anticipated hearing that the DNA samples came back as no match.

"We are not sending the samples to Texas after all, Vic. It came back that you are not a law enforcement agency and the powers that be scratched it. The people at Vidocq concur with this decision."

Vic took a deep breath.

"You are kidding me, right, Collin? Not a law enforcement agency? What's that about?"

"Look, don't shoot the messenger. This is what I've been told. That's how it is."

"We are a licensed investigatory agency, certified and approved by the States of New York, New Jersey, Connecticut, and Florida. The Feds are using us on a major espionage case, we have a global reach, and the PPD thinks we are not reliable? That's totally unacceptable."

"These DNA tests have to be taken by someone who knows what they are doing, I guess."

"I hired a lab who instructed us on how to take a simple cheek swab. Sterile Q-Tip swabs, using sterile surgical gloves, placed in sterile envelopes. Nice and easy. It's not rocket science, my friend. So, some detective from PPD knows better? Or some jerk-off at the morgue who has a certificate from some online training school knows better than two ex-NYPD cops? My lab ran the samples without any mention of this bullshit."

"What can I say, Vic? I'm only taking orders," Collin said. He didn't sound like he was upset by these orders.

"That's what those German generals said after they killed millions of people at the death camps: "We were only following orders." Nobody bought that crap then, and I'm not buying it now," Vic said. Raquel's mouth was wide open. She was shocked and beyond speechless.

"What can I do? This is what I was told. I only work here, Vic," Collin said

"I'm coming down there. I want someone in authority, some-one above your pay grade, to say this to my face. I have half a mind to bring my lawyer or sue for the original DNA tests of the boy. Oh, and fuck the Vidocq Society. If they were any good, this case would have been solved years ago."

"I can't stop you from coming, but don't expect things to change or for a warm reception," Collin said.

"What are you trying to say? I'm not welcome to solve the longest cold case of child murder in the history of Philadelphia?"

"No, I'm just trying to explain the position of PPD. Is there any other route you can take?"

"Not without the kid's DNA we can't. You guys have that, I need that, and I can have a test result in the time it takes to eat one of those cheese steak sandwiches," Vic said. He was starting to lose his composure. Raquel signed him to calm himself down.

"I doubt if they will release that evidence," Collin said.

"Evidence now? Evidence that hasn't been used correctly in decades? For Christ's sake, Collin, do you hear what you are say-ing?"

"What do you want from me? I'm just telling you what I've been told to tell you."

"And I'm telling you it's unacceptable! Is it they don't want the dago from New York to solve the case for fear of them looking bad?"

"Honestly, Vic, I don't think that anyone here feels that. I also don't think there is anyone here who gives a shit about this case. Plain and simple."

"Now that is not what we thought the first day we came down there with all of the drama. Photographs, autographs, back slapping, ass kissing. When did this turn into the worst case of gonorrhea I've ever seen?"

"I really don't know. Maybe you need to let dead dogs lie. Chalk this one up."

"Collin! That boy is no dog. He was a real, living person who was abused and murdered and dumped in a fucking cardboard box in a vacant garbage lot," Vic said. He was fuming.

"Sorry, I guess that was a bad choice of words. Vic, there are some things that just can never be solved. This is one of them. Just walk away."

"What am I wasting my time with you for? Let your bosses know that Vic Gonnella never takes no for an answer. I'm insulted beyond what words can express. I'm going to see my attorney and probably take this to the national media who loves stories like this. I have that kind of clout you know. I can just see the articles. 'Hero of the Deegan murders told to go and fuck himself by the Philadelphia Police Department, news at 7 and 11.'"

CHAPTER 45

The walk over to attorney Jim Wexler's office took only five minutes. From the sound of Vic's voice, Wexler knew he had to clear his schedule. Vic and Wexler had met at the Police Academy and were assigned to their first job together in the Bronx. They became close friends, Vic climbing the ladder a bit quicker than his pal. Vic was married and had started a family. Wexler spent most of his off time taking courses at St. John's University Law School and studying. Wexler spent ten years on the job, all in a squad car. He liked the job but didn't love it. What he did love was the law. Wexler joined a small law firm and made his reputation by litigating impossible-to-win cases. He became a sought-after commodity among several large, white-shoe law firms. He joined the prestigious law firm Thomson Hine with a fabulous monetary offer. He quickly became partner with all of the trappings and benefits attached.

Vic and Raquel used Wexler and his firm exclusively for all the firm's legal work. As Centurion grew, so did their legal billable hours.

Short, dark, and handsome with slicked back, salt and pepper hair, Brioni-suited Wexler was a no-nonsense, ballsy attorney who made minced meat out of his opponents, largely because of his computer-quick brain and his street savvy. He left nothing to chance and took notes while Vic and Raquel outlined the facts of the Boy in the Box debacle. Wexler listened intently and paused before he started speaking.

"What I'm hearing is that the Philadelphia Police Department has turned on you. The Vidocq Society people, whoever they are, threw you under the bus and perhaps are looking to take any glory surrounding the potential solving of this case. I'm not certain what the police department's motivation is, but it's clear these Vidocq folks smell money or attention, perhaps both. Here is the basic problem. We can demand the evidence. I'm not certain if the Freedom of Information Act will trump the position the PPD will likely take. They can claim the DNA evidence is part of an active investigation. We can go in front of a judge in Philadelphia and lose any motion forthwith. If we take it federal, we have a better chance of being heard, but this will take months to get anything going. You tell me, for whatever reason you have, that time is critical, so, we don't have a lot of wiggle room. If I petition the Philadelphia court for a change of venue, they can sit on this for a while, reject it, we appeal, and even more time can pass. So, my opinion, for what it's worth, is one of two avenues of attack. Get to someone high up in the PPD and reason with them before you take your plight to the press. You are better off trying to win them over and discover what their real, underlying reason for stonewalling you is, or make them an offer they can't refuse."

"What would that be, Jimmy?" Vic said.

"This legal action will cost you a small fortune. We bill out at nine hundred and fifty dollars an hour. Not that I don't want to make money, but, as your friend, I would hate to see you spend this kind of dough and potentially lose. It will be more cost effective for you to offer the PPD full payment of whomever they want to fly down to Memphis, retake the DNA samples, fly those samples and the technician to Texas, pay for the analysis, and see if your theory is correct. So, you're looking at five grand against sixty or seventy grand minimum. At the same time, you meet your self-imposed time limitation. Bring in Vidocq, telling them you are willing to share in the credit of solving the case. Everyone wins. Philly gets what they want, Vidocq wins as does their thing, and you have the satisfaction of knowing whom the boy was. And not letting these pricks beat you."

"Can you come to Philadelphia with us?" Raquel said.

"Of course I can, but the moment a New York lawyer from a big firm shows us at their doorstep, they will shut down like a bodega on Christmas day. You don't want me there at this point. There is always time for the lawyers to fuck things up and start billing hours on both sides down the road."

"They sound like they don't want to see us," Vic said.

"And when did that ever stop you, Gonnella? Are you getting soft on me, buddy?"

"How did I know you were going to say that?" Vic laughed.

"What are friends for? By the way, this conversation is on me. Let's go over to the Union Club and have lunch; I'm starved," Wexler said.

"Thanks, Jimmy, but we have to get back down to Philadelphia. We'll take a rain check," Vic said.

"How did I know you were going to say that?" Wexler said. He shot Raquel a quick wink.

CHAPTER 46

"Can we smoke 'em peace pipe, Kemosabe?" Vic said.

"This was a call I wasn't expecting this late in the day. I was waiting for six lawyers and four mobile news units to be waiting outside my house this morning," Collin Frank said.

"C'mon, Collin, you know my Italian temper. I'm like Santino Corleone sometimes."

"You know what happened to him?"

"I should learn from that, shouldn't I?" Vic said. He grimaced at the sight of the Godfather's son being chopped down by machine guns at the tollbooth.

"Are we okay now, Vic?"

"Listen, I really want a chance to come down to the Round House and hash things out. I get it about not being a law enforcement agency and all that. I'm a little hurt, but I'm over it. Rules are rules, and we all need to bring our egos into check. I apologize for anything I said that insulted you, Collin."

"I knew you were pissed off and hot under the collar. I didn't mention anything to anyone at PPD about the news media and stuff. Nobody likes threats, and I figured you needed some time to digest the bad news. All is forgiven," Collin said.

"I'm glad about that. Good friends are hard to find and even harder to keep these days. Tell me, can you set up a meeting with whoever you think has the authority to help. I didn't want to go to the new NYPD commissioner and ask a favor. He's up to his ass in alligators and kissing every black reverend's ass who cries racial profiling. I figured you would tell me the best way to go forward," Vic said.

"Vic, I'm not sure they are willing to bend on this ruling. Besides, there is a huge corruption scandal that just hit the papers down here. Have you heard about it? Everyone is looking over his or her shoulders. The commissioner is on the warpath. 'Worst case of police corruption I've seen in forty years,' he said. And the Republicans want his ass. If he were a white guy, he'd been gone already."

"What were these knuckleheads thinking? Shaking down drug dealers is nothing new in this world. I'm sure that Sean was very involved with this bust. And he never whispered that the FBI was into anything about PPD," Vic said.

"Yeah, and I'm glad he didn't. One of the guys is my Kaitlin's godfather. That would have fucked me up if I had known anything about an investigation on his squad," Collin said.

"Would you have told him to lay low if you knew about it?" Vic asked.

"Without a doubt. Professionalism and a career are one thing, but this is family. That's why I'm glad Sean didn't say a word. And he shouldn't."

"We digressed. So, who do you think I should meet with?" Vic asked.

"It's true, you don't take no for an answer. Let me nose around and feel the temperature of this place. Lots of call outs this week. People are lying low, so, it's crazy. At any rate, they are not going to budge on this thing you want."

"I get that. I do have a plan that may work for all concerned. If you get me an appointment, I'm certain we can all come out with what we are looking for, even those mutts at Vidocq," Vic said.

"C'mon, Vic, they are good people. There you go again, getting all Bronxy."

"Sorry… sorry, you're right. Geez, Raquel is always telling me I need a filter on my mouth."

"Raquel is very beautiful and very wise."

CHAPTER 47

Collin Frank called Vic a few hours later, telling him Inspector Tony Scarpa would see Vic and Raquel the next day at 11 in the morning. Vic fought the urge to negotiate an earlier time.

"I feel like a ping pong ball that got stuck on the New Jersey Turnpike," Raquel said.

"What's really scary is that I'm getting used to the acrid aroma," Vic said.

"It smells like ass, Vic."

"That's it! I've been trying to figure out where I got that whiff before!"

"So, forget ass sniffing. Let's go up to the Bronx this afternoon. I'm missing Dominick's salad and that pork chop pizziola dish. I could use some pastry, too," Raquel said.

"Great, tell the doorman to get us a cab. I'm not bringing the new car anywhere near the Bronx with the temporary license plates that say, 'Yo, steal this new Benz,'" Vic said.

"I hear that!"

Vic's cell phone rang. It was Deegan. Vic motioned to Raquel and put the call on speaker.

"Hello, John. Enjoying the Big Apple?" Vic said.

"Hello, Vic, hello, Raquel. Wasn't sure if you were at the office or at home, so, I called the cell number."

"Liar. You probably know exactly where we are and where we are having dinner tonight," Vic said.

"I couldn't care less. I'm more interested in helping you solve this case. It's dragging on much too long for my liking," Deegan said.

"I don't remember that we ever asked for help, John," Raquel said.

"I realized that you would never ask and why you never call me. I'm that mad serial killer whom you shouldn't associate with. Better to hang around those fakers in Philadelphia. Have you figured out why they are stalling you?"

Vic looked at Raquel with a face that can only be described as amazed.

"What brings you to that conclusion?"

"As Sherlock would say, 'Academic, my dear Watson.' You would be done with the case if they were being forthcoming. It's very clear to me that they are hiding some deep, dark secret."

"Such as?" Raquel asked.

"Not entirely sure, just yet. That will have to present itself in due time. Suffice it to say, they have more secrets then the Vatican. Well, not really, no cop has ever taken a vow to keep confession sacrosanct. Someone will give the answer you need before long. There is a Judas Iscariot among them."

"Your religious analogies are epic, John. That's all you have for us?" Vic said.

"At the moment, yes. You guys have a nice dinner."

John ended the call.

"Cryptic as always," Raquel said.

"I'm calling Sal Angrisani. I want this place and the office swept for bugs. The car, too. Deegan knows too much. How the hell does he figure these things out?" Vic said.

"You keep reminding me that he is a genius and that this is a game of chess to Deegan. I wish I could think seven moves ahead like he does."

"Seven moves is an insult to his intelligence."

The yellow cab dropped Vic and Raquel in front of Dominick's on Arthur Avenue. The place was packed as usual. Charlie, the owner, reached over the bar to shake the couple's hands. The four waiters and two busboys came over to shake hands and tell Raquel how gorgeous she was.

"You're number forty-two, Vic," Charlie said.

"How long a wait?" Vic asked.

"We're on number twelve now. It goes fast. Maybe an hour, maybe less. Go upstairs, and have a drink. I'll call your number."

"We'll go next door to the Parisian and have espresso. I see some familiar faces sitting outside. Ask Jack to call us. That Sardinian needs to step outside for a minute anyway," Vic said. Charlie laughed.

Four men were sitting at one outdoor table, two at another. They were all smoking something, cigars, cigarettes, totally ignoring the "No Smoking" sign in the window, which faced the bustling street. When Vic and Raquel stepped in, the men all stood up at once. Handshakes and kisses on both cheeks is the traditional Albanian greeting. Some of the men put their right hand to their hearts in a sign of respect and admiration. They would pick up the tab; of that, there was no doubt.

Vic ordered espresso with anisette for himself and an espresso with Sambuca for Raquel. The waiter scurried inside to place their order.

The usual locals passed by as did some tourists. Some of the locals waved at the men. The tourists looked at the men as if they were viewing a mob movie. Some were even bold enough to take photos with their cell phones.

"Who would have ever thought that this place would be a tourist attraction with those tour busses lined up and down Arthur Avenue? When I grew up here, no busses were allowed. Busses brought in the undesirables," Vic said.

"I guess my people were among the great unwashed in this neighborhood," Raquel said.

"Puerto Ricans and blacks were the enemy. I'm happy that hatred has changed over the years. More Hispanics live in the neighborhood than any other group right now. Very few Italians left. And, of course, the Albanians are strong here. The neighborhood works; it just works differently," Vic said.

A street person pulling a shopping cart that was loaded with old clothing, random rags, and empty bottles for deposit money stopped in front of the Parisian. He looked as if he smelled badly. Scraggly beard, open, oil-stained sneakers, his fingernails long and filthy, his hair badly matted.

"Can anyone spare some change for a hungry man?" The street urchin begged.

"Go, keep walking. Too many beggars on this street," One of the Albanians said, waving the homeless man away.

The waiter ran out onto the sidewalk, standing between the man and the seated patrons.

"Get the hell out of here. Go away; don't come back here, or I'll kick in your fecken' ass," the waiter said.

"Wait a second. Hold on," Raquel said. She reached for her purse.

"Miss, with all respect to you, we have these people pass all day long. If you give to them, they keep coming back. Give him nothing. Let him get a job," a thickly accented Albanian man at the next table said.

"Get out of here, you filthy *rrugaq*," another said.

Raquel ignored the advice, stood from her chair, and handed the disheveled man a twenty. The man lowered his head.

"Thank you, miss. God will bless your kindness," the homeless man said. He took his shopping cart and his belongings and quickly walked away.

"Honey, I know that you have a good heart, but these men are exposed to this kind of thing all day every day. Women with small children begging for food, drug addicts asking for food when they will put junk in their veins. It's terrible, and it never ends," Vic said.

"Okay, and your point is?" Raquel said.

"My point is to ignore these people and let the locals live by their own code."

"My code is different. That man needed food. And a bath. Maybe he will be happy for a day or two with my twenty."

"Mr. Vic, you are number twenty one, right?" Jack, the waiter from Dominick's, came out and approached the outdoor table where Vic and Raquel were nursing their second round of espresso and *aperitivos.*

"No, we are number forty-two," Raquel said.

"Yes, Jack, we are twenty-one. Thank you, we will be right in," Vic said to the waiter.

"Raquel, the fix is always in around here. Charlie had an opening, and here we go," Vic said.

"Is that part of the neighborhood code you are referring to?"

"Now, you're getting it!" Vic said.

"But I don't have to like it."

Vic and Raquel entered Dominick's and were ushered to a table in the back of the restaurant. They ordered a bottle of red wine. Jack took their order. No menu, just Jack explaining today's fare. Veal parmigiano, veal *cacciatore*, chicken parmigiano, steak, chicken scarpariello on the bone, calamari, lasagna, snapper marechiara.

"Any pork chop pizziola?" Raquel asked.

"For the pretty woman, of course," Jack said.

There was some excitement at the entrance to the restaurant. Charlie stepped from the bar and started to shoo away the homeless man. Charlie turned and walked back to Vic and Raquel's table.

"Sorry, Vic, this bum wants to see your lady."

"See, I told you, honey. Now, he wants a date," Vic said.

Raquel walked with Charlie toward the door. Two waiters, both of them trying to pull the homeless man away from the door, surrounded the street urchin.

"Just a second," Raquel said.

The man smiled broadly when Raquel came to the door. He handed a plastic shopping bag to her. His eyes were sparkling. In the bag was a stuffed toy: a bunny rabbit.

Raquel took the toy and thanked the man. The waiters escorted the man away from the restaurant. Raquel walked back to the table. Everyone in the place followed her moves, especially the men.

"Wasn't that the sweetest thing you've ever seen? The poor man wanted to thank me in his own way," Raquel said. Her eyes were moist with tears.

"Nice move," Vic said.

The famous Dominick's salad arrived. Vic placed the salad into his and Raquel's white, oval dishes. They dug in with gusto.

Just before the salad was finished and their entrées were presented, Vic's phone rang.

"Deegan," Vic said.

"Hello, John," Vic said. His voice betrayed his annoyance. "That was so nice of Raquel. You have a keeper there. I wasn't expecting a twenty."

CHAPTER 48

"Jesus Christ Almighty! That street bum was Deegan," Vic said.

"What? You're kidding right?" Raquel said.

"He is fucking with us now. That was him! Did you notice anything about that guy that was familiar?"

"No, except his eyes were clear. Crystal blue. Usually, homeless are all bloodshot and veiny. Holy shit, Vic! It was him. I should have realized it was him."

"And he has the balls to come right up to us. He knows he is a master of disguise, and he is laughing right in our face. Man, he is good!" Vic said.

"But why? What is his motivation?"

"Because he can. And he gets off on it. It's fun to him. Like I said, it's a game to him."

"Should we look for him?" Raquel said.

"Are you kidding? He's probably back in whichever hole he is hiding in. Probably the Pierre Hotel or some other place where they think he's an Arab prince. Deegan is simply an artist of disguise."

"And you're sure we aren't in any danger?"

"I don't think so. If he wanted us dead, we would be at Ferranga Brothers right now, laid out head to head. No, honey, in his own way, he admires us and still feels obligated to me."

"Maybe, now, we should meet with him."

"Don't think so. He knows we shouldn't. He said so himself. Let's be happy to play as pawns on his chessboard and watch the game unfold."

The dinner was served. Jack brought the steaming hot dishes and sides of pasta.

"I can't eat now," Raquel said.

"Do you mind if I do? Nothing will happen until we get to Philadelphia tomorrow, and I'm starved."

"Well, I guess you're right. I can taste a little."

Vic and Raquel finished their meal. Dominick's not only doesn't have a menu, but there is no check either. Vic motioned to Jack the waiter for the amount of their tab. Jack walked over to their table.

"Mr. Vic, a limo driver came in here and handed Charlie three hundred dollars to pay for your meal," Jack said.

"A limo driver now! I bet that was Deegan, too," Vic said to Raquel.

"Jack, what was the bill?" Vic said.

"One twenty, Mr. Vic."

"Keep the change. It's all yours."

Vic and Raquel strolled around to 187th Street for coffee and cannoli at DeLillo's Pastry Shop. After desert, Vic hailed a gypsy cab for their trip back to their apartment in Manhattan.

"Your name isn't John Deegan by any chance?" Vic asked the driver.

"No, sir. Raul. Raul Sanchez, at your service."

"Raquel laughed loudly.

"This is why I love you, Gonnella. You always have the best one-liners."

"And here I thought it was my big, brown eyes."

"See! See what I mean?"

Back at their apartment, Sal Angrisani left a message on Vic and Raquel's answering machine. Every inch of the apartment, office, and the new Mercedes was swept. No bugs, no cameras, and no wiretaps on any of the telephones. The coast was clear. If Deegan was listening in on conversations, he was using equipment that even the CIA didn't have.

"That's certainly a relief," Raquel said.

"I was actually hoping we would have found something. Now, we are still guessing. I guess Deegan's talents extend to the meta-physical," Vic said. He was being facetious. Vic is a meat and po-tatoes kind of guy. Until he saw the apparitions of the boy, all that kind of thing was total nonsense.

"Vic, seriously, do you think he has clairvoyant abilities? I don't believe in coincidences, and I know you don't either."

"I chased this guy half-way around the world. There was nothing psychic or telepathic in his MO. He was just one giant step ahead of us-until he no longer wanted to be."

"I don't care what you say, I'm locked and loaded. Two guns like when I was on the job. If he gets the drop on us, he'd better move quickly."

"Guns or no guns, if he wanted us, we are practically defenseless. He is a trained killer, trained by the best on earth: the United States Government. Stop worrying about it, will you?"

"What's our next step?"

"We are going to find out where PPD went off track with us. I will not leave that place until I have a reasonable explanation or they take those samples themselves."

Vic and Raquel turned in early but didn't get to sleep for hours. They enjoyed a love-making session as if they were honeymooners.

CHAPTER 49

"Good morning, Vic, Raquel. Nice to see you two again," Inspector Tony Scarpa said. His rapid speech was the same as the last time they met, maybe a tad faster. His countenance betrayed nothing in an attitude change. Scarpa's expression was identical to the time when they had arrived at PPD that first time, when they had been welcomed like Caesar and Cleopatra entering Rome.

"Good to see you, Inspector. I suppose Detective Frank filled you in on why we are anxious to see you," Vic said. Vic knew that getting straight to business was the best tactic to take with Scarpa, especially in light of the pressure he was feeling over the latest corruption scandal that plagued PPD.

"He did, Vic, and I have to tell you, we are not flexible on our position. Any private investigator, you included, with all due respect, is not a bona-fide law enforcement agency. We would be exposed to a great deal of criticism if we set this precedent with you and your firm."

"We are past that, Inspector. We came here today hopefully to come to an amicable understanding, one that would not cost your department one penny. We get on with our investigation, and you get shared credit in solving this homicide," Vic said.

"I'm listening," Scarpa said.

"You send down whomever you want to get DNA swab samples from Mr. Jordan in Memphis, and we pay for everything. The man hours, overtime, flights, ground transportation, and meals. The full monty," Vic said.

"Now, I have to ask you a simple question. Why?"

"We want to solve this case. It's important that this boy has a name on his gravestone," Vic said.

"Not enough. What is your real motive behind this case?"

"Inspector, please put our motive aside for a moment. Why would you not want to accept our offer?" Raquel said.

"Because your motivation smells like you guys may be opportunists looking to cash in on a case that has no urgent need to be solved. For Christ's sake, this case is older than the three of us. Forgive me for speaking so frankly. It's certainly not for justice at this point." Scapa said. He placed both of his hands behind his head while his rapid speech was accompanied by rapid eye blinking.

Scarpa's body language was very telling. Vic knew that anyone who placed his hands behind his head was not taking him and Raquel seriously. The eye movement conveyed that he was lying.

"We will sign any document that will prevent us from doing any interviews, book or movie rights, television programs, anything that you think may add to the ringing of our cash register," Vic said. Vic put his two hands behind his head in mock similarity to Scarpa's.

"I'm not comfortable with this scenario, and I can speak for the PPD administration on this matter. We are far too busy to be dealing with this case at this point in time. Basically, we have other fish to fry. Vic, I would love to help you out, but my answer is no. Find another way."

"Can we have the DNA evidence?" Raquel said.

"We can't do that."

"Why not? What is the big secret? Are we missing something here?" Raquel said. She felt her head getting warm with the beginnings of anger.

"This is an open case. That evidence is confidential," Scarpa said. His body language tells escalated. Scarpa folded both of his arms in front of his chest. He was shutting down. Scarpa had made up his mind and was clearly protecting something.

"PPD sent the evidence box almost in its entirety to Jim Hoffmann, who wrote a book about the case. Why all of a sudden is the evidence of a fifty-seven year old homicide case so confidential?" Vic said.

Scarpa was clearly annoyed at Vic and Raquel peppering him with logic.

"Look, my answer is final. I'm sorry that you came down here for a fifteen minute meeting. I have a full schedule today, and I need to get going. I wish you both the best."

"Thanks for your time today, Inspector Scarpa. I have to tell you that we intend to get to why the position of PPD is so rigid. You will be hearing from us again," Vic said.

"Is that some kind of threat, Gonnella?"

"Threat? Only someone trying to hide something would take what I just said as a threat."

Scarpa got up from his chair and left his office.

"Like a petulant child," Vic said to Raquel.

"He is hiding something for sure," Raquel said.

"And he just threw down the gauntlet."

"Honey, let's go home. I'm feeling really nauseous all of a sudden."

Raquel was feeling quite ill. Maybe the stress of dealing with Scarpa or maybe just exhaustion, a flu, or something else made her sleep for the two-hour drive back. Vic decided somewhere on the turnpike to make a call that he didn't really want to make.

CHAPTER 50

The gray Manhattan skyline was visible against a clear, blue sky. The view of the city resembled a photograph on a postcard as Vic and Raquel got closer to the city. Raquel was feeling better, or, at least, she said she was. Her color was good, but she was very quiet, almost solemn. There was no Sinatra or Elvis singing on this trip. In fifteen minutes, they would be home, and Raquel would take to her bed. Vic was still upset with the treatment they received from Inspector Scarpa but did not verbalize his feelings. Vic never called Collin, nor did Collin call them.

It took Vic a full hour of driving for his fury to subside. Now, he was just out to get the PPD.

Once Raquel was fast asleep in their darkened bedroom, Vic went into his study and made the call.

"Well, hello, Vic. I was awaiting your call. I know you didn't want my counsel on this case, but I think it's in all of our best interest that we chat for a while," John Deegan said.

"How did you know I was going to call you after all?" Vic said.

"The time for my cryptic hints and messages are over now, Vic. At the moment, we have to work together to get this case solved. Three heads are better than one. Is Raquel on the line with us?"

"She's not feeling well right now. It's just me and you."

"I'm sure she is as upset as you are. I hear the tension in your voice, Vic. She'll be fine. Raquel is a strong woman. Let me answer your question. I knew you would call because you've hit a stone wall. I knew this would happen."

"I have to ask the same question, John. How do you know this?"

"A bit of geometric logic, some life experience, a dash of intuition. It's not black and white. There is something fundamentally wrong with why the PPD and that Vidocq Society have set up a sort of Maginot line to prevent the case from being solved," Deegan said.

"I'm at a loss. Can you shed some light for me?"

"When people are hiding something that makes no sense, there are three things that always, always come into play: money, sex, or religion, sometimes all three."

"Hmmm, so, by process of elimination?" Vic said.

"Good, now you're thinking clearly again. Your voice even sounds better. You are back from the edge of anger. Now that the anger is gone, your good judgment has returned. So, go ahead, and analyze the situation."

"Religion? I don't think so. I don't get that from the PPD. It seems they are reading from the same hymnal but not because of religion," Vic said.

"I agree. No blind faith or phony dogma is indicated," Deegan said. His response was quick and to the point.

"Money? They may want the sole glory of solving the case, and some money could follow. Do you believe that their egos are as good as money in this case?" Vic said.

"Take that one step further."

"If they solve the case, will they all benefit financially? I don't think so. Scarpa and the rest of the PPD are not even smart enough to spin this story into gold. They are civil servants, trapped in the pension treadmill. They are all marking time with no entrepreneurial spirit. The Vidocq guys are all well past their prime. They are more like guys in the front pew waiting for their check-out call. Therefore, I would have to say no," Vic said.

"Again, I agree, but only somewhat. Protecting their reputation and pride, in a sense, is just like money," Deegan said.

"Sex? I can't connect the dots on this one, John," Vic said. He was fishing for the genius to help him here.

"Our generation did not invent sex and its trappings. I remember once visiting the destroyed ruins of Pompeii. They had wonderful brothels with a large penis and balls that pointed into the entrance, advertising their location. The walls of these whorehouses were decorated with the most explicit, multi-positioned ceramic tiles. Some of the scenes would make the Kama Sutra blush. This was in 77 A.D. By the 1950s, people were still having kinky sex, just not so readily advertised in this puritanical country."

"I'm missing the point," Vic said.

"Martha's mother was a whore plain and simple. And a kinky one at that. What she didn't get to satisfy her normal sex drive, she took out on the boy and her daughter. There was no easy means to find sex partners in those days. Sex was not as readily available as it is today. Women like Martha's mother did it the old-fashioned way. They got involved with men who had more to lose than she did. It was paramount for these men to keep their assignations from going public. I have a suspicion that the PPD and the Vidocq know something about Lillian Jameson. Some scandal they are still wanting to cover up. Shame and dishonor are very embarrassing things, and sex scandals have a long and dirty memory. The

Roman Church has proven this for a long, long time, Vic. Even though most of the people that were around when the boy was found are dead, there are still a few players who are alive."

"John, are you saying that someone was banging Lillian James-on and covered up for her?" Vic said.

"No. I'm saying they covered up for themselves."

"The question is who?"

"That's what we have to discover. I suggest it's someone close to the PPD, someone willing to protect a murderess from being exposed rather than face humiliation and loss of position."

"So, that may answer the question as to why Martha's testimony was ignored," Vic said.

"Precisely. Elementary, my dear Watson."

"Impossible to prove at this point."

"I'll borrow a line from the Godfather, my Italian friend. 'Difficult but not impossible.'"

"John, this is the longest conversation we've ever had. By now, you would have hung up, leaving me scratching my head."

"We're partners now, Vic. Just ask Tia Carmen. Now, remember what Tia Carmen said to you about slippery serpents? We are together in a snake pit. We need to fight our way out. Now, I hang up."

CHAPTER 51

A few hours later, Raquel woke and walked into Vic's study. Vic was looking over their notes and jotting down names on a large, yellow legal pad.

"Hey, sleeping beauty. How are you feeling?"

"So much better. I guess I needed the sleep. I haven't felt so tired since I was in grad school and had to cram for exams. What's cooking?" Raquel said.

"You look much better, too. Your color was pretty piqued this afternoon. Glad you are yourself again. I have a confession to make, honey."

"You called Justine, and you're leaving me and moving to Cincinnati."

"Would you get off that, Raquel? I thought we put that behind us."

"Only kidding, Mr. Sensitive. For joke."

"Very funny. I decided it was time to call Deegan."

"What? You did? I thought we agreed that wouldn't be a good idea."

"I just thought we don't have many options, and, frankly, his advice was amazing. He thinks PPD is hiding some deep, dark secret probably tied to Lillian Jameson and some sex scandal that surrounded her. The guy is brilliant. I'll give you the whole run-down.

Vic explained Deegan's theory in full detail.

"It's better than what we have on the table at the moment. It's very plausible. So, where do we start?" Raquel said.

"One more thing. Deegan said we should ask Tia Carmen about us being partners now. He also made reference to her slippery serpents. That was the only vague statement he made. I'd like to go see her and get details of their conversation."

"No time like the present. Let's go."

"I'll get the car and meet you in front of the building."

"I thought you were done with bringing your car up to the Bronx. We don't want this new Benz winding up in Kuwait."

"The wheelchair man will watch it for us. If he's sleeping, I'll wake up his fat ass. I'm sure he can use the money."

On the way to Tia Carmen's place, Vic and Raquel played "What if?" What if one of the detectives on the case and Lillian Jameson were doing the nasty? What if one of the big police honchos was involved with her and that ex-nun, ex-priest couple, the Nelsons? What if the boy was part of some weird child porn thing?

Vic made a left turn on Tremont Avenue and Southern Boulevard up in the Bronx. They could see flashing red and white lights of an Emergency Services Unit and two patrol cars in front of Tia Carmen's building.

"*Ay, Dios Mío*, its Tia Carmen," Raquel said.

"Doesn't look good," Vic said.

Vic parked thirty feet behind the EMS ambulance. He and Raquel got out of the car quickly and simultaneously as cops do. The EMS people were wheeling a covered body toward the open rear doors of the ambulance.

Raquel put both hands to her mouth and started to cry.

Vic knew one of the cops at the scene, a sergeant from the forty-eighth precinct, and approached him.

"What do you have, Jimmy?" Vic asked.

"DOA, this big guy died in that wheelchair over there. Evidently, from the locals, he just fell asleep and died. Coroner said it looked like a massive coronary. The guy was in really bad shape. A shame. Local street fixture, only thirty-eight years old."

"I knew that guy. He used to watch my car when my girl and I visited a lady in the building," Vic said.

"Better find someone else. He's headed downtown for an autopsy to confirm cause of death," Jimmy said.

Vic turned to Raquel who was being comforted by two older women. They were Tia Carmen's prayer ladies and remembered her from the apartment and hospital when she and Vic had visited.

"Thank God it wasn't Tia Carmen. It was poor Pablito. He was not doing so good lately. He was always in a lot of pain. He is with Our Lady and Jesus now. His suffering is over," one of the ladies said. Both women blessed themselves and kissed the rosary beads in their hands.

The look on Raquel's face changed from despair to sadness. She was glad it wasn't Tia Carmen yet sad that the wheelchair guy was dead.

As the ambulance was pulling away without lights and sirens, Vic called over a guy who was watching a game of dominos.

"My friend, will you watch my car for me? I have a twenty in my pocket for you," Vic said.

"For twenty, I will wash and wax it for you."

"I heard that same thing from another guy. That's okay. Just stand by the car. I'll be back soon."

"Oh, my god, Vic. How sad," Raquel said.

"Just goes to show you, there is always someone ready to take your job," Vic said.

"Very sensitive, Gonnella."

Tia Carmen was not doing well. Idalis escorted the couple into the bedroom where Tia Carmen's head was propped up on two pillows. She was covered by a hand-woven quilt. The old woman was staring into the light of a lamp that was on a bureau. The rest of the apartment was dark. There were no prayerful women to be seen at the moment.

"Ah, little one. Victor, how are you both?" Tia Carmen said. Her voice was low. She sounded and looked very weak.

"We need a moment, my dear Tia Carmen," Raquel said.

"What is on your mind, little one?"

"That man who came to visit you, that man John. Can you tell us more about what you and he talked about?" Raquel said.

"He is a good man. We spoke of his difficult and tortured life. I could see his damaged energy. He is better now than before in his life, but he needs more time to help himself."

"Did he speak of his past? Did he say how he knew us?" Raquel said.

"He didn't have to say those words. I knew his story from light in his eyes. I've connected his energy with the boy. John will help you now. He is very strong, little one. His purpose is to enlighten you and Victor, and you must trust him. John will see the boy through his journey for a little while longer. My energy is almost done. I am ready to pass on to the next level."

"But, Tia Carmen, if you go, who can I…" Raquel stopped her thought. She suddenly felt very selfish and light headed.

"Little one, you were ill today, yes?

"Yes, yes, I was, Tia Carmen. And suddenly, I'm feeling poorly again. Why do you ask?"

"This will pass soon, my child. You have the morning sickness."

CHAPTER 52

Raquel was dumfounded by the bomb Tia Carmen dropped on her. Vic was numb. The morning sickness reference didn't register with him at first. After a short while, Vic and Raquel left Tia Carmen but not until Raquel showered her in kisses and "thank you"s in Spanish and English. The Spanish, for whatever reason, seemed to have more meaning.

The dominos guy did his job. The new car was still there, and Vic paid him with a crisp twenty.

"Vic, are you okay? I thought you would be ecstatic about having a child with me," Raquel said.

"It hasn't hit me yet. You know my feelings about bringing kids into this cesspool of a world. Of course, I'm happy to have a child with the woman I love. This will be a whole new experience for me. I'm just not in the mood to jump up and down at the moment," Vic said.

"I guess I understand."

"You can't imagine the feelings of someone who has been abused as I was. I'm glad you can't. I was never huggy, kissy with my kids. I wanted to be but could never bring myself to do any of that."

"This one will be different, I promise."

"I'll try, Raquel, I really will. So, what about the other bomb Tia Carmen dropped on us? The John Deegan thing?"

"I'm trying to understand what that means. So, Deegan is now attached to the boy?"

"I guess so. He is like a surrogate of Tia Carmen, I imagine. He will be the one who helps the boy's spirit or energy or whatever the fuck it's called to move on. This stuff is mind boggling to me still," Vic said.

"What now?"

"I haven't the faintest clue. We start looking for cribs and stuff?" Vic said. Raquel and he both laughed aloud.

Raquel leaned over and kissed him on his cheek as he drove back to Manhattan.

Vic was very irritated that he hadn't heard from Collin Frank. The guy seemed as if he couldn't care less. Vic wasn't going to let that stand. He gathered his emotions to keep himself in check and called Collin's cell phone. Raquel listened in.

"Hey, buddy. Raquel is having a baby!" Vic said.

"Wonderful news, Vic! Congratulations to both of you. Any leads on who the father is?" Collin said.

"Not just yet, but we have our entire team on it," Vic said.

"Seriously, Vic, all the best. You deserve it. This opens up a whole new chapter in your life."

"Thanks, Collin. How you been?"

"Same ole, same ole. Working OT on a few cases. The mood here is bleak. The upper tier is merciless right now. By the book, if you know what I mean."

"Let me ask you a question. You didn't call me to see how my meeting with Scarpa went. How come, Collin?"

"I need to back away, Vic. I'm sorry; I guess I should have called you. Scarpa opened me a new asshole. It's like my fault that I opened this old wound again."

"Old wound?"

"Yeah, and it sucks big time. He's making it seem that I'm not loyal to the department; he calls it 'the brotherhood.' Real douche bag. He flat out said this case would affect my future here. What future? I want my twenty, and I'm outta here."

"I don't get it. What is he hiding, and for whom?"

"I'm glad you called my cell. I can't discuss this in the office. I'm sure my phone is being listened to. When you left, he called me in and had the deputy commissioner with him. They wanted to know what you were up to and what I thought your next moves would be."

"What did you tell them?" Vic asked. He voice was matter of fact, without emotion.

"I told him I had absolutely no idea. And you know what he had the balls to say?"

"No clue."

"That you need to be spoken to. Scarpa said that you need to be told to stop your investigation. I told him I advised you to walk away and that you were not the type to quit."

"Why does he want me to quit? Any idea?"

"I flat out asked him that same question. He said, 'For the good of the department.' Then, he continued to berate me like I had had something to do with this fucked-up case to begin with."

"Are they just embarrassed that this poor kid's murder has not been solved for so long?"

"No. I really think they don't give a shit about that at all. It's not that the Boy in the Box case is even talked about," Collin said.

"Collin, what else do you know? It's just me and you talking here. What's up their ass?"

"I have no idea. There must be some deep, dark secret that they are not willing to bring to the surface. It's just that obvious to me. What it is, I'm totally in the dark."

"I think I may have an idea what it might be."

"I'm all ears. Vic, you can trust me. I loathe these guys for the way they are treating you and Raquel as the enemy and how they have treated me."

"I may need some stealth information from you. Will you help?"

"To the extent that I can, absolutely. I need to tell you the evidence in the case has now been sealed. It needs the commissioner's approval to release any facts attached to the case."

"So, it goes all the way to the top?"

"Looks that way to me. What are you thinking?"

"Someone at PPD back in the day, someone involved with the investigation, was compromised. Somehow, that person was implicated in covering up for the killer. He may have been attached to that Lillian Jameson lady somehow."

"Any idea who?" Collin asked.

"Not yet. Can you access old personnel files?"

"I can try. I have an old drinking buddy who may be able to help me."

"I'll let you know if and when I need something."

"If someone was tangled up with Jameson, that certainly will not show up in a personnel jacket."

"Of course not. But there may be some intricate details about a guy's background or career path that will throw off something. I'm just hearing myself think at this point."

"I'll do what I can. But you have to know, I need my job. I need that pension even more. I have to protect my family."

"I get that. If you feel at any time that you can't do something to help me, I will totally understand. And the job offer when you leave PPD stands, no matter what."

CHAPTER 53

The next morning, Raquel took the early pregnancy test just to verify Tia Carmen's diagnosis scientifically. Sure enough, the double line showed she was expecting a child. She was officially pregnant. Not that she doubted the old lady; she just wanted to see it for herself. Raquel planned to make a doctor's appointment, call her mother with the news, and go to the office and make the announcement to the staff.

Just before 8 o'clock, the telephone rang.

"Hello, Raquel this is Idalis. I wanted to tell you that Tia Carmen passed on early this morning peacefully."

"Idalis, I am so, so sorry for your loss."

"For everyone's loss, Raquel. You were very special to her. Would you pass this news on to your family for me?" Idalis said. There were no tears that Raquel could tell.

"How are you holding up, Idalis?"

"I was prepared for a while, but I'm sure the reality will set in soon. Tia Carmen gave specific instructions. No wake, no funeral, no prayers at the gravesite, which will be back home in Puerto Rico. I will attend to all of her wishes. I have been with her my entire life. She said to everyone around her many times that we are only borrowed to one another. Our energy is to be shared until we must share it again in another time and place. I'm finding great comfort in her words."

"What can we do for you?"

"I would like for you to keep in touch with me from time to time. Tia Carmen told me to tell you something. Your baby will be born healthy and strong. She wanted you to try to help the boy's energy the best you can."

"I will, Idalis. Did she say if my baby is a boy or a girl?"

"Yes. She told me, but I am not to tell you. That is for you to share with Victor."

"I will call you soon. I feel as though a member of my own family has died," Raquel said. She was fighting her tears.

"Tia Carmen has not died. She just moved on. It was her time."

CHAPTER 54

Vic started to line up the names of everyone at the PPD who was associated with the investigation from the time the boy's body was found until he was first buried. He also charted the names of the people around the Jamesons: the owners of the foster home, the Nicolettis, and any else who was investigated by the PPD that he had on file.

There was a chance that some of these people were still alive. He was determined to speak with any and all of the survivors. This was no small task, but he had to start somewhere. Vic also needed to confer again with Special Agent Sean Lewandowski and John Deegan. Vic left a message for Lewandowski at his office and on his cell phone. The call from Deegan came moments before he dialed Deegan's number.

"Hello, Daddy. Congratulations," Deegan said.

"Good news travels fast I see."

"I knew from Tia Carmen before she passed. Then, I got drafted into the big leagues."

"Can you handle it, John?"

"Piece of cake. The boy and I have met a few times already. He is anxious to move on. What are you up to?"

"I'm looking to find out if any of the players are still around. It may take some time, but I have already begun making lists."

"Been there, done that," Deegan said.

Vic laughed. "Why am I not surprised? Always a step ahead of me."

"Maybe two or three steps, Vic. I've narrowed it down to two potential persons of interest. That's what you cop types call them, correct? One is a detective who was on the case, and other is that former nun, Sister Mary of the Crown of Thorns, AKA Mrs. Maggie Nelson."

"She's still alive?"

"Yes, she is and still living in Philadelphia. Father Jimbo has been dead for some time and hopefully rotting in hell if you believe in such a place."

"How can I see her?"

"Not so fast, buckaroo, not so fast. The question is when will WE see her? I'm going with you on this one."

"Have you completely lost your mind? How can we go together? You are a wanted murderer. Every law enforcement agency on the planet is still looking for you, and we show up, me, the good guy investigator who didn't shoot you dead, and you, the fugitive of the century. You have to be nuts."

"Who said we are going together? I'll meet you there. No funny business. You're going to need me on this one."

"And what, may I ask, do we expect to find out from the ninety-year-old, dried-up prune?"

"Eighty-eight, Vic. She just celebrated her birthday. We may just discover who Lillian Jameson was holding hostage, so to speak."

"I have to think about this one, Deegan. I want to speak with my partner and see what she thinks. I'm not so sure if this is going to work."

"Sure, it will, Vic. Stop thinking inside that cop's box, will ya? Call me in the morning for details. Time is very much of the essence, my doubting Thomas."

"He wants to do WHAT? Is he crazy?" Raquel said.

"You heard me correctly. Maggie Nelson is still alive, and he wants to go interview her with me. And, yes, he is crazy."

"This can close us down, Vic. It can ruin us."

"I thought of that."

"I can just see it now. 'Hero Investigator and Pregnant Girl-friend, Cavorting with Serial Killer, Try to Cash in on Dead Kid.' The PPD will have a field day with this one."

"Well, what else you got, honey?"

"We can do the research ourselves and handle it like any other case. What's the end game for Deegan?" Raquel said.

"The whole fucking thing is a game to him. He doesn't need fame or fortune. He already has that. The world will not forgive his murders. He doesn't want to be in a prison for whatever time he has left."

"So, why is he insisting on partnering on this interview?"

"He said I needed him on this one. Look, we meet him there, we do our thing, he does his, and we walk away smarter. Maybe even with the answer to this entire case."

"So, you are all for it?"

"I'm not all for it. In the absence of other ideas or leads and in the interest of time, I don't think we have many reasonable options."

"So, when do we do this?" Raquel asked.

"We? I wasn't planning on you coming along."

"Okay, this is going to be a good one. May I ask why?"

"You're pregnant, honey. You need to stay home and rest."

"I'm pregnant, yes, but I'm not eight and a half months pregnant with a belly out to here. I don't even have a bump. Wait a minute, Vic. You are trapping me into agreeing with this craziness."

"I need to call Deegan and say we are on. The sooner, the better. Better pack for another trip to Philly."

"I suddenly have an urge for cheese steak," Raquel said.

CHAPTER 55

FBI Special Agent Sean Lewandowski called Vic from LAX.

"Hey, Vic. How's it going?"

"Sean! Where in the world are you? We miss you like you can't believe," Vic said.

"Heading back home from Los Angeles. I hope you guys understand that I couldn't say a word about that mess at PPD," Sean said.

"Areyoukiddenmeorwhat? No way would you do that, and anyone who expected you to talk about it doesn't know you. We have another issue with PPD that I want to discuss with you."

"I'm getting on the plane now. Can it keep until I get back? Should be in Philly in six hours, give or take. But how about just a hint?"

"Here is a teaser. PPD is hiding something from us on the Boy in the Box case, something that may be big," Vic said.

"No shit? I can't imagine why, but nothing surprises me anymore. I've become the classic, jaded law enforcement douche I promised myself would never happen. Can't wait to hear the whole story."

"Okay, see you later. Oh, one more thing. Raquel is pregnant," Vic said.

"Nice. Congratulations to both of you. If that kid has her looks and brains and your balls, watch out, world!"

Maggie Nelson still lived in the Fox Chase section of Philadelphia. She and her husband, the former Father James Nelson, lived in a small house in the Northern Philadelphia section until his death from stomach cancer twenty-six years ago. A few years ago, Maggie moved into a small apartment at the Villages at Pine Valley, a development for senior citizens. She spent her days praying and volunteering at Cola Services, a center that offers professional human services to children and their families.

Vic and Raquel were waiting in their car outside the gates of the Villages. John Deegan was expected within five minutes.

"This is so ironic," Raquel said.

"What is? That this woman is still alive and we are going to scare her shitless?"

"No, you goofball. What's ironic is that we are on Susquehanna Road. The boy's body was found a few blocks from here before this place was developed, and this bitch lives where that home for wayward girls was years ago. To top it off, irony of all ironies, Maggie volunteers at a place that helps kids," Raquel said.

"Where do you expect people like her to be? Of course, she wants to be around young kids. All of these abusing lunatics do."

"But she's nearly ninety years old for Christ's sake."

"It's all about control, Raquel."

Walking up Susquehanna Road from Verree Road, a short, slightly stooped over man could be seen from a distance of two hundred yards.

"This could be Deegan," Vic said.

"I don't think so. He looks older, and, if I'm not mistaken, it's a priest," Raquel said.

"Trust me, its Deegan. And it's a bishop."

As the man got closer, he smiled broadly at Vic and Raquel. Raquel put her right hand behind her back, loosened the strap on her holster, and switched the safety off. She was leaving nothing to chance. As far as she was concerned, they were taking too many chances already.

Deegan was indeed dressed as a bishop. A long, black cassock with cerise buttons and trimmings was finished by a matching color sash, neatly knotted on the left side. A solid gold pectoral cross hung down to Deegan's belly, adorned with a ruby red sapphire in its center. A zucchetto, a vivid, reddish-pink skullcap, that matched the sash sat on Deegan's head.

Raquel and Vic exited the car and approached the "bishop." Deegan offered his right hand, exposing a gold ring encrusted with diamonds with a matching, red sapphire in its center, as if he expected it to be kissed. His gesture was more of a joke to Deegan, which was ignored by Vic and Raquel.

"I am Bishop Francesco Cali, from *Roma*. So nice to meet you both. Did we not meet before once before, perhaps in Vatican city, no?" Deegan said. He was speaking in an elegant Italian-accented English.

"Where the hell did you get this get-up, John?" Vic said.

"It was made for me by the same people who make the vestments for His Holiness. You like?"

"Adorable. And you expect Maggie Nelson to think you are for real?" Raquel said.

"I am for real. You just, how do you say in English, play along. I will hear her confession," Deegan said.

"You wouldn't!" Vic said.

"Oh, but I would. We are fighting *i serpenti*, the slippery serpents, remember?"

"So, now what?" Raquel said.

"So now, we face this Sister Mary of the Crown of Thorns on her own, as you say, turf. Allow me." Deegan pointed the way down a sidewalk that led to a group of apartments surrounded by manicured lawns and flower beds.

"*Allora,* here we are, *numero quindici,* number fifteen. *Una bella casa,*" Deegan said. He had become Bishop Cali. Deegan invited Raquel to ring the doorbell. He took a step behind the couple. Raquel stood sideways so that she could see Deegan and not have her back to him. Vic watched Deegan's reflection in the brass knocker plate.

"Just a moment please." A woman's voice came from inside the apartment. Shuffling, slippered footsteps could be heard approaching the door.

The old woman opened the door. She looked surprised to see three people. Her eyes went right to the bishop.

"Mrs. Nelson, my name is Raquel Ruiz, and this is my partner Vic Gonnella. We were wondering if we may have a chat with you?"

Deegan stepped between the couple and introduced himself.

"And I am Bishop Francesco Cali from *Roma*, my child," Deegan offered his ringed hand. Maggie Nelson, as she was trained to do, curtsied unsteadily on her old legs. She took Deegan's hand and gently kissed his ring." Vic and Raquel glanced at each other in disbelief.

"Please come in, Your Excellency."

"Preggo. " Deegan said.

Maggie offered her living room area for her guests.

"May I ask why you are visiting me?" Maggie spoke to Raquel and turned her gaze back to the bishop.

"We would like to speak with you about the dead boy whose body was found many years ago not far from here," Raquel said.

"Oh, yes. What a tragedy. Can I offer you some tea?"

"Delightful, no sugar for me," Deegan said.

Maggie scurried to her kitchen, which was just off the living room area.

"May I bless your home, Sister Mary?" Deegan said.

"But of course, Excellency. No one has called me that in many, many years. How did you know I was a nun?"

"We keep information on all of our clergy, Sister, in *il Vaticano*. Once you are a nun, to us, you are always of the cloth," Deegan said in his perfect Italian accent.

"Oh, my, I never knew that. The tea will be ready in a few minutes." Maggie sat in her Stratolounger while the others sat cramped on her sofa.

"Ah, but, before we begin, I will give my blessing to your home." Deegan, in a dramatic flourish, took his right hand and made the sign of the cross. He took a small vile of "holy" water from inside his suit. Deegan spoke in perfect Latin, pronouncing an appropriate blessing upon the apartment and upon Maggie. He had never forgotten his Catholic training and fervent prayers.

"Were you living here when the boy was found, Mrs. Nelson?" Raquel asked.

"Oh, yes. My late husband, Jim, and I were here for just a short time when this happened. We were very upset as you can imagine."

"And the boy's death still remains a mystery," Raquel said.

"Yes, I know. Why are you asking me about this?"

"We have been led to believe that your husband, the late Father James Nelson, perhaps knew something about the child and his foster parents," Raquel said.

"Oh…no, we were not part of this, no," Maggie said.

"My child, it is better for your soul to speak the truth now. How do you say in English, to face the Lord with a clean soul in the state of grace," Deegan said.

"Oh, my. It was a difficult time for me. And for my husband," Maggie said.

"Confession is good for the soul as you know, Sister Mary. I will grant you absolution here and now," Deegan said.

Vic was almost stunned. He watched Deegan do his magic. The charade could work, he thought.

"But we had nothing to do with the boy's death. Really nothing at all," Maggie said.

"Of course, but we believe his adoptive mother, Lillian Jameson, committed the murder and…"

Maggie Nelson put her head in both hands and began to cry. Deegan got up from the sofa and approached her. He knelt down beside her."

"Lord, this is a good woman, give her the strength to say the truth and remove her great burden," Deegan said.

"Excellency, there were terrible things that happened in my life but none to compare with the death of this poor boy."

"Tell these good people what you know, and lift your soul to the Holy Trinity," Deegan said.

"May God forgive me. That woman was Satan himself. Yes, the boy was her adopted son. She did so many evil things. When the child died, she acted as if he was never with her, like he was never alive."

"Go on, my child," Deegan said.

"We knew the boy that was found was hers, but we never came forward. We never went to the authorities. We did nothing," Maggie said. She was still crying. She took a set of rosary beads from a table that was next to her chair. She held the beads tightly in both hands.

"Why didn't you say something?" Raquel said.

"We were ashamed. And worried."

"About what, my child? You know that the Lord protects the righteous," Deegan said. He remained kneeling next to her chair.

"Yes, but our sins were so many."

"Now is your chance to cleanse yourself. Our Blessed Lord is all forgiving, Sister," Deegan said.

"Oh, my God, forgive me. Forgive the soul of my husband."

"You will both be forgiven. Of that, I promise you," Deegan said.

The teapot began to whistle. Vic got up and went into the kitchen so as not to lessen the conversation. The thought of tea and the aroma of the teapot's steam turned Raquel stomach. She fought the urge to run to the bathroom and continued her interrogation.

"We were involved with her. She entrapped us both. The woman was totally evil. She enticed us to her bed. Please forgive me, Your Excellency."

"Yes, of course, my child."

"Were you worried that you would be exposed for this?" Raquel said.

"Of course we were. We left the Church because our bodies were weak. Where would we have gone? To prison? Perhaps, that was the punishment we deserved."

"Did your relationship continue?" Raquel said.

"For a time, yes, it did. Lillian threatened us with going to the police, to confessing to the murder. And her poor daughter. That child saw so many horrible things, unspeakable things."

"Such as?" Raquel said.

"She was forced into Satan's own bed. She was forced to watch and listen to her mother's debauchery. That woman had no morals whatsoever."

"Tell me, Maggie, was anyone else involved with this woman?"

"Yes, there were many men whom she entertained."

"Her husband, did he know of her behavior?" Raquel asked.

"He must have, but he did not participate in these mortal sins," Maggie said. She began twisting the rosary beads in her hands.

"Do you recall any of the men whom you refer to?" Raquel said. Deegan was blessing her for the tenth time.

"I do. Yes, I do. One man was a policeman. Another was a politician. Oh, merciful Jesus, forgive me for the things that I have done and not done."

CHAPTER 56

Vic, Raquel and John Deegan left Maggie Nelson's apartment and walked in the direction of the car. Deegan finally broke from his role as Bishop Francesco Cali.

"Well, now we have it straight from the horse's mouth."

"Your performance was award winning," Vic said.

"And Raquel touched all of the bases. I'm happy to see that you stayed quiet, Vic. Raquel handled her with aplomb-woman to woman," Deegan said.

"And you gave her absolution? Do you have no shame, Deegan?" Vic snorted.

"None whatsoever. The whole thing is smoke and mirrors. Selling indulgences to build the Vatican was no less fraudulent. We needed her testimony, and we have it. The old lady will go to her grave in peace. I did her a favor," Deegan said.

"She's been harboring this guilt for fifty-seven years. She must feel relieved, telling us the story," Raquel said.

"Without a doubt," Vic said.

"What made you think of the bishop angle? It was brilliant," Raquel said.

"Thank you. Once again, it's elementary. We are taught from when we are little children to respect and obey men of the cloth. Sister Mary of the Crown of Thorns had this embedded in her psyche. She immediately returned to her familiar. After all, the bishop came from Rome to see her. She was putty in my hands. Like I said, smoke-and-mirrors trickery. The real guys with their so-called religious calling know the power and sway they have over the faithful. They use it for the greater good of their Church and for their own self-aggrandizement."

"Do we report her to that place where she volunteers? You know, about the reason she left the nuns?" Raquel said.

"She is harmless, especially now. The old lady wants to get into heaven. Let her be," Deegan said.

"And there is no reason to divulge where we obtained our information," Vic said.

"Now what?" Raquel said.

"Here is where I walk away and go about my business. My wife is surely missing me. *Buona fortuna a tutti.*"

Deegan walked down Susquehanna Road toward Verree Road, stoop shouldered, his cape blowing in the wind.

Vic and Raquel stood in front of their car, watching the fugitive from global justice, bishop's garb and all, stroll down the street.

"Do you think we will ever see him again?" Raquel said.

"I sure hope not. Talking to him on the phone is tough enough; being in the same room with him was surrealistic," Vic said.

"You're not kidding. My heart was racing the whole time. Now, I can put the safety back on my handgun."

Vic and Raquel had unfinished business in Philadelphia. Sean was back from his assignment, and the couple wanted to lay out what they had discovered. They also wanted to confront Collin Frank.

The couple checked into their regular hotel. Sean was meeting them at the bar that evening. Raquel needed a nap. She was exhausted from the stress of the day. She could feel that her energy level was fluctuating. Right now, she was spent. Vic could tell his lady needed her rest and her space. He decided to take a long stroll and clear his head.

When he returned two hours later, sweaty and spent from his walk, Vic found Raquel on the sofa in the suite, watching a Phillies game.

"Who's winning?" Vic said.

"Who cares? It's just background noise. Besides, if it's not the Yankees, I have no interest," Raquel said.

"How was your nap?"

"Maybe a half hour. Then Jonathan came to me."

"And you are sitting here calm as a cucumber?"

"He was with Deegan. They were walking on that same beach where I saw the boy before. They were strolling along the shore, hand-in-hand. The boy was smiling and skipping over the foam of the waves. He looked different," Raquel said.

"Different how?"

"I don't know, different. Happy maybe; the bruises were gone, and he tried to talk to me. I couldn't make out what he was saying."

"And Deegan?"

"Like a grandfather walking with his grandson."

"Did he say anything?"

"No, nothing. But he turned to me and tapped his watch a few times. Then, I woke."

"We need to move quickly now. He's telling us time is short just as Tia Carmen did."

Vic and Raquel met Sean at the hotel bar as planned. They took a table after all of the congratulatory hugs and kisses about the baby. The men ordered a drink, and Raquel a club soda with lime.

"Tell me what the hell is going on," Sean said.

"These bastards at PPD have kept this case going in circles for decades. The hint should have been when Martha Jameson came forward and implicated her mother as the boy's murderer. Who-ever coined the phrase, "You can't see the forest from the trees," was a smart son of a bitch. They found a reason not to believe her, some stupid, unacceptable testimony that had more holes in it than a wheel of Swiss cheese. The latest hint was when they rejected our samples because we are not a law enforcement agency," Vic said. His face developed a reddish hue of anger.

"Hold on, back up a bit. I'm lost," Sean said

Vic and Raquel laid out the events of the past few weeks for Sean, including their meeting with Maggie Nelson. They omitted anything about John Deegan. After all, Sean was with the FBI, and it was better that he didn't know anything about the Deegan connection.

Sean was flabbergasted.

"How can I help? Do I report this to the Bureau?"

"I don't think so, but I have a plan if you are game," Vic said.

"If I don't break any laws, I will do what I can for you guys."

CHAPTER 57

It was good for Vic and Raquel to know they could count on Sean, at least up to the extent that he would help them. The funny thing about most FBI agents is that they go running to papa bear the minute the going gets a bit rough. The looming federal penitentiary thing along with loss of pension and never working ever again seems to bolster this behavior.

Now, Vic and Raquel had to test their relationship with Collin Frank. Vic heard him say yes to helping them with insider information. Problem for the moment: Vic no longer trusted Collin.

"Why, honey? Why don't you trust Collin? I thought you were friends, almost like family," Raquel said.

"I'll remind you what my *Nonna* Lena used to say. 'When it comes to money, there is no mother, no father, no sister, no brother.' I've lived by that for my entire life."

"So, what does that mean in English?"

"He will do what's right for him and his family and throw us under the bus if he needs to."

Vic called Collin and set a meeting for the next morning. It was Collin's day off. He had something to do with his daughter in the afternoon, so, they made breakfast plans.

"So, how is mommy feeling?" Collin asked.

"I thought you would at least say I looked radiant. When I wake up, I feel like I already ran a 5K race. I'm exhausted."

"And maybe a bit touchy?" Vic joked.

"Just a little. I'm sorry, honey, but it's a brave new world for me."

"I know, honey. That's ok. You are beautiful. Anyway, enough of the pre-natal evaluation. We have information to share with you, Collin, something that we discovered implicating the PPD in a cover up of the boy's murder," Vic said.

Collin was nonplussed. Vic's words were heard, but it took a few seconds for them to register. He had to find the words to express himself.

"You're saying…you mean to tell me …the department has sat on information for almost six decades? Come on, really? How can that be?"

"Look, Collin, I want to put our cards on the table. Were you at all aware that Lillian Jameson was involved with one of those detectives who were investigating the case?" Vic asked.

"What? No fucking way. I think it's outrageous that you would even ask me that question," Collin said. His face reddened.

"And she was also sexually involved in kinky group sex with a powerful member of the city council who was known as a power broker in Philadelphia for nearly thirty years," Raquel said.

"So, you're both saying that Lillian Jameson was definitely the boy's killer and members of the police department let her get away with murder. What kind of crazy theory is that? I know you guys are upset about the DNA test thing, but this is way off the reservation."

"Not a theory, Collin. It's a fact. We have an eyewitness who played an intricate role in this whole psychosexual cabal," Raquel said.

"What's his name?" Collin said.

"He is a she, but we are not at liberty to divulge her name, at least, not at the moment," Vic said.

"And you expect someone to listen to this crazy woman?" Collin said.

"Look, the department should have solved this case within a week or two after the boy was found. That obviously didn't happen. When Martha Jameson came forward and said her mother murdered the boy, the investigators found that she was not credible. Both the PPD and the Vidocq guys decided that Martha was a loose marble and that she made up the story from information she obtained about the investigation."

"Maybe she is a nutcase," Collin said.

"Who would have specific details about the boy and blame her own mother?" Raquel said.

"Someone who hated her mother very badly," Collin said.

"Or someone who needed to get a homicide off her conscience, someone who knew a little too much perhaps," Vic said.

"I can't believe any of this. So, why would they cover this up for so long?" Collin said.

"Maybe because the people who were hiding the truth hung around on the job for many years after the murder," Raquel said.

"And they were afraid that a scandal would ruin their lives and destroy their families' lives. Put them in prison for any number of legal reasons," Vic said.

"A scandal that could have toppled an entire police department and political machine that sucked tax money into God-knows-whose pockets," Raquel said.

"Hold on just a minute. I feel like you guys are giving me the third degree. All that's missing is a glaring overhead light bulb and a rubber hose," Collin said.

"Sorry, buddy. If we are overly emotional, it's because we don't want to see this boy's very existence thrown on the garbage heap like his body was," Vic said.

"Vic, you need to come up with evidence to back these allegations. That's cop work 101," Collin said.

"We have an eyewitness account that one detective and one councilman were hooking up with Lillian Jameson on a regular basis both before and after the boy was murdered. This person saw the boy in Lillian's home. When the boy came up dead, our witness was threatened by Lillian to out her and her husband as sex degenerates. Those same threats were likely used against the cop and the politician. We're talking about the 1950s here, Collin. Christ, they didn't even show full tits in Playboy back then," Vic quipped.

"How old is this witness?"

"What does that matter? She's almost ninety. She was there, she saw the whole thing unfold, and she knew the players. She fucked them," Raquel said.

"So, why now? Why did she come forward now?"

"She didn't come forward. We brought out her testimony as part of our investigation," Vic said.

"Okay, let's just say I buy into this whole mess. Why would my bosses, who probably weren't even born when the kid was killed, want to keep this a deep, dark secret?" Collin said.

"That's where we need your help Collin. That is the missing link. This charade about us not being a law enforcement agency simply does not hold water. Why do the brass at PPD not want to solve this case? Why not run the fucking DNA tests that we brought in against the sample taken from the boy? Is it just pride, or are they embarrassed that they blew a case? We don't think so," Vic said.

"We want information on the cop. We want to know what happened to him during his career on the job. We want to know what happened to him after he left the PPD. We want to know if he had a legacy in the department," Raquel said.

"The question is, Collin, are you still willing to help us?" Raquel asked.

CHAPTER 58

That afternoon, while Raquel was resting at the hotel suite, Vic decided to take a ride up to the Ivy Hill Cemetery to pay his respects to the boy. As with any grave visit, there is an emptiness that only memory can soothe. Vic, not knowing the boy but only the horrific story of his short life and brutal death, stood by the grave, his mind racing. There were several small toy trains and toy cars left by previous visitors now embedded into the earth around the tombstone. The sight of these remnants was unsettling.

On the ride to the cemetery, Vic was pondering his next few moves with Collin, Sean, and the PPD. Was Collin to be trusted? Was he already unfolding to his superiors the potential damage that was about to fall upon the PPD? Could Sean be relied upon to be there if and when he was needed? Would being a father be something he could handle at this point in his life? Was any of this investigation actually worth all the time and effort that he and Raquel had expended?

Vic parked his car a few feet away from the boy's grave. He sat on the bench next to the plot. He spoke out loud.

"Tell me, Jonathan, are we on the right track? I'm so sorry that you had to go through what happened to you. Life is really not that bad. If you had had a few good breaks, a good family would have loved you and made you a happy little boy. Please hold on a little longer, buddy. Sorry that it's taken us so long to give you a last name, but I think we're close. I tasted abuse when I was a boy. Sometimes, the memory is too much for me to take. There were times that I wish I had died young, not to live with the guilt that lingered in my brain. Look at how silly I am, Jonathan. I'm talking to your grave when all that's here are some bones. I want to see you come to me again before you leave, and I want you to be able to smile... forever."

Vic felt an emptiness inside of him, which made him sense the fruitlessness of talking to a granite tombstone. He felt foolish for coming to the boy's grave. His visit was senseless and a waste of precious time. Vic realized that the boy wasn't here. Now, he understood that the boy's energy, as Tia Carmen was saying, was somewhere else, somewhere on a plane that he could not even imagine. Vic turned and walked back to his car. He fought the urge to turn and look at the grave for the last time.

It took a solid fifteen minutes for Vic to remove the sadness of the boy's gravesite from his mind. He drove at a slow and somber pace back to the center of Philadelphia.

Getting back to the hotel to be with Raquel helped for a couple of reasons. He wanted to share his gravesite experience with her. Not one to share feelings readily, Vic was comfortable enough with Raquel to bare his soul to her. She had become his strength on many levels. Vic realized for the first time in his life what love really was. Vic also wanted her. For some reason, since they had discovered Raquel was pregnant, Vic found her especially arousing. Just thinking about being with her gave Vic an erection. He was looking forward to some afternoon delight.

Vic's cell phone rang. It was Collin Frank.

"Hey, Vic. What's up?"

"I just went to see the kid's grave. I know it's a place I will only go back to when we put his name on the stone. Other than that, visiting graves is not for me. It leaves me cold," Vic said.

"I hear that. Listen, Scarpa and the deputy commish want to see you again. You busy?"

Vic was momentarily taken aback.

"Ah, no, not really. I'm headed back to see Raquel and make a few calls. Lots to do to get to the bottom of things."

"How about this afternoon? Tell me what's comfortable for you."

"What's on their mind, pal? Why the sudden interest in talking to the brash New York dick?"

"I'm really not sure. They just asked me to reach out," Collin said.

Vic knew he was lying.

"Did you mention anything to them about what we uncovered?" Vic said.

"No, no way. They just wanted me to set up a meet."

Vic could feel his face redden with anger. He kept his composure.

"Sure, let's say 3, 3:30," Vic said.

"Great, I'll let them know."

"One thing, Collin: tell them I want you there."

"I dunno, Vic. I'll mention it."

"No, Collin, tell them I want you there, period," Vic hit the end button on his phone.

CHAPTER 59

"That son of a bitch. He just lied to you," Raquel said.

"Oh, yeah. I wish I were a fly on that wall when he told them about our witness. Now, we will flush them out."

"I think you should call Deegan."

"Why's that?"

"Let's get his take and not let our ego get in the way. He thinks like a damn computer. Let's get his advice."

"I had other thoughts for the moment."

Vic smiled and raised his eyebrows up and down.

"Yeah, I'm as horny as a Cocker Spaniel in heat, but it has to wait. Let's get this thing done first," Raquel said.

Vic picked up his cell phone and began dialing.

"I can't believe you are making me hang for you."

"I promise you will not be disappointed," Raquel said coyly. She put her index finger into her mouth. Vic felt himself quiver. The call connected.

"Mr. Gonnella, how was your visit at Mount Ivy this morning?" Deegan said.

"How in the fuck did you know that, John?"

"The boy told me. Well, not in those exact words. He communicates with symbols."

"Forget that for now. PPD brass has called me in. What do you think?"

"I think desperate men make desperate moves. They want to know where and when you will attack them. Play along, but give them only what you think they can't use against us. I expected them to react like this. Very transparent," Deegan said.

"And Collin?"

"He went over to the dark side, I'm afraid. Give him disinformation."

"Are you still around if we need you?"

"You're on auto pilot now, Vic. My relationship with Jonathan is pure energy. It's like advanced telecommunicating. Very cool."

Vic and Raquel arrived at the Round House at 3:45. Their lateness was intentional. Collin ushered them into the large conference room where they had been greeted as royalty on their first visit.

"Vic, Raquel, I hope we can start over. Our last meeting was not productive," Scarpa said. The deputy commissioner was clearly letting Scarpa be the voice of the PPD.

"That's behind us," Vic said. Raquel had a dispassionate look that was unsettling to the three cops, who sat across from them.

"We are hoping that we can resolve our issues amicably," Scarpa said.

"That's the goal. Only thing is, we have uncovered some very disheartening information of late," Vic said.

"Such as?"

"An eyewitness we discovered who was involved in a sexual relationship with the boy's killer. She also implicated a detective and a powerful political player as part of their circle of friendship," Vic said.

"And who is that person?" Scarpa asked. The deputy moved uneasily in his seat. Collin's eyes were flashing between his two superiors. The tells were obvious.

"I wouldn't tell Detective Frank, and I will not tell you. She will remain anonymous for her privacy and protection," Vic said.

"These are strong allegations. As we can't verify her story, we are relying on you to play as a team with us," Scarpa said. Scarpa was working hard at keeping his cool. That was becoming difficult for the fast-talking, brash inspector who was used to using intimidation to get what he wanted.

"I need to remind you that we are private investigators, Inspector. We are not part of any law enforcement agency, so, we work from a different set of rules," Vic said.

Scarpa stared at Vic for a few seconds. He was gathering his thoughts for a reasonable rebuttal.

"Okay, what if we ran the DNA tests like you originally wanted? Would that work for you?" Scarpa asked.

"That's one step in the right direction, Inspector, but now we have the matter of a fifty-seven year cover up that your department has seemingly sustained," Vic said.

"Now, hold on for a minute, Vic. I've been sitting here holding my tongue. You are accusing us of something that none of us had anything to do with. What is your end game in all this?" The deputy said.

"And all this time I thought you were just here as a witness to the proceedings. Our end game? Raquel, why don't you answer the man in the nice uniform?" Vic said.

"With pleasure. Our end game, as you so eloquently put it, is justice. Justice for a dead little boy and for the people who we believe are complicit in a cover up."

"If there was a cover up, those people you are referring to may all be dead. Then what?" Scarpa said.

"Then we expose anyone who isn't dead that kept this charade going to this day," Raquel said flatly.

"And, may I add, do you now think that we would believe your DNA test results you would report back to us? One lie becomes twenty, gentlemen. Just like the lie Collin told me that he never told you both about our findings," Vic said.

"C'mon, Vic. This is my life we are talking about over here. I work for the PPD not you," Collin said. He was clearly furious.

"And you will now never work for us, Detective," Vic said.

"Settle down please. Let's figure out how we can prove your theory. Then you can go back to what you do in New York," Scarpa said.

"Very simple. We want the actual DNA samples of the boy's bones, verified by an independent laboratory of our choosing. And we want the PPD to issue a statement regarding the past indiscretions of your fucking department. I'm certain your public relations people can spin a nice tale," Vic said.

"And you have twenty four hours to give us your answer," Raquel said.

"Or?" The deputy said.

Vic cut in. No one was going to challenge his lady, even on the job. "...or we go to the media with our story or the feds or both. This will make your current corruption scandal seem like child's play. A few scumbag cops taking money from drug dealers is one thing. Hiding the truth about a murdered four-year-old boy is something quite different," Vic said.

"And if your theory about the DNA test is wrong and you can't prove who the boy's family is and your case is done, then you are both a smacked ass. That's a big risk even for the famous Vic Gonnella," the Deputy said.

"I guess that's a chance we are willing to take," Raquel said.

"Think of the potential embarrassment before you get so glib, Miss," Scarpa said.

Raquel replied, "It's 'Ms. Ruiz' to you, Inspector. Twenty-four hours, 'gentlemen.' Let's see who blinks first."

CHAPTER 60

Someone blinked first.

Soon after Vic and Raquel arrived back at their suite, the room telephone rang. It was Collin Frank. He was in the hotel's lobby. He wanted to talk.

"The plot thickens," Raquel said.

"I can't wait to hear what he has to say, but let's make him bust a few minutes. You go down, make up some bullshit. Tell him I'll be there when I can. In the meantime, find out what filth is under his fingernails," Vic said.

Raquel entered the lobby, saw Collin, and pointed to the bar area. He scurried there quickly.

"Raquel, I don't know what to say. Where's Vic?"

"He's taking a shower. He said he feels dirty after meeting you and those two jerky bosses you have. Then he's calling the FBI to line things up. What's on your mind?" Raquel said. Gone was her friendly tone and smiling face. She always liked Collin, but, now, she was showing him a side of her that he didn't know existed.

"Can he hold off on that call until he hears what I have to say?"

"Why, so you can turn on us again? That was really messed up, Collin. We trusted you."

"Look, I want to make things right. Just hear me out is all I'm asking. I know I fucked up."

"Wait here. I'll see if I can get him to hold that call for a while."

Raquel walked toward the elevator. Collin couldn't even bring himself to look at her ass. Raquel was back in the suite within minutes.

"He's a mess. Let's hear what he has to say," Raquel said.

"Absolutely. Our bluff may have worked. They have no idea we are not willing to risk our names on a theory that could be dead wrong. Let's go listen to that Benedict Arnold."

Vic and Raquel walked toward the bar. Vic's gait was like a peacock strut, confident, unwavering, and bold. Raquel walked beside her man; she had an air of self-assurance and poise that exuded power.

"I feel like Michael Corleone in the Godfather. 'Freddo, you broke my heart,'" Vic said.

"I want to make things right with you two. I have no balls. I was worried about my own ass. My job, pension, all that shit. My conscience will not allow me not to do the right thing."

"Do you even know what the right thing is anymore, Collin?" Raquel said.

"I've known from day one that they were hiding something. When I went to them about you guys coming here on this case, they basically told me to humor you. They had no idea that you were as good as you are. What I didn't know until now is why."

"So, you are here to tell us what we already may know?" Vic said.

"I don't think you know the real reason behind the whole mess that was created back in 1957."

"We're all ears," Raquel said.

"Lillian Jameson held the PPD and city hall hostage. No one was willing to deal with the embarrassment of a scandal. The truth would have toppled the department and city hall, so, they intentionally bungled the investigation. They knew she killed the boy. Only a few individuals knew the truth, and they stonewalled the investigation. Guys were promoted and paid off by Jim Slade, the power broker who spread a lot of money around. Like you said, one lie became twenty. They figured the boy was nobody, so, why risk careers and millions of dollars of corruption money that was made by the politicians? The thinking was, 'Squash the case; it will go away.' One of the key detectives, a Tom Anselm, got a bit too close to the truth for Slade's comfort. Anselm was set up and arrested on a drug charge, lost his job and pension, copped a plea, and stayed out of jail. He moved to Arizona, never to be heard from again. No one on the job, that is, no one in their right mind, was willing to take on the power that Slade wielded. This case has been a black mark on the department ever since day one."

"So, that's why Martha Jameson's statements against her mother were crushed?" Vic asked.

"There is no other explanation. They found a reason not to believe her. No one expected Martha to come forward. The brass in charge now were coming up in the department. They were aware of the mess when Martha came forward. They decided to perpetuate the cover up to save a scandal. Martha's testimony was simply added to the mountain of other dead end leads. They saw no upside in destroying the PPD's reputation and credibility. Lillian was dead, the kid was dead, and, so, it was better for everyone that things be left as they were."

"So, Mata Hari was dead, her daughter was deemed to be a wacko, and life went on," Vic said.

"And Martha was advised to keep her mouth shut or her career and her life would be destroyed. The woman had nothing to live for but her work. That's why she will not say a word," Collin said.

"And Scarpa and that vile deputy commissioner told you all of this?" Raquel asked.

"They did. And now they want to make a deal."

"Let me guess. We go away. We put a name on the kid's grave, and the lie and life continue," Vic said.

"Why not? All you ever wanted was to find out who the boy was. After all, what benefit is there to soiling the name of the PPD and ruining the department's name? Every organization has its ugly secrets.

"What about our consciences? We have to spend the rest of our lives being part of a murder cover-up. I don't think we can live with ourselves that way," Vic said.

"So, what do you want?"

"We want the original DNA samples and an admission from the department," Raquel said.

"One more thing that may change your minds. Jim Slade, the multi-millionaire politician. He is Martha's real father. The father she knew was just Lillian's husband, a patsy. Slade paid for Martha's education and left her a blind trust. Evidently, Lillian was screwing these guys and others for years before and after the shit hit the fan," Collin said.

Vic and Raquel looked into each other's eyes for a long moment.

CHAPTER 61

Sean Lewandowski called Vic to check on the status of events. He also had his own news to tell.

"How are things, Vic? Any news?" Sean asked.

"We have a few things going on. Looks like the PPD in its infinite wisdom will make the DNA samples available to us after all."

"What do you need me to do, Vic?"

"My threat of taking this to the feds was enough for now, Sean. I never used your name per se. They know we have a good relationship, so, that worked wonders."

"Good. Just call if you need me. I have other news."

"Good or bad?"

"One is great news; the other may be good news. Too soon to tell."

"The suspense is killing me, Sean."

"The good news is that I'm being transferred back top to New York. Division Chief, Counter Terrorism will be under me."

"Climbing the ladder to the stars. Congratulations, my friend. I know we will be seeing each other in the Apple."

"And the great news is, my wife is also expecting."

"Look, I was nowhere near her, Mr. Division Chief. I have an ironclad alibi."

"I deserved that from my tasteless comment," Sean said. He laughed out loud. Turn around is fair play.

"I'm thrilled for you guys, Sean. Looks like our kids will be hanging out together in that park over near Gracie Mansion. Wonderful news!"

Vic would not put Sean in a position to tell him what they really uncovered. There was no reason to ratchet this scandal up to the FBI. After all, the Bureau had bigger fish to fry. The world is a powder keg with maniac fundamentalists blowing up anything they can and lopping heads off in the desert.

They made soft plans for a get-together with the expectant mothers in Manhattan once everyone was settled in. Vic enjoyed Sean and knew him to be a friend, but business was business, and there was no percentage in asking the newly appointed Division Chief to break any FBI rules. Sean's help on this case would no longer be needed.

Vic and Raquel reviewed their options on the case. They agreed to contact Collin Frank again but not until they spoke with John Deegan.

Vic called Deegan's number and got an answer on the first ring. Deegan was back with Gjuliana at their lakefront home in Switzerland.

"How wonderful to hear from you, Vic. How is Raquel feeling?" Deegan said.

"I'm doing well, John. You're on speaker," Raquel said.

"I was a bit nervous when you were fingering your nine millimeter at Maggie Nelson's apartment. With all of your hormones out of whack, I thought it could be curtains for me," Deegan laughed at his comment. Raquel mouthed to Vic, 'How did he know?'

"Don't take it personal, John. She is overly cautious these days," Vic said.

"As she should be," Deegan said.

"Just wanted to fill you in on the details. We hope to be wrapping things up in the next day or so," Vic said.

"Before we get into that, John, I would like to ask about Jonathan. Is he in touch with you?" Raquel asked.

"Of course, many times today. He is very anxious. More so than I have seen before. It's anticipation, I suppose. I don't know how long he will be attached to me. I'm new at this thing as you know," John said.

"We are trying our best," Raquel said.

"And you are calling because you're not sure if you should simply be happy with the DNA results or blow a whistle on your fellow law enforcement types."

"What brings you to that conclusion?" Raquel asked.

"The case should have been solved back in '57. Your theory on the boy's family was accurate. My theory about the corruption is the only supposition that is rational. There was money and sex involved. Religion shockingly was not involved. Am I correct?" Deegan said.

"Why do you ask a question to which you already know the answer?" Vic said.

"Old habit, I suppose. Now, you want an opinion. Do you bring the matter to a conclusion, or shall you keep beating the horse?"

"If you must put it that way, the answer is yes. We are in a conflict of conscience," Vic said.

"Ask yourself the following questions: Do you reveal Sister Mary of the Crown of Thorns, Maggie Nelson, and destroy what life she has left? Is ruining the rest of Martha Jameson's life, if you call it a life, important enough for you to expose her as at this point?"

"And let these motherless mutts get a free ride?" Vic said.

"Vic, Raquel, I gave up being an interpreter of moral issues a long time ago when I decided to leave the clerical world. It's all on you guys now."

"So, we need to decide if we do what's right for a dead boy or for the two survivors of human frailties," Raquel said.

"Or just flip a coin," Vic said.

"If it were only that simple. Vic, you are no longer choosing sides for a stickball game. Make a decision, and live with it for better or worse," Deegan said.

"So, give us a break, and tell us which way are you leaning, O Wizard of the Lake?" Vic asked.

"My love is waiting for me to take a boat ride across that lake into Italy." Deegan ended the call.

CHAPTER 62

Vic and Raquel ruminated over their quandary for some time before they decided to place a call to Collin Frank. He called them before they had the chance.

"Vic, the brass wants another sit down. They have the DNA test results," Collin said.

"What are they, Collin? Is this another bullshit three card Monte scam you guys want to run on us? My grandfather always told me, 'You can trust a thief but not a liar.' So, why should we trust you or them for one second?" Vic said.

"They haven't told me the results. I'm in the dark on this, I swear on my kids."

Raquel, listening in on the conversation, squinted her eyes, nodding her head yes to Vic.

"Sure, we will listen to them, Collin, but on our turf. We are not coming to that den of inequity so we can be put in that good-cop/bad- cop opera. I'll get a conference room here at our hotel. Be here in an hour. We have other meetings scheduled," Vic said. He didn't wait for an excuse or an answer.

"One thing, Vic. I think you need to know something. They figured out who your eyewitness is. They are all over it like stink on shit," Collin said.

"What do you mean?" Vic said.

"I mean they are doing a thorough investigation. I'm not privy to any of the discussions. Just wanted you to know," Collin said.

"It changes nothing. As they say, it is what it is," Vic said.

Collin, Scarpa, and the deputy commissioner arrived on schedule. The conference room, unlike the fancy board room at the Round House, consisted of a white-tablecloth-covered table with five uncomfortable, gray, metal folding chairs. Three on one side of the table, two on the other. Vic and Raquel sat across from the cops. They were visibly uncomfortable. Noticeable moisture could be seen on Scarpa's upper lip. Collin's eyes were darting around the room, looking at the ceiling and four walls. The deputy looked pale, almost ill.

"So, the results, please," Raquel said.

"We want to apologize first for things getting out of hand between us. There was no disrespect intended," The deputy said.

"Apology accepted, please move on," Vic said. His response was curt and unemotional. Raquel fought herself not to roll her eyes.

"Yes, we have the results in this envelope for you. Before we hand them over, we would like to know what you have in store for us. There is a potential for a lot of bad to come out of this information," Scarpa said.

"Bad for whom?" Raquel asked.

"Our department can lose a lot of respect and credibility, and maybe we deserve that. We are talking about a scandal that can hurt a lot of people. People with careers, families, I think you get the picture," The deputy said.

"Once we get the results, we will let you know exactly what our plans are," Raquel said. She extended her right hand toward the deputy, who was holding a sealed manila envelope.

The deputy handed the envelope to Raquel, never taking his eyes from hers. Raquel took the envelope without any tell on her face at all. Vic leaned back, raising the front of his folding chair a few inches from the floor.

"Would you like the honors, Vic?" Raquel asked. She offered the envelope to her partner.

"I defer to you. After all, this was your case, Raquel. You deserve to see it more than anyone," Vic said.

Raquel smiled at Vic and turned the envelope so the flap was exposed. She slowly ran the nail on her index finger under the flap. Raquel slowly removed one sheet of paper and placed it flat on the table. All the while, she was glancing at the three men sitting across the table.

After a few pregnant moments, Raquel picked up the document and read it. Again without giving away her emotion, she handed it to Vic. He scanned the page quickly.

"Positive match. Well, I'll be dipped in shit!" Vic said.

"You're theory was correct, Gonnella. Congratulations," Scarpa said. He looked like he was about to be sick.

Collin smiled broadly at Vic and Raquel. The deputy's face was drenched in sweat. He dabbed his handkerchief to his forehead and mouth.

"How are we supposed to believe you? Maybe you faked the test just to give us what we wanted in the hope that we will just disappear," Raquel said.

"The chain of custody is perfect. The University of Texas sent technicians to our office to verify each sample. They flew back to their lab and ran the tests at our expense. They will attest to the veracity of the testing. I would give you my word, but I know that is meaningless to you," the deputy said.

"I want to see the documents that you are referring to. I will take you at your word for the moment. In the meantime, please wait here. We have a call to make. When we come back, we'll discuss the next steps," Vic said.

Vic and Raquel left the three cops sitting in their chairs with expressions of wonder on their faces. There is always a dumbfounded and amazed look to a person when he thinks his life may be changed in a split second.

Raquel waited to get into the elevator before she put her arms around Vic's neck and planted a wet, passionate kiss on him. Vic responded by putting both of his hands on her ass and leaning into her.

"We did it, baby! That little boy was a real person. Jonathan Jordan. My god, how happy Tia Carmen would have been," Raquel said.

"I'm pretty happy, too," Vic said. He pointed to the obvious bulge in his pants.

"You are a crazy bastard," Raquel said. Her laughter seemed to resonate up and down the elevator shaft.

"Tia Carmen is delighted wherever her energy is. I'm still not a one hundred percent believer, but I'm sure she is doing a Puerto Rican dance."

Arms around each other's waists, Vic and Raquel reached the hotel suite. Vic lifted Raquel off her feet in the proverbial wedding gesture. Raquel swept the key card with a flourish, and they were in the room.

"I have to call Deegan one last time," Vic said. Raquel sat on the sofa in the living area of the suite.

"And I have to pee so bad I can taste it," Raquel said. She headed off quickly to the bathroom.

Vic dialed Deegan's number and got a fast busy followed by a recorded message. "You have called a non-working number. Please check the listing and dial again." Vic pressed the redial button on his phone achieving the same result.

"Vic? Honey?" Raquel said. She was standing in entrance to the living room. Raquel had a strange look about her.

Vic jumped to his feet, thinking the worst.

"Raquel, what's wrong? Are you okay? Is the baby ok?"

"He's in the tub," Raquel said.

"What? Who is?"

"Jonathan. He is in the tub taking a bath, playing with some toys."

Vic led the couple to the door of the large bathroom. There was a round Jacuzzi in the middle of the room. The spa was surrounded by a circular teak bench, which was adorned with bath towels, soaps, lotions, and candles. This was not to be a romantic getaway by any means.

Jonathan was happily splashing the water with a small truck in one hand and a tiny train in another. The boy stopped his play for a moment, looked up at Vic and Raquel, and smiled. For the first time, the boy no longer looked like the dead child in the morgue shot. Jonathan looked like any other little boy happily playing in his bath with his toys.

Suddenly, the bath water began to recede. As the water ran to the drain, Jonathan began to fade. Within a minute, all that was left were the toy car and train.

"Don't tell me you still don't believe," Raquel said.

"I'm getting there… I'm getting there," Vic said.

EPILOGUE

John Deegan had intentionally removed his phone from service. He knew that Vic and Raquel would make the choice that was proper and fitting for all concerned. He busied himself with daily chores with Gjuliana while keeping tabs on the outside world through the news media and still very active contacts. In his mind, he had earned a slight reprieve from the intense world of private investigators.

The second call Vic and Raquel made was to Bobby Jordan. When he learned that the Boy in the Box was indeed his brother, Bobby asked that the boy's remains be sent to the family circle gravesite of the Memphis Jordans. Bobby was to be buried there. Vic and Raquel also asked to speak with Phillip Logan Jordan. Phil was home studying and heard the news when Bobby was told.

"Hi, Phil. Pretty amazing, don't you think?" Raquel said.

"Yeah, amazing and sad at the same time. That boy was my uncle, and his life was snuffed out when he was so young. My life, all of our lives, would have been different had he been able to grow and become a man. Warts and all, he was still ours," Phil said.

"I hear that," Vic said.

"Ah, Phil, we have some other news for you that you may or may not want to share right now," Raquel said.

"Let me guess. My dad is not my dad, right?"

"You indicated that might be the case. We were almost not going to give you this news. We were thinking about saying the test was not taken correctly to save you any grief," Raquel said.

"Bobby was my dad, he is my dad, and he will always be my dad. A tiny sperm makes a father, a real man makes a dad. I love him to death," Phil said.

"You're making my mascara run, Phil," Raquel said.

"Hey, buddy, say goodbye to your dad for us. See you guys again sometime," Vic said.

Now, the tough part. Vic and Raquel headed for the door of the suite. They needed to go back to the conference room to see Collin and his superiors.

"We need to see these guys right now?" Vic said.

"What else do we have to do?" Raquel said.

"Thought we'd, you know, celebrate," Vic motioned with his head toward the bedroom.

"Oh, no, nothing doing. It's not that I don't want to, but I'm still reeling from seeing Jonathan. Besides, I just can't wait to see the three stooges, live and in person."

"Rain check?"

"Without a doubt."

Vic and Raquel entered the conference room to see Collin, Scarpa, and the deputy sitting pretty much in the same positions as when they had left. They hadn't even left the room for coffee or water.

"Gentlemen, we are prepared to inform you of our decision," Vic said.

"There are some details that we must request first. Is that reasonable to you?" Raquel said.

"Yes, so long as the demands are indeed reasonable," the deputy said.

"Demands? Well, you make it sound like we are holding hostages," Vic said.

"Gonnella, with all due respect, you are holding an entire police department hostage whether you know it or not," Scarpa said. He spoke so quickly his last six words came out as one.

"If you put it that way, I guess you are right," Vic said.

"The Jordan family, the family of Jonathan Jordan, has requested the boy's remains be exhumed and reburied in their family plot, in Memphis. We, Raquel and I, will pay for an appropriate stone bearing the boy's name. Any problems?"

"None that I can imagine. We just need to get an order of exhumation and arrange for a funeral director to transfer the remains," the deputy said.

"Spoken like a true civil servant, Deputy. I'm certain you can fill out the right form to pay for that service as well," Raquel said. Vic looked at her as if to say, "Bitchy, bitchy."

"Secondly, all rights to any books, articles, movies, and the rest be granted to Mr. Robert Jordan of Memphis Tennessee, the boy's brother. Our attorney will draw up the documents. Any issues here?" Vic said.

"None. The PPD wants nothing to do with any of that," Scarpa said.

"Lastly, you motherfuckers have an inspector's funeral when this boy's body is removed from Mt. Ivy Cemetery," Raquel said.

"And what happens to the department? Are you going public?" the deputy asked.

"We both feel, after discussing this with each other and with a trusted confidant, that Martha Jacobson has suffered enough in her lifetime. We also feel that our never-to-be-named eyewitness can live out her days repenting her sins that surrounded this situation. She certainly belongs in jail for helping in covering up that poor boy's abuse and murder, but we are going to respect Martha's wishes for privacy and not release our source so as not to cause Martha any more unnecessary publicity and its accompanying pain. We will release a joint statement from our firm, which will indicate that an anonymous person led to the DNA samples being taken, and a positive match was made. Nice and easy," Vic said.

"We will write the press release. The PPD is happy that the case has been solved after all these years, and so on," Raquel said.

"There will not be an inspector's funeral, and there will not be any fanfare, and there will certainly not be any press release of any kind from PPD. The case is solved, hooray for you guys," the deputy said.

"You don't seem to understand. We are not suggesting these things; they are demands," Raquel said.

"Let's put our cards on the table so we can end this little dance we've been having. You guys are not the only smart people in the game. It took us a while, but we figured out who your eyewitness was. We interviewed Mrs. Maggie Nelson, and we didn't bring any so-called bishop or cardinal with us. She told us how you questioned her and used the fear and intimidation of her religion to coerce information. Funny thing was, we didn't get her to tell us what she told you. She was a very nice old lady," Scarpa said.

"Look, Scarpa, we have her testimony, and she will make a formidable witness, so, go fuck yourself," Vic said.

"Yeah, she would have made a great witness. Only thing is, when we went for a follow up interview, we found her hanging with her dainty wash in the bathroom," Scarpa said.

Vic's face drained. Raquel went from playing the tough cop to showing her shock. She brought both hands to her open mouth, inhaling deeply. Collin, true to not being in the loop and equally as shocked, let out his emotions.

"Holy shit!" Collin said.

"She never would have killed herself! That woman lived to redeem herself and get into heaven," Vic said.

"Are you implying something, Gonnella?" Scarpa said.

"I sure am!"

"Before you go off half-cocked and start making asshole accusations, I think you should look at her suicide note. It says nothing about the case," the deputy said. "Better yet, I'll read you her note. 'I've had enough of this life. I want to join my husband and my Savior and Lord, Jesus Christ. I leave this world in the state of grace, my sins forgiven by a bishop. I know that my church will have a funeral mass for me and that Jesus will accept my soul into heaven, for my conscience is clear.' There you have it. No implications at all," Scarpa said.

"So convenient. You can actually sit there, looking smug, and expect us to believe that Maggie Nelson wasn't killed," Raquel said.

"I would be careful of making accusations, Ms. Ruiz. The walls can come tumbling down on you," Scarpa said.

"Watch your mouth, Scarpa. I take that as a threat!" Vic shouted.

"Conspiracy theory, threats, very cloak and dagger stuff. Sounds paranoid to me, Gonnella," Scarpa said in rat-like, smug fashion.

"Everyone, just calm down. Can I go off the record?" the deputy said.

Vic and Raquel both nodded in the affirmative.

"You two have done a magnificent job in bringing this ugly, festering sore on the PPD to a head. I, for one, and I know others within the department, are truly grateful for your great detective work. Thank you. Please accept our profound apology. Now, I think it's best for all concerned that you take your ball and jacks and go back to making a fortune in your business."

"Classic stalemate?" Vic asked.

"No, I don't think so. I think everyone wins. Now, we need to get out of here and keep this city from going to the dogs," Scarpa said.

Scarpa and the deputy left the room without a smile or a handshake.

Collin lagged behind. He approached Vic, man to man.

"Sorry, pal. Once again, I have no words. I don't know what to say," Collin said.

"Just remember I'm still your friend. Call me anytime," Vic said.

Collin turned to Raquel, his lower lip quivered as he fought back tears.

"You were a great mother to Jonathan. This baby is very lucky," he said as he patted her stomach.

"Get out of here before what's left of my makeup winds up on my top," Raquel said. She hugged Collin hard, holding him close for a few seconds.

Back in their New York apartment, Vic poured two tall glasses of lemonade. He put some Saltine crackers in a dish for Raquel to ease her persistent morning sickness.

They sat together on the sofa, enjoying the view of the city lights and the East River. Alicia Keys' song "Like You'll Never See Me Again" was on the CD system.

Vic put his glass down on the coffee table and removed Raquel's glass from her hand, placing it next to his. He offered his hand and asked her if she would like to dance.

Raquel rose from the sofa, and she and Vic moved into each other slowly. They more hugged than danced as Alicia's mellow voice waffled through the room.

If I had no more time
No more time left to be here,
Would you cherish what we had?
Was it everything that you were looking for?
If I couldn't feel your touch
And no longer were you with me,
I'd be wishing you were here
To be everything that I'd be looking for.

I don't wanna forget the present is a gift
And I don't wanna take for granted the time you may have here
with me
'Cause Lord only knows another day is not really guaranteed.

So, every time you hold me,
Hold me like this is the last time.
Every time you kiss me,
Kiss me like you'll never see me again.
Every time you touch me,
Touch me like this is the last time.
Promise that you'll love me,
Love me like you'll never see me again.

Oh, oh, oh

How many really know what love is?
Millions never will.
Do you know until you lose it
That it's everything that we are looking for?
When I wake up in the morning,
You're beside me.
I'm so thankful that I found
Everything that I been looking for.

I don't wanna forget the present is a gift,
And I don't wanna take for granted the time you may have here
with me
'Cause Lord only knows another day is not really guaranteed.

So, every time you hold me,
Hold me like this is the last time.
Every time you kiss me,
Kiss me like you'll never see me again.

(Can you do that for me, baby?)
Every time you touch me,
(See, we don't really know.)
Touch me like this is the last time.
(See, every day we never know.)
Promise that you'll love me.
(I want you to promise me.)
Love me like you'll never see me again,
(like you'll never see me again.)

Oh, oh, oh, oh, oh

When the song was over, Vic and Raquel stood together as if the music were unnecessary. They were one.

Vic parted from Raquel to retrieve something from his inside jacket pocket, which draped a dining room chair. It was an envelope. He handed it to Raquel. The envelope said, "We need a getaway." Inside were two first-class plane tickets to Bermuda with accommodations at the Reefs.

"Mmm, Bermuda," Raquel said, "I'm sure there will be nothing but relaxation there..."

About the Author

Louis Romano was born in The Bronx, New York in 1950. He began writing urban poetry at the age of 18 and, in addition, started writing fiction in 2010.

To connect with the author:

https://www.facebook.com/LouisRomanoAuthor

https://twitter.com/LRomanoSrAuthor

http://instagram.com/louis_romano_author/

https://www.pinterest.com/louisromano/

His debut mob novel FISH FARM, a favorite of his fans, introduces Gino Ranno and his buddies, who are also seen in Mr. Romano's 2nd mob book, the 5-time award winning BESA. A third book in this series will be released in 2016.

BESA is currently under film production. Follow the making of the BESA movie at:

https://www.facebook.com/pages/
BESA/1527054917580749

About the Author, cont.:

Romano's first book in this Detective Vic Gonnella series, the smash hit INTERCESSION, is a
semi-fictional novel set in 2012 involving the re-
venge of a psychologically damaged man who was
abused by his priest as a young boy. The screenplay
for this novel has also won numerous awards.

Been abused? Please contact Road-to-Recovery,
a non-profit on which Louis Romano is a board
member:

https://www.facebook.com/roadtorecovery.in-
fo?ref=br_tf

Follow Detective Vic Gonnella and his squeeze,
Ruiz here:

https://www.facebook.com/DetectiveVicGonnella

For conversation on justifiable murders, and information on giveaways:

https://www.facebook.com/IntercessionbyLouRo-
manoSr

CPSIA information can be obtained at www.ICGtesting.com
Printed in the USA
BVOW04s1627210515

401240BV00008B/6/P